COUNTY

Mark Brewster

To Emma & Peter
with best wishes

[signature]

Published, printed and bound by Gipping Press Ltd.
Units 1-2, Lion Barn Industrial Estate, Needham Market, Suffolk IP6 8NZ

© Mark Brewster
50 Ash Road, Onehouse, Stowmarket, Suffolk IP14 3HB

First impression January 2015

ISBN: 978-0-9931108-2-5

The right of Mark Brewster to be identified as the Author of this work has been asserted by him in accordance with the Copyright, Designs and Patents Acts 1988.

All rights reserved. No part of this publication may be reproduced, stored in a retrieval system, or transmitted in any form or by any means, electronic, mechanical, photocopying, recorded or otherwise without the prior permission of the author and publishers.

CONTENTS

1. INTRODUCTION (page 4)
2. TOWN AND COUNTRY (page 6)
3. TEENAGE KICKS (page 8)
4. BANK NOTES (page 14)
5. AN OFFER I COULDN'T REFUSE (page 16)
6. FEELING COOPERATIVE (page 22)
7. PEDIGREE AND PELLET PASTE (page 29)
8. TROUT TALES (page 37)
9. IRELAND (page 42)
10. RADIO AND TV TIMES (page 50)
11. HOLME PIERREPONT HISTORY (page 54)
12. CLUB CATCHES AND MEMORABLE MATCHES (page 60)
13. WHOLE LOTTA ROSIE (page 93)
14. FROM WILLOW PARK TO WARRINGTON (page 105)
15. BACK ON THE BANK (page 117)
16. A YEAR OF MIXED FORTUNES (page 124)
17. LINDHOLME LESSONS (page 132)
18. TAKE THREE GIRLS… (page 140)
19. DENTS DIARY (page 146)
20. SOUTH HOLLAND SUCCESS (page 157)
21. LINCOLNSHIRE POACHERS (page 167)
22. MILTON KEYNES HAT-TRICK (page 171)
23. WINNING AT THE WATER PARK (page 178)
24. WESTWOOD HO! (page 200)
25. A TRUST TROPHY (page 213)
26. STAINFORTH SILVERWARE (page 222)
27. DRAIN DOMINATION (page 230)
28. BACK TO BOSTON (page 244)
29. THE ONLY WAY IS ESSEX (page 256)

30. COVENTRY CAPERS (page 268)
31. A WINTER OF DISCONTENT (page 278)
32. GIRLS ON FILM (page 282)
33. REFLECTIONS (page 296)
34. SUFFOLK COUNTY SILVERWARE (2007 TO 2014) (page 300)

INTRODUCTION

The reader will be aware, I'm sure, that I've not won any world championships medals, nor have I fished, let alone won, countless open matches. As far as books on angling tuition are concerned, there are numerous publications that cover all manner of techniques and which satisfy even the most discerning practitioner. This is not a book therefore, for someone looking to read either gripping accounts of a high profile angler fishing top-flight competitions, or page after page of in-depth instruction. If, on the other hand, you'd consider a publication that chronicles the life of a less-than-perfect, but nonetheless, successful club match angler, who chose to pass on what he'd learnt to others; then you may just find this book acceptable, occasionally informative and sometimes amusing. The reader whose child, grandchild, niece or nephew represented Suffolk County will perhaps, find my detailed accounts of national events of particular interest, as will, I'm sure, the anglers themselves.

A member of the Gipping Angling Preservation Society in the mid-seventies, I also fished matches with British Steel Piling. I joined Gipping Valley Angling Club shortly after they were founded in 1984 and accepted a proposal to become their treasurer in 1992, a position I held until 2013.

GVAC's 'Have a Go' days and well attended junior events fuelled a local demand for coaches. Taking the opportunity to gain a recognised coaching qualification in 2004 proved invaluable when my full-time work in financial services came to an end in 2009 and I was able to spend a lot more time on the bank, as opposed to where I started work when I left school: in one!

I worked for National Westminster between 1977 and 1984 and represented them on a local level at football and on one occasion even made the region's mixed hockey team. Nat West also held two annual angling contests and I experienced fishing on the Trent, the King's Sedgemoor Drain in Somerset and the Great Ouse near Bedford. In those days, when unable to secure a lift with a colleague who owned a car, I arrived at various venues (including the King's Sedgemoor) on a Kawasaki Z400 motorcycle. Later, a move to Prudential meant that a reliable car was a necessity and my Toyota Corolla estate was much more fit-for-purpose. An increase in income meant that I was able to sample fishing further afield and I enjoyed several trips to Ireland. I married Hazel in 1988 and our (quite unexpected) triplets, Abigail, Bethany and Cameron, arrived in 1992. Sadly, Bethany died just two weeks old.

In 1995 I left Prudential for Cooperative Insurance, for whom I worked until 2009 when effectively, I became a self-employed coarse angling coach. In 2006 I'd been diagnosed with Hereditary Motor and Sensory Neuropathy (also known as Charcot-Marie-Tooth disease), so the change of direction work-wise, albeit much earlier than expected, was perhaps, a welcome one.

Whilst fishing hasn't exactly taken me around the globe, I have fished rivers and lakes in Ireland, fly-fished for trout in Scotland and sampled sea fishing from beach and boat around the coasts of England. When catching and coaching, I've visited counties between Cornwall and Cumbria and have been fortunate enough to meet some very successful and indeed, famous anglers whilst doing the latter. In more recent years the young anglers of Suffolk County picked up national trophies and medals on a regular basis. The path to this level of achievement hasn't been easy, but as the former NFL coach, Vince Lombardi, once said, 'The dictionary is the only place success comes before work.'

TOWN AND COUNTRY

The 19th August 1959 saw the arrival of young Brewster at Ilford Maternity Hospital, Essex. *Dixon of Dock Green* was four years into its twenty-one-year run and Cliff Richard was at number-one with *Living Doll*.

William Torbitt School was a short bus ride from our Chadwell Heath home and it was there that I spent the first few years of my education. Living close to London didn't see me exposed immediately, to the potential joys of fishing, but a family move to Suffolk saw that change.

Being a young lad attending Claydon Primary School in the late sixties meant having to use open-air urinals in the playground and occasionally retrieving one's football from the entrance of an old air raid shelter. Having passed my 11 plus, I was rewarded with an early alarm call for another daily bus trip, this time to Stowmarket Grammar School (which became Stowmarket High soon after). The journey along what was then the A45 meant a twice-daily crossing of the River Gipping. With several youngsters from the village seemingly familiar with the basic skills required to land small perch from close to the brick piles near the Ben Cooper garage, it wasn't long before curiosity and playground conversation resulted in my first proper fishing trip.

The Gipping at Claydon offered sport in the shape of the aforementioned small perch, as well as the occasional roach and much larger pike. The stretch of river that I, along with a few school friends, chose for our first organized trip however, was the weir pool at Needham Market. The weir has since been reconstructed and fenced off and has changed in appearance greatly. In 1974 though, the pool was relatively deep and home to pike, roach, perch and a couple of other species. The agreed weekend meeting time was early and before the local buses were out on the road. At that time, following my parents' separation there was no family car to transport my minimal load of fishing equipment or, more importantly, to transport me. What some youngsters would make today of walking the five miles from where we lived then, carrying fishing gear etc. to the pool at Needham, I can only imagine. Then however, I had no other option. Drink, packed lunch and whatever equipment I had, all went into my *Ipswich Extra* newspaper delivery bag and I left home early before we all met up on the bank, as arranged.

I recall the session itself being largely uneventful and I believe the only two fish landed, came to me. I have a longstanding aversion (putting it mildly) to eels, but the two I caught that day and that were surely unhooked by one of my companions, seemingly didn't put me off fishing. After much ribbing from my friends, I caught the bus back to Claydon, anticipating no doubt, another day's fishing very soon. We later had many trips to Needham and I acquired a decent second-hand bicycle. I became the proud owner of a Craddock float rod, an ABU Cardinal 40 reel and a six-legged basket. Being able to strap my rod and rod-rests to my crossbar and carry my basket across my back, gave me the independence to undertake trips to Barham Pits and the Gipping at Great Blakenham, Sproughton and Bramford, as well as Needham. However, it wasn't always fishing that took up my time when I was a teenager.

TEENAGE KICKS

My early school years at Stowmarket were reasonably uneventful, although I do remember winning the Captain's Prize for Art on a school cruise around the Mediterranean in 1972. Work Experience at the Tackle Box (now Breakaway Tackle), in Bramford Road, Ipswich followed my first forays along the Gipping and my initial acquaintances with Barham Pits. My education competed for my full attention as fishing proved a continual distraction. Thankfully though, my O level results were more than acceptable. In addition to local fishing excursions, I was later fortunate enough to be taken to Weybread Pits with friends, stopping off at the garage in Brockdish on the way to buy our day tickets. I remember discarding the maggots during one session and catching small bream on bread flake. I also remember running out of bread and delving into my lunchbox for my strawberry jam sandwiches. In the warm weather, it was easy to form a pink paste from these and I continued to catch skimmers, rather than revert to being pestered by small rudd on maggot.

My fishing log confirms that by the time I came to leave school in 1977, I'd caught 14 species of fish, all from venues a short bus journey or manageable bike ride from home. The most notable entry is a 1lb 13oz roach taken whilst float fishing by the road bridge on the Gipping at Bramford on Boxing Day, 1975. The pages also detail capture of a 13lb pike from Sharmford Lock. I recall ditching the geography revision the night before an A level exam and grabbing a couple of hours' fishing on C pit at Barham (this was before further landscaping and excavation saw B, C and D pits merged to form one water). The larger of the two tench taken that evening took the scales round to just beyond 4lb 6oz - I also scraped an A level pass at geography!

The free stretch of the Gipping at Great Blakenham drew me, along with my school friends, to its banks throughout the season. Roach to over a pound came to our float rods and dace too, that often weren't that much smaller. We'd also walk the stretch between Blakenham and Claydon, fishing floating crust or a juicy black slug for chub in the warmer months and changing to lobworm in the autumn and winter.

Many nights were spent fishing Barham Pits and I recall Tim Ostler's nocturnal diet of lemon curd sandwiches and Gary Harris having to drink all the contents of his flask as soon as we arrived as it was damaged and wouldn't keep his drinks hot! Night fishing provided the opportunity for us to enjoy, on occasion, quite hectic sport in the shape of hard-fighting tench and good-sized bream. Prior to a night session at Barham, I'd meet up with my mates and we'd make our way, on foot, to the venue. I even recall us pulling our trolleys along the A14 before it was open to traffic. We'd drag our kit up the bank and on to the newly laid dual carriageway at Claydon, before walking to Barham A or B pit. This seemed a lot easier than crossing roads and negotiating numerous kerbs when walking via Great Blakenham, or through Barham and along the badly lit and narrow pavements of the A140.

Lucky Strike!

One particular session was, I recall, no different as far as our preparation was concerned. We arrived at B pit and were lucky enough to get some prime pegs on the spits that face the south bank and look across to the Gipping. The pegs on the end of these spits were particularly prolific. Later in the evening and well after sunset, a thunderstorm befell us. We were used to fishing in rain; what angler isn't? But that night, it was truly torrential and our umbrellas offered little protection. The pegs soon became awash and we took the decision to abort the fishing and take temporary shelter under the railway bridge a couple of hundred yards away. The Stowmarket-Ipswich line crosses the Gipping at the downstream end of the free stretch at Great Blakenham and continues today, to provide shelter today for anglers, dog-walkers and shall we say, ne'er do wells. It was pitch dark and we made our way through the mud and along the path between A and B pits to the bridge. By then, the thunder had become almost deafening and the lightening lit up the whole area. We remained under the bridge for some time, shouting to each other over the noise of the rain. With no cessation in the downpour, we decided to return to our pegs and collect our gear. We trudged back along the pathway to where we'd set up and began tackling down as the rain fell and the water and mud washed around our feet. Suddenly, we heard a tremendously loud clap of thunder and simultaneously, a lightning strike illuminated our efforts to get cleared away. For a second or two, we stopped and stared at each other in the temporary, and extreme bright light, too frightened and stunned to move. A short time later and back in darkness once again, we gathered both our tackle and our wits. We realised immediately, that the bridge had been struck; we could smell the charred wood and brickwork. Completely drenched and laden with wet fishing equipment, we inspected the bridge before making our way home somewhat earlier than expected and feeling not quite as cocky as we were when we arrived.

Sport was particularly fast and furious at Barham after the carp were introduced. The newly stocked fish were suckers (sorry!) for floating crust and we caught them under our rod tips at night, watching our silver paper bite indicators anxiously as the fish circled and nosed our baits just feet from where we sat. By day we often anchored crust in open water over gravel bars. I remember running out of bait during one session and placing half a bap from my packed lunch on the hook, with the obligatory piece of grass placed in the gape. This was cast out and obviously had no trouble pulling line through the eye of the small Arlesey bomb as the bread rose to the surface. The huge bait was not difficult to see and it bobbed proudly in the drift until engulfed by a pair of rather large lips. The carp in question however, was no monster and whilst we caught many, my log shows none in excess of 10lb. My log also indicates that during the hot summer of 1976, we also took fish on sweetcorn. My first experiments with corn as bait were after reading an article by the late Fred J. Taylor. I remember buying bags of it frozen, from of all places, Woolworth's. Long since closed down, Woolworth's in Ipswich then had a food hall and the fish counter was also where we purchased sprats for our pike fishing. We won't claim to be main players in the 'sweetcorn revolution', but we'll all tell you that locally, there weren't many others fishing with it at that time.

    I didn't venture too far down the road of becoming an avid carp angler, although I subsequently purchased some Optonic bite alarms and made my own rods from fibreglass blanks. I did though, enjoy reading about carp and other species. The Osprey Anglers' publications *Carp* and *Pike* by Jim Gibbinson remain in my book collection today, having been signed by the author and given to me just before my 17th birthday by his close friend, Ian Gillespie. Ian lived not far from us and his son, Lindsay was also a fellow pupil at both Claydon and Stowmarket. I shared a few fishing trips with Lindsay, or 'Gilly' as the family still know him, and after one visit to the Gipping at Blakenham was grateful for a lift home in the back of his dad's Renault 16. I say grateful, as I fell in, and not for the last time, I'll add! This was, I recall, a great source of amusement for Ian in particular and the fact that I was made to share the rear of his car with his spaniel and a dead pheasant or two only prolonged the entertainment for all concerned!

    Almost a year later I finished my schooling and 1977 also saw me collect my first fishing trophy: a cup for winning the BSP Freshwater league. This competition was a series of three matches fished on local venues. Juniors would fish with seniors in the same competition, with many events being held on Barham C pit, where BSP shared the fishing rights with GAPS. A knockout competition also took place on occasion, in which anglers drew for choice of venue. I recall fishing the Gipping at Elton Bank and West End Road in Ipswich, among others. Silverware confirms that I took part in these events between 1977 and 1983. During this period I often used my first pole: a telescopic Shakespeare International with an allow crook at the tip to which a short length of elastic was attached. Armed with this, my Ray Mumford pole floats, Bayer Perlon line and Pegley Davies hooks to nylon purchased from the village shop at Claydon; I verily plundered the local roach populations! Whilst it seems I spent countless days fishing the Gipping, Barham Pits and local ponds, I was also playing quite a bit of football.

The 1st Claydon Scout group had, as far as football was concerned, strength in-depth. In just a few years our teams won both the under-14 and under-16 seven-a-side competitions, as well as the area's cup and league. I'd signed for Stowupland whilst still at school and played for them on a Saturday, before also joining Northam Celtic where I played Sunday morning games. Later, I transferred and played for both of Claydon's weekend teams and enjoyed five-a-side during the week. As is the case with circles of friends of such an age, some of those I fished with were often with me on the football pitch at the weekend. Even those that fished, but didn't play, were supporting us from the touchline - and were with us in the bar of the Claydon Crown after the match!

I continued to play football regularly until my early thirties, at full-back or centre-back and as a stand-in goalkeeper. Football was very popular among the young men of Claydon and in addition to the two Saturday sides, a second Sunday team was eventually formed and which I captained for a couple of seasons. We enjoyed immediate success, winning Division 11 at the first attempt and then finishing runners-up in Division 9 as the first team progressed in much higher divisions. Whilst football and the consequent socialising took up much of my time in the seventies and eighties, I always found some time to fish.

Fishing even played a part in my choice of first, full-time employment, which began shortly after my 18th birthday. Despite having achieved seven O levels and a top CSE grade in art, my subsequent efforts with A levels didn't go entirely as planned – apart from the geography! Not wishing to rely on passing all subjects - let alone getting good grades - it was suggested by an angling acquaintance that I apply for a job in a bank. I did so and was offered positions with two. After choosing to take a job at the Town Hall branch of Nat West in Ipswich, I stomached no more than a year of bus rides into work before purchasing a brand new Suzuki A100 from Revetts. This was the first of around a dozen motor cycles I would own, the largest being a splendid, shaft-drive Yamaha XS750.

From my days of playing football for Claydon, I'll always remember the sense of camaraderie and team spirit, both on and off the pitch. When I stopped playing, these, along with the collective sense of achievement were things I'd not experience to the same extent until a quarter of a century later, when standing on the bank of the Grand Union Canal in Milton Keynes as a county angling coach.

BANK NOTES

Nat West's fishing competitions then were not as we've come to know matches today. Back in the late seventies and early eighties, such events involved travelling and an overnight stay on a Thursday, followed by fishing on the Friday. These matches, I recall, usually lasted seven hours and a packed lunch was delivered to all the anglers on the bank, courtesy of the hotel we were all staying in. In those days, participation in such events was encouraged by all within the organization it seemed, except one's branch superiors who were tasked with arranging cover for those away. Perhaps this was also connected with a reluctance to accept fishing as a 'proper' sport - a debate that continues today.

    I can't recall catching more than a handful of very small fish in any of my matches with Nat West, but I wasn't alone. The King's Sedgemoor competition was a real grueller and another on the Great Ouse near Bedford, wasn't much better. In addition to an annual match on various venues around the country, we also fished for the Trent Trophy every year. It would be fair to say that I was punching above my weight on the Trent and the block-end feeder techniques employed by some were far removed from the light float fishing styles I used on the Gipping. I recall one match though, where my work colleague and then, Ipswich Wasp angler, Graham Howe saw off many of the locals to secure individual third place.

    The most vivid memory I have from those Nat West matches is of having to transport and store large quantities of bronze maggots for the competitions on the Trent. After checking in at one Nottingham hotel, I remember taking, or rather smuggling, several large bait tubs up the fire escape. Whilst running cold water in the bath, I removed the lids from all of the tubs. I then floated these tubs of maggots in the bath overnight. I believe all of my teammates did the exact same. I don't recall any mishaps, but it seems that we all went without a bath from the time we arrived until after the match!

Ruddy Marvellous!

My employment with Nat West saw me work in Felixstowe and Tavern Street, Ipswich, in addition to the Town Hall branch. Shortly after leaving for a job in insurance, I found the time to accept an offer from Iain Burgess, an acquaintance at Barclays. He'd invited me to fish Kingsfleet, just up river from Felixstowe Ferry. To this day I prefer tench to carp and I looked forward then, to visiting this fishery with the hope of landing a few of the former.

My host and guide was eager to see us enjoy good sport and we tackled up with great anticipation. Although odd rudd found our baits soon after we'd started fishing, as the session progressed, it was evident that the tench were going to prove conspicuous by their absence. Eventually though, I did connect with a fish that took me to the far side of the fishery and it was a good while before I gained any kind of control. The previously unseen specimen was eventually netted and yes, we'd finally landed a tench, although it wasn't sadly, of specimen-size. The fish that graced my landing net after such a long and dogged fight was of modest proportions and hooked right in the middle of its tail! Despite Iain's obvious disappointment that none of its friends or relations put in an appearance by the time we packed up, I'd thoroughly enjoyed myself, as quality rudd had continually fed in the bright and windy conditions. I'd caught the species before, but not from a natural venue and in the number and consistent size that we'd taken at Kingsfleet. No huge fish were landed, but the experience of catching a good net of quality silver fish on float tackle wasn't wasted on me that day.

AN OFFER I COULDN'T REFUSE

Nat West had transferred me to Felixstowe a few years after I started in Ipswich and it was at the coastal branch that I met Hazel. A couple of years later, another move took me back to Ipswich. We were then asked to consider a move to Lowestoft, King's Lynn or Great Yarmouth. This was whilst we were still courting (to use an old-fashioned phrase) and the prospect of setting up our first home so soon and possibly in the next county wasn't that attractive. Mind you, if I'd have appreciated fully then, the quality and variety of fishing available in Norfolk, things might have been very different!

My parents had separated and divorced some time previously and with my two sisters married (not to each other, obviously) and living elsewhere, a house move from Claydon to Needham Market saw my mother receive a visit from the local Prudential manager, Doug Virr. It transpired that Doug, whilst an agent, had called on Mum in Chadwell Heath, Essex over 20 years before. It also transpired that I worked with Doug's son, Nick, at Nat West – in-between his cricket and my fishing that is! With an unofficial reference obtained from Nick, Doug called back to offer me a vacant agency. Given the prospects of much higher earnings and that I'd be able to work from home, I accepted. After a successful interview and discussions with Hazel, I took the position and started working for Prudential in September 1984. Sadly, Doug passed away during the time I was working on this book and I, along with a few old work colleagues, attended his funeral.

I'd purchased my first car, a Toyota van, some years earlier, but had reverted back to two wheels after writing it off along the Felixstowe Road. I recall that this was during the close season, but it didn't curtail my fishing on June 16th, when I walked to the Hawks Mill stretch of the Gipping close to home and banked three modest chub. A few weeks into my new job and after a short period of borrowing Mum's Renault 5, I took possession of a brown Toyota Corolla estate. This would not only prove to be reliable transport for my insurance rounds, but would also do sterling work as a fishing car. My annual mileage as an insurance agent however, took its toll and I changed vehicles several times during my new career with Prudential and later, Co-op Insurance.

I wasn't fishing too many matches around this time, but two reasonable incomes enabled Hazel and I to enjoy regular holidays whilst still saving. We enjoyed fishing breaks in Lincolnshire during the close season and also discovered Cransley Hall between Kettering and Northampton. This was an idyllic holiday destination for us with good fishing, good food and a pub within easy walking distance. Hazel's parents, John and Gwen joined us on some of these trips where we all appreciated the tranquil surroundings and consistent sport from the carp-filled estate lake (and the cask ale available at the hostelry just along the road!).

Hazel and I married in July 1988 and we celebrated with perhaps, more footballers than fishermen. We set up home in Onehouse, near Stowmarket, where my CX500 Eurosport motorcycle eventually made way in the garage for Hazel's Vauxhall Astra. We were both members of Gipping Valley Angling Club by then, but also enjoyed excursions further afield, to venues such as Horncastle Golf and Country Club in Lincolnshire. In 1990 I made my first visit to Ireland with John, staying just outside Mullingar and fishing the River Inny, the Feorish and Lough Ramor. I later went back with friends, staying just outside Portumna and sampling sport on stretches of the Shannon, several stillwaters and the odd length of canal.

The odds against a natural conception of triplets were, we found out some time before Abigail, Bethany and Cameron were born in March 1992, around 10,000:1. I was Assistant

Match Secretary at GVAC at the time and football had finally given way to my match fishing. The children had arrived early on a Thursday morning, after Hazel had been kept in hospital overnight following a check-up. With all three children in the Special Care Baby Unit, Hazel had suggested that I should run the final event in the Matchman League on the Saturday as, she said, by the time I'd found someone else to do it, I might as well have run it myself. Hazel was to stay in hospital for a week or more and at that time, permitted visiting times were to be observed. Saturday arrived and the match was fished at Needham Lake. I recall catching, and thus avoiding a hefty points penalty. Martin Wood won not only the match, but the league, with a last gasp and sizeable tench.

The newly established Club Angler of the Year title however, was to be awarded to the angler with the best aggregate score from both the Matchman League and Evening Series. I'd tied on points with the since departed and much missed Terry Keymer in the Evening Series and I remember buying him a pint of bitter shandy in the Onehouse Shepherd and Dog on the way home. Martin, having beaten me in similar fashion in the Matchman was afforded similar courtesy in the shape of a can of Guinness, delivered on my way to the hospital after I dropped all my fishing gear off at Mum's and had washed and changed.

Late that night, Hazel underwent an emergency operation and Bethany died 11 days later. I travelled between home and hospital most days and even on occasion, did paperwork at Hazel's bedside with the constraints of set visiting times being relaxed, given the circumstances. She was later discharged from hospital and we took Abigail and Cameron home when they were around five weeks old. I'd won the inaugural Club Angler of the Year competition and earned the club captaincy for the following season. These achievements were put into perspective obviously, by what Hazel and I, with the support of family and close friends, were dealing with at home.

Whilst I recall some of that final match of the season, more vivid is the memory of that night. I remember close friends, Lindsey and Michael driving - not slowly, I suggest - to the hospital in their XR3i. They brought freshly made tuna sandwiches for me to eat, along with considerable moral support whilst Hazel was being operated on. I also remember Steve Gilbert, GVAC's then Match Secretary, phoning me soon after Bethany died and Martin's wife, Sally making me sandwiches on more than one occasion when I called in on the way home from hospital.

Over the next year or two, my competitive match fishing frequently took a back seat as Hazel and I made around a dozen trips to Great Ormond Street Hospital with Abi for specialist treatment; visited Addenbrooke's with Cameron and as we took both for their three-monthly checks back at Ipswich. My log confirms that I did manage to wet a line occasionally and I still gave my club colleagues a run for their pools money, albeit a little less often.

Stone Me!

One of the matches I did find time to fish when the children were young was the GVAC Matchman League leg at Needham Lake on 10th October 1992. The winner of this match would go forward to compete in the final of the Stones Ginger Wine Club Angler of the Year competition on the famous Warwickshire Avon.

In the car park at Needham Lake that October morning I drew peg 18 and chose to set my stall out to win the match with bream. The weather had turned cold and we were all aware of how the fishing could be affected. Nonetheless, I recall taking a fish reasonably early on and a second, late in the match after scaling down to a very small hook and long, fine hooklength. Next-door to me, Dave Trautner returned two bream and a perch for 4lb 3oz and second place. Only three anglers broke the pound and my 4lb 9oz net was good enough for me to start planning for my trip to the Avon. This was probably the one and only occasion that I managed to beat Dave off the next peg!

After practising on the Manor Farm stretch, it was a foregone conclusion that I would draw Twyford in the final! I stayed overnight nearby, arrived early and remember being at my peg with around two hours to set up. I commented to a local about the number of fish topping, but had my enthusiasm dampened after he explained how many matches were held on that stretch and how the fish would seemingly disappear once the match was underway. Undeterred, I set up stick float and waggler rods, a bomb and maggot feeder, as well as long pole rigs. I fine-tuned the shotting on my stick float rig and applied Vaseline to the line immediately above the float in readiness. I looked forward to emulating another, somewhat more famous Prudential employee at the time, Dave Harrell, who'd won countless matches on the stretch.

The match started and I looked to execute a text book underarm cast with my trusty 14-foot Shimano XMA. As I attempted this procedure however, its tip found temporary residence in the ivy of a tree branch above my head and my subsequent attempt to flick it deftly from the foliage resulted in my intricate 'shirt button' shotting reform into a small and very tight tangle. I managed to pull everything free, only for several leaves and small pieces of branch to fall on my head. That was the end of that and out went the waggler! This induced no bites at all, but to be fair, this was not a cultured display of float fishing in the style of Mr Harrell and the response from the fish was, looking back, quite appropriate (and there was me thinking the bloke next-door under the Tuborg umbrella wouldn't know what he was doing!).

During the match I managed just four small fish, dropping one of these on to the platform before it fell between the wooden slats (I did say they were small!) and back into the river. I wasn't alone in struggling and there were several blanks in my section which was won with, I was told, an eel of around a pound. Somewhat disappointed, after tackling down all my rods and clearing away my kit, I didn't hang around to take part in any communal inquest. Still, I'd travelled to the renowned and picturesque Twyford Farm section of the River Avon and caught a few fish. I enjoy a glass of Stone's Ginger Wine now and again and sip it from a sherry glass with a smile as I recall how I once fished a prestigious match on a classic stretch of a famous river... like a complete numpty!

Later in 1992 I agreed to take the position of Treasurer at GVAC, after a short period assisting Steve Gilbert with running their matches. I was, it seemed, a natural choice, given my work background. By this time, changes were afoot at Prudential, and my workload was reducing. In December 1995, I accepted an offer of another insurance agency, this time with the Co-op and following three days' induction at Watford; I started work officially on Christmas Day.

FEELING COOPERATIVE

Working for Co-op Insurance as an agent required the purchase of the existing business or 'book'. Subsequently, business written on the agency increased one's book value, whilst contracts lapsing or maturing devalued it. Regular deductions were made from agents' earnings, enabling them to buy their business via a loan. Later, when an agent left, they received the net value of their business and his or her replacement began the purchase procedure once again. Sometime after I started work however, the majority of the agency values began to fall and few years before I left them, the Co-op bought these businesses back off their employees and a more conventional wage package was introduced. This resulted in cash payments for a lot of employees, including me. The credit cards were paid off, a little was stuck away and enough remained for me to buy a new television for Cameron's computer gaming and Hazel received a laptop computer; Abi and I took possession of brand new 16-metre poles!

The agency I agreed to take on was based in and around Needham Market. From the moment I started with the Co-op it was evident that above-average earnings were available to an agent that worked hard and methodically. With a young and growing family, I really had no option, other than to make work my priority.

The introduction of the Financial Planning Certificate examinations saw me spend a good deal of time studying and attending courses away from home. Most Saturday mornings I was at my desk and many Sundays were spent revising. With several courses being week-long and culminating in an exam, I'd often travel to a hotel on a Sunday afternoon and spend an hour or two in the gym before enjoying an evening meal. I'd stopped playing football in my early thirties, but had taken up running to keep fit. Although working hours with the CIS were unsociable, there was plenty of opportunity during the week to run. I completed several half-marathons, including the Great North Run with a Co-op colleague in 1997. I completed the Felixstowe and Stowmarket half-marathons twice, a few local 10-mile races and several 10km events. Despite regularly running in excess of 25 miles-a-week in training, my times were nothing special. I did manage a sub-eight-minute-mile average for the 1995 City of Norwich half-marathon though. I finished in around 1 hour 43 minutes, crossing the line as Rob Andrew kicked England to victory against Australia in their quarter-final match of the Rugby World Cup in South Africa.

    I also entered a few triathlons and recall driving to my first with the temperature outside only just above freezing. After 32 lengths of the Stowmarket Leisure Centre pool, I remember running barefoot to my bike, leaving footprints on the frosty tarmac. The 10km bike ride was followed by a 4-mile run and after finishing and showering, I headed for the bar where I downed two consecutive pints of bitter shandy whilst consuming no fewer than three Mars Bars!

    Whilst there was plenty to distract me from my fishing, I didn't neglect my GVAC duties. Despite missing matches, I remained responsible for collecting annually-presented silverware, purchase of new trophies and for arranging the engraving of both senior and junior awards.

    GVAC anglers and guests would enjoy a somewhat lavish, three-course meal in a large room at the Limes Hotel in Needham Market. Afterwards, trophies were presented before the more energetic took to the floor for a disco. In more recent years however, presentation evenings as such, have been devoted entirely to the youngsters with senior prize-giving being incorporated within the formalities of the AGM. Junior ceremonies have continued to be very popular though, although the disco has made way for fundraising draw and digital slideshows. In addition to the trophies awarded to anglers from the Junior Academy, commemorative medals have been presented to Suffolk County squad members.

Since GVAC's formation, the two most prestigious competitions have been the Evening Series and the Matchman League. Following its inauguration in the 1991/92 season however, winning the Club Angler of the Year trophy has been the aim of the club's more competitive members. As mentioned in the previous chapter, scores from the Evening Series and Matchman League are added together to determine the winner of the Club Angler of the Year trophy. In the early days of GVAC, the winner of the Matchman League received the honour of captaining the club team the following season. Later, this role fell to the Club Angler of the Year, before committee discussions resulted in the skipper being nominated and the position decided by vote. The structure and format of the Club Angler of the Year competition remains though, and a more appropriate cup has replaced the original, inexpensive shield. All the winners' names from the original trophy were engraved on the new cup's base before it was presented.

In more recent years and prior to me finally stepping down; committee and club duties, coaching commitments and ultimately deteriorating health saw me unable to compete as effectively in club leagues. I have though, had my moments. I'm proud to say that my name is the first on the Club Angler of the Year trophy and it appears again for the 2002/03 season. I've been fortunate enough to win the Matchman League on a few occasions, but a win in the Evening Series eluded me, although I finished runner-up at least three times.

Castle Ashby Cash

One of my Matchman League wins provided an opportunity for me to raise my game and whilst continuing with my studies for insurance industry exams, I found myself considering the prospects of lining up for the 1996 Daiwa

Club Angler of the Year semi-final. The match was scheduled for Castle Ashby Lakes in Northamptonshire, a venue I'd not seen before. Because of work commitments, courses and exam preparations, not to mention other priorities at home with the family; I'd not be able to find time to practise. Nonetheless, I prepared the best I could otherwise, for the forthcoming fixture.

Section winners at Castle Ashby would be treated to an all-expenses-paid trip to Ireland for the final itself. Unfortunately, I was in Barnsley the week before. I say unfortunately, as I wasn't there fishing among the famous local match anglers, but on a course with work. Each day I travelled with colleagues, between our hotel and the local CIS office by taxi. As ever, I was in a minority as far as fishing was concerned and would bore my companions each morning and afternoon, asking the taxi drivers whether they knew of the likes of Tom Pickering, Alan Scotthorne and Denis White. For four days, my quizzing of each driver received a similar response to the J. R. Hartley character in the old Yellow Pages advert as he searched for his own book on fly fishing. Only on the final morning did we have a driver who joined me in enthusing about the famous Barnsley Blacks and my fellow passengers breathed a collective sigh of relief. With the course completed, an early departure from Barnsley saw me travel south again on the Friday afternoon and call at Bosmere Tackle in Needham Market for fresh bait, before I made final preparations for the match the next day.

Having set my alarm for around 5 a.m., I left home and eventually arrived at the venue in good time for the draw. I enjoyed a cooked breakfast on site and with that consumed in a somewhat smoky match headquarters (this was before the national ban on smoking in such public places); I joined the long draw queue second-from-last. I chatted to the only angler behind me: Fred Jones, from Dalston. With the draw queue diminished, we were left with two pegs on Brickyard Pond. At just two acres, this was the smallest lake on the complex. Fred had a corner peg and I was a couple along, but in the next section. Pulling my peg number from the draw bag, I'd been advised to fish a waggler, or bomb if it was too windy and I set up both, along with my pole. Despite being told several times by anglers in my section to forget the latter, we had plenty of time and I've never been one to waste it; as a result though, I usually take longer than most to pack up! I'd also been given some advice before leaving home and that was to stick to what I knew, tactically.

    As the match began, it was evident that with an overnight frost, sport was going to be slower than expected. The wind also, would present problems with presentation and only a handful of anglers were able to fish a waggler, but to my left, Fred was one of them. I did indeed, stick to what I knew and fished a bomb with a three-foot-plus hooklength. I alternated between combinations of sinking and floating red maggots on the hook and, after regularly loose-feeding samples of the same over the top, eventually had some indications. I'd learnt how to fish slow sinking maggot baits at Alton Reservoir when after bream and in the opens at the Bury St. Edmunds Sugar Beet factory pits for carp. I'd found the method particularly good when fish are reluctant to get their heads down properly and feed with confidence and a bait falling very slowly through the water, rather than nailed to the bottom, is sometimes what's required to tempt them.

    With a few small carp in my net, bank-walkers confirmed that I was doing okay, but not as well as the anglers on the corner pegs. I recall several blanks in my section and one angler from Hull packing up very early and walking past me as I played another carp - he was one of those that were full of advice before the start!

    I ended with six carp for 12lb-plus, but a previous winner of the competition had taken the section from the corner peg along the bank to my right. I also knew that Fred to my left had won his section. With the tackle packed up and the car loaded, despite having missed out on a free trip to Ireland, I thought I'd stay and hear the results. As I made my way to the presentations, I was asked by a section winner from the opposite bank how I'd done and what I'd weighed in. After I replied he explained, quite excitedly, that no decent weights had come from Scotland Pond and top weight on Grendon was only around 9lb! Fred had won the adjacent section easily with just over 23lb and the three of us joined the large group awaiting the announcements.

On more than one occasion, I've fished matches where organisers have never heard of GVAC when announcing the prize-winners. To this day, membership numbers are modest, so perhaps it was no real surprise that when the fifth placed angler stepped forward to receive his winnings for a return of 12lb 9oz 8dr, the applause was not exactly spontaneous and far from rapturous. Nonetheless, I received a pat on the back from my new friends as I pocketed quite a thickly packed brown envelope. I had no caddy or bank-runner with me and no mobile phone (this was 1996 remember). I drove back down the A14 with a satisfying smile on my face, knowing that although I wouldn't be heading to Ireland for the final, we'd have a bit more spending money on the family holiday we'd already booked for that same week.

Back home in Finborough I pulled up at the village stores before driving the short distance home. On entering the shop, Trevor, the proprietor, began explaining that I was in the doghouse. I'd been away all week on a course and no sooner had I returned home, I'd messed off again fishing – it transpired that Hazel had been in for the paper and they'd got chatting! I then casually explained that I'd had a reasonably successful day and also, that I'd received the biggest payout of my match fishing career. I advised Trevor that I'd called in to pick up a bottle of wine and some chocolates before I got home. '…You've just been forgiven!' shouted Trevor's wife, Jackie, from the top of the stairs!

Whilst still with CIS and as mentioned in my introduction at the start of the book, I was fortunate enough to gain my Level 2 coaching qualification in 2004. The course involved classroom and home study, a written examination, practical demonstrations and an interview. A few years later, with increasing competition for business from the internet and with customers able to arrange business over the phone, it became evident that the job I knew at the Co-op was changing. In 2009, I was offered a modest financial package and left their employment the day after my fiftieth birthday and following a short period of garden leave.

Shortly before leaving CIS, I'd attended a union conference in Blackpool. Standing in my hotel room at the Hilton, looking out to sea, I chatted to GVAC Chairman, Steve Barnes, about the prospects of coaching youngsters from Springfield Junior School in Ipswich. The school had been pointed in our direction by Roy Startup, after his own children had attended GVAC Junior Academy events. After returning home, Steve and I met with Michael Lynch, the school's headmaster and I was on the bank with their pupils within a few weeks of leaving my last job in financial services. After family discussions, I chose to take available pensions and clear most of our mortgage. With a few quid tucked away and a new bathroom ordered, I treated myself to some new, top-of-the-range Shimano luggage (it was reduced in a sale, honestly); Abi and I also became proud owners of new and interchangeable Fox Stax seat-box systems.

Within a year, GVAC had forged links with seven schools and I'd become a less than lithe, not exactly young and perhaps not the fittest ever, self-employed sports coach.

PEDIGREE AND PELLET PASTE

Cransley Hall is a 16th century country manor house set in 17 acres of its own grounds in Northamptonshire. In the eighties and nineties, anglers staying there were able to fish its lake which was originally dug and stocked by monks. Given the tranquillity of the surroundings and quality of the fishing, the hall was an ideal place for a hardworking insurance agent and his wife to spend an early summer break. Hazel and I visited Cransley Hall several times and it was one place that we fished, where the consistency of the sport really was, of secondary importance. Hazel's parents, John and Gwen, joined us on occasion and whilst we caught no monsters, as ever, there was a lot more to the fishing than just catching fish. Pre-internet, we'd come across the fishing breaks available when trawling through advertisements in the angling press. The journey from Suffolk wasn't a long one and with fishing permitted from 2 p.m. on the afternoon of arrival, we'd be on the bank with rods set up and lines wet, within a few hours of setting off after breakfast.

      Fishing-wise, it was evident from the start, that we wouldn't be catching any huge carp. The shallow estate lake had a substantial covering of lily pads and was teaming with small roach and rudd. Seemingly thousands of small carp of just ounces also inhabited the water, but there appeared to be a good few modest-sized mirrors and commons, as well as some approaching double figures or more. A large tackle shed was situated close to the dam wall end of the lake, and as evening approached, we'd walk our equipment over and place our rods on the racks, without the need even, to break them down.

      Standing on the close cut lawns that slope down to the water, the views across the lake, with its wooden boat shed and surrounding trees, were eclipsed only perhaps, by the grandeur and splendour of the hall itself. Cransley was certainly stark contrast to some venues I've had cause to visit since.

Originally built by Dame Alice Owen around 1580, subsequent owners have included, among others, the Chancellor of the Exchequer. The dining room boasted a long banquet table where guests enjoyed their evening meals and cooked breakfasts. Vegetables grown in the grounds were served with evening roasts and even honey for the toast in the mornings came from hives in the hall grounds.

The library had a stock of appropriate and befitting angling publications and there was even a snooker and billiards room with a full sized table. Unfortunately however, I found there was no such thing as 'a quick game of snooker before we go to the pub', given my lack of prowess with a cue.

The guest rooms were everything one would imagine and I recall being faced with a walk of several paces to the toilet after entering the bathroom – no chance of sitting on the loo with your foot against the door here!

For those so inclined (and we definitely were) a short walk to the local pub was rewarded with a pint or two of Marston's Pedigree. One hears stories of pubs where the landlord doesn't call last orders and the local policeman walks in just before closing time with his pint being served just as he places his helmet on the bar; well this was one of those. In fact, I recall Sandy, the landlord at the time, rising from his evening nap only just in time to serve said bobby with his pint! John, Gwen, Hazel and I never took too much advantage of the apparent, localised relaxation of licensing laws and two or three rounds were more than enough to satisfy our thirst ahead of another day's fishing.

Sandy isn't the only character I recall fondly from the times we spent at Cransley. Among the guests that we shared a bank with, were Bob and Alan. Whilst Alan seemed the more determined and perhaps serious angler, his pal evidently, had different priorities. Bob would spend longer than most, chatting to proprietors, Brian and Margaret after breakfast. Once he'd made it to the lake, he'd set up his quiver-tip rod and cast out. His bait wouldn't be in the water for an awfully long time and once the church bell chimed 11 o'clock, Bob would make his way to the pub for his game, or rather games, of dominoes. A long lunch break would see him return for a short spell of fishing in the afternoon, prior to departing, he'd tell us, for a bath before dinner. I'm sure Bob enjoyed his fishing breaks at Cransley every bit as much, and possibly more, than the rest of us.

Meanwhile, back on the bank, I found some difficulty in catching anything other than the aforementioned small carp and only an occasional larger fish graced my landing net. Hazel's weapon of choice was a floating boilie and whilst she didn't catch large numbers of fish, she definitely got to grips with how to pick out the better specimens from one or two areas of the lake. In those days, we made our own boilies and I remember strawberry, ethyl-alcohol baits being particularly productive. Gwen however, chose a much less labour-intensive bait and always nurtured a large piece of Cheddar for a good few months before our trips to Cransley. It worked too, as she caught the largest fish we saw during our many visits in the shape of a sparsely scaled mirror of very nearly 10lb from near the dam wall. It seemed then, that as a match angler at heart, I wasn't prepared to sit it out for the larger fish. As I went through a variety of baits and methods, it was noticeable however, that one angler's float rod was bent alarmingly with some regularity throughout the day.

Out of the corner of my eye, I could see that Alan, some distance away, was obviously casting very close to the lilies and hardly ever did I see him bring in a small fish. In the relaxed surroundings and with the sun shining however, curiosity never got the better of me. Rather he, being the perfect gentleman, asked how I'd got on as we packed away one afternoon and then, after I'd explained my frustrations, he offered assistance. He told me to meet him by his car with a bait tub before we headed indoors for our evening meal. As he opened the back of his car, I noticed a large Cramphorn Garden Centre bag. Alan then took my bait tub and almost filled it with what the bag contained. He passed the tub back to me and I saw that he'd given me a supply of trout pellets. I was instructed to boil a kettle back in our room and just cover the pellets with hot water. He then asked whether I could add anything to bind the paste that formed, the following day. Given the carp fishing that Hazel and I occasionally did, we had some basic ingredients with us, including a jar of Horlicks.

The next morning, I mixed the trout pellet paste with some Horlicks and a few other ingredients until it was of a consistency that would keep it on a large hook fished under a waggler rig. Alan's successful tactics involved casting the weight of the bait, rather than the float and shot, and positioning it as close as possible to the lilies. A lump of paste around the size of a golf ball was rolled in the palm of one's hand and the hooklength line laid tightly across, and then within it. The mainline was pulled slowly through until the hook disappeared into the ball, with the paste then moulded to cover the split left by the line.

I found the best way to get the bait very close to the lilies was to cast quite high overhead and allow the paste to land with a discernible 'splat', on top of a one of the broad, green leaves. The float would then sit, half-cocked between rod tip and bait, until the paste was pulled gently back, so it fell from the lily leaf and sank slowly. As it did so, the float would be pulled towards and up quite very close to the lilies themselves, given the size and weight of the bait, the small waggler and its light shotting. The paste effectively acted as a plummet, with the float set at dead depth. As the large ball of paste had fallen vertically and laid as close to the lily pads as one could fish, Alan's tactic was obviously to lure the better fish from their sanctuary to the edge of the open water with a bait that wouldn't hopefully, attract the attentions of small fish.

A few knocks on the float were followed eventually, by it disappearing under the pads. A low half-sweep of the rod was usually met with stubborn resistance and, with the right hand on the rod handle and the left cupped over the reel spool, buttocks were clenched as the tussle between angler and fish began. Eventually, with the rod almost past semi-circle and its tip absorbing the pressure of the carp's lunges, the fish could be coaxed away from the lilies and the rest of the fight would be somewhat less frantic, before it was finally netted.

Alan had fished the same swim close to a large tree that provided plenty of shade throughout the first few days that we'd been at Cransley. One afternoon however, a group of, shall we say, 'bivvy boy' wannabe carp anglers arrived. Whilst those of us already at the hall were more than happy to allow Alan continual use of his favourite swim, one of the new arrivals, on seeing how many good-sized fish he was catching, chose to set his gear up there on the day I was to try out the paste. This was of no real concern to Alan, who promptly set up down the bank from me and, needless to say, said carp angler caught nothing like what Alan amassed on the previous days. Whilst Hazel spent the day stalking fish close to the dam wall, freelining her floating boilie for the most part; Alan and I enjoyed a day's waggler-and-paste fishing near the sluice. By late afternoon, whilst we hadn't exactly emptied the place, we'd finished with a similar number of better carp – and we'd certainly done better than our friend by the tree!

Unfortunately, as is so often the case with some baits on certain waters; the tactic of fishing with large balls of pellet paste to deter the small carp didn't work for ever. We enjoyed good sport for a year or two before it then lost its selective effectiveness. After changing from the standard approach with a float rod to freelining ever-increasing sizes of paste baits on later visits; I also switched to fishing with a pair of light carp rods. On occasion, I would pull two bobbins, on the same rod, but placed between consecutive pairs of rings, to ground level and laid them across the grass. Even after waiting for all of this slack line to be taken up and for the line to tighten, I would not connect with fish. Eventually we realised that even small carp would nose the paste balls, pick them up between their lips and move off. The only truly selective bait by then was Hazel's floating boilie.

Nowadays of course, pellets specifically designed for carp are marketed and these are of lower oil content than those fed to trout, thus ensuring the carp are able to digest the feed easily. All manner of pastes are also available, but many anglers still prefer to make their own. As well as the obvious satisfaction gained by catching on bait prepared yourself, anglers fishing their own, often unique combination of flavours and colour, will often have an edge, particularly it seems, in matches.

Beer Tent Bonus!

Now, just when we thought that we'd found everything we'd ever want in a fishing holiday destination, we were made aware of a completely unexpected attraction, one that would see us booking our breaks at specific times of the year in the future.

One morning, as several guests enjoyed the usual post-breakfast conversation, Brian, in his usual laid-back manner, passed comment regarding the fact that our fishing that day might be disturbed. In fact he apologised for what was to take place in the grounds. It transpired that Cransley Hall was the venue for the village fête; its sprawling, pristine lawns an ideal location for this quaintest of English village summer traditions. There would be the usual stalls and we could take a break from fishing if we wished, to visit the tombola stand, purchase some homemade chutney or even – and this was almost an afterthought tagged on to the end of the apology – pop up from the lake to the beer tent! Now at that point in the conversation, I wasn't the only one to look up from my third or fourth cup of tea and give a half-smile glancing up and down the table.

So, several hours later, there we were, sitting comfortably by the lake, in the sunshine, being visited occasionally by those that chose to wander down from the fête and engage us in pleasant conversation. The grass was freshly mown, the lake was calm and the carp were topping. To my right was my float rod, placed in its rests and temporarily redundant with my hook in the butt ring. To my left, nestled in the grass close by my feet, was a freshly poured pint of cask ale and it's somewhat ironic that one of my fondest angling memories is of sitting by a lake, where the fish weren't that big and where catches were modest, and where I seemingly spent quite some time not actually fishing!

To bring the reader - and indeed the author - back to reality however, I'll end this chapter with a recollection of one particular day at Cransley that remains memorable for all the *wrong* reasons…

On 22nd June 1986, Hazel and I had enjoyed breakfast, and indeed the fishing, like we had done on many other days. We'd packed our gear away somewhat earlier than usual though and made our way back to our room. That afternoon, a World Cup quarter-final was taking place between England and Argentina. To say the least, Hazel's never been the most enthusiastic football fan, but this was the World Cup and a quarter-final at that. I'll not labour over the story of the match itself, as even those with a limited knowledge of football will recall that England lost. They may recall also, that one of the two Argentinean goals wasn't scored off a head or a boot.

The mood at dinner that night was not what we'd become accustomed to. Given both the game's result and the manner by which England had been knocked out of the tournament; those of us that had packed up fishing early, wished we hadn't. This was the last occasion where watching a football match took priority over my fishing. Since then there have been many GVAC club matches that have taken place at the same time as World Cup games and the former have usually been well attended. In recent years I've also found on such occasions that my favourite chub swims on the Gipping are always free!

TROUT TALES

I suspect quite a few coarse anglers of my generation took up trout fishing for the same reason me: it provided a means by which one could continue wetting a line during the close season. For younger readers that may be unaware, the original close season applied not only to rivers, but also to canals and stillwaters. This meant that a young lad living in Suffolk in the early eighties had an enforced break from his fishing for three months of the year. Whilst I undertook trips to fish land-locked waters in Cornwall, Devon and Lincolnshire on occasion, where coarse angling was still permitted; trout fishing seemed like an attractive alternative. Trout fight very well, the equipment required to game-fish is minimal and one can actually eat what one catches. The fact that coarse anglers spend so much time putting together a net of fish, only to put them all back again at the end of the day is something that still mystifies many, it seems.

I've always enjoyed reading and when I considered taking up trout fishing I bought a publication that I found so informative that I've read it again since. *The Pursuit of Stillwater Trout* by Brian Clarke is, I feel, worth the asking price just for the author's short passage referring to an encounter with a fly fisherman in Ireland where he details a particularly laid-back, but very effective use of a green drake Mayfly during a daddy-long-legs hatch.

Having read the book and equipped myself with a fly rod, trout reel, floating line and landing net etc. I practised my casting on a suitably large area of grass behind my house. My first experience of catching both brown and rainbow trout was whilst on holiday at Worthing in Norfolk. There, I fished a lake of approximately an acre in size, close to the River Blackwater, a tributary of the Wensum. The most enjoyable method I found was to fish a floating line with a long leader and a single nymph - fishing a team of flies has always seemed to me, like asking for trouble! I took several fish on my first outing and more during other sessions later in the week. Whilst I enjoy eating trout, particularly those I catch myself, fishing for them was never going to be anything other than an occasional deviation from coarse angling. Since first casting a fly though, trout have provided me with fond and vivid memories of fishing trips around the British Isles.

One year at Cransley Hall, it quickly became evident that the fishing on the tranquil estate lake wasn't exactly what Hazel and I were used to. Whilst we began our fishing break catching carp, very soon, a different fish altogether was gate crashing the party.

Brian, the proprietor, explained that during the early spring, a local farmer had stocked a number of trout with the intention of catching a good few, if not perhaps all of them over time, for the table. Unfortunately, although I'm sure many were taken and later consumed, there remained a good number in the lake come June 16th. No matter what bait we tried, trout would make an appearance and usually sooner rather than later. Their presence graduated from being a pleasant surprise to a blasted nuisance very quickly. It wasn't only us that were being pestered and conversation at the evening meal centred mostly around trout, rather than carp. Having slept on it, one morning at breakfast I promptly announced that I was to spend the day deliberately fishing for trout - my statement of intent met with great amusement. What tactics would a coarse angler on holiday use to lure these game fish? Why, waggler and sweetcorn obviously! I had some corn with me and we often dyed and flavoured our baits. For those that remember it, I'm sure my corn would have had a good dose of Duncan Kay's Carptract 3.

Given that the trout is a predator, I chose to fish corn, on-the-drop, on a waggler rig at dead depth and with very little shot down the line. The idea was to cast out to an area that I'd loose-feed sparingly, encouraging the trout to home in on the noise of the corn hitting the water, before taking the bait as it dropped enticingly through the few feet to the bottom. As the float settled at depth, I'd catapult more grains of corn, retrieve and cast the hookbait over the top again. The tactics, I have to say, worked a treat and with use of a keepnet permitted, more and more trout were retained - and fewer remained to swim around the lake and pick up carp baits! Catching them on a float rod and waggler set-up was, I found, somewhat different to taking them on a fly rod. Within seconds of hitting the bite, I'd find myself with rod bent, main line running down from its tip and into the lake and then up and out again to the fish as it tried to shed the hook by leaping from the water. This was very active fishing and my antics provided an entertaining spectacle for the other guests that were using more acknowledged tactics.

I ended up with around 30lb of trout and the carp anglers had, I'm sure, more carp than they would have had otherwise. I have to say, it wasn't the most addictive or enjoyable day's fishing I've ever experienced and the following day my sanity seemingly returned and I was back targeting carp with more traditional, species-specific methods. It wasn't too long before most, if not all of the trout were landed, and obviously eaten, as the fishing in the following years returned to what guests expected.

A Trip to Turnberry

On one or two occasions whilst working for CIS, I was fortunate enough to travel with colleagues to the Society's annual sales conferences. These gatherings were usually arranged for top performers and I recall one December, taking a call from my manager at the time, Bob Morgan. He'd phoned to congratulate me and confirm that I'd booked my place on that year's conference and successful agents were due to spend two nights at the Turnberry Resort in Scotland, during the week before Christmas. Most famous for its golf courses and indeed for hosting several Open

Championships; Turnberry also offers other activities to tourists and visitors, including archery, quad-biking and shooting. None of these really appealed to me however; it was the fly fishing on the itinerary that caught my eye.

Whilst many colleagues chose to drive up with their golf clubs in the back of their Volvos and BMWs, I opted to let the plane take the strain and my second-hand half-set of clubs remained under the stairs and my Vauxhall Astra estate on the drive. The two days' activities included the usual syndicate work with other agents and managers of various levels, but on the second day of the trip, we were free to indulge our sporting passion of choice. The resort boasts a two-and-a-half acre loch, stocked with both brown and rainbow trout and it was these I was going to have a crack at catching with a few of my more hardy colleagues. I say hardy, as when we eventually touched down on the Tuesday night at Prestwick Airport, it was several degrees below freezing and it remained almost as cold for the whole break.

We assembled on the bank of the loch shortly after lunch on the Wednesday and were met by three gillies in traditional attire. They explained the tactics we'd be employing and also demonstrated casting with a double-handed salmon rod, as the mist thickened and the ice worked its way down the loch. I have to say, I was about as good with the salmon rod as I was coping with the sub-zero temperatures: not very! One of the gillies explained his technique for getting his hands accustomed to the cold on such days. He'd plunge them into the icy water in the morning and they'd feel warm, he assured us, for the rest of the day. As an angler with medically certified, extremely poor circulation (a classic symptom of CMT), I'll not repeat on these pages, exactly what I thought of his idea, but to be fair to the gentleman and his comrades-in-tweed, it seemed to work for them.

We fished with floating lines and reasonably long leaders and worked our leaded flies down the loch, ahead of the ice. The gillies showed their casting prowess by sending the lines out into the deeper water where the trout lay, as some of us struggled to reach the required distance.

To use the accepted match fishing term, I didn't exactly bag up. I did though, eventually connect with a hard fighting Scottish loch rainbow trout. After a dogged fight and, as it approached the bank, my gillie squatted down and began breaking up the marginal ice… with his fingers! As I drew the fish closer, he banked it with his bare hands at the first attempt. It was, I was told, in excess of 5lb and whilst we had the option to retain our trout, I chose to release mine and, job done, headed for a warm bar and a late afternoon, if rather expensive pint.

Following a black tie dinner that evening and a rather short night's sleep, we flew home on the Thursday, sometime after breakfast. I remember a small group of us taking morning tea as we waited for our lift to the airport for the flight home. My colleague, Mike Cole picked up the tab for that particular round, just as he'd done several times during our visit. A year or two later, between Christmas and New Year, I took a call on my mobile phone whilst fishing for roach on the Gipping. It was Mike's brother, Kev, whom I also worked with at CIS. Kev informed me that Mike had sadly died in a motor accident whilst on holiday in South Africa. Shortly after, I met with the family and was proud to be asked to write an ode as a tribute to Mike, which I read out at the funeral with the support of Kev's wife, Suzanne.

I have many angling memories and I'll not forget that call from Kev. I shall always remember too, taking morning tea at Turnberry, looking out on the Irish Sea as the sun shone and as Mike complained characteristically, about the cost of the round which, I explained, was down to the view, and not the price of the tea bags!

IRELAND

The trips I've taken to Ireland came about for much the same reason as my taking up fly fishing inasmuch as they provided a means by which I could continue to fish during the close season. But whilst fly fishing invariably involved sticking just a rod, reel, landing net and small bag of kit in the car, jaunts across the Irish Sea were planned with almost military precision as our vehicles – which included the occasional mini-bus - were crammed with seat-boxes, platforms, groundbait buckets and every other conceivable item of coarse kit one could imagine. The one concession though, was bait. Whilst we usually stuffed a few bags of our favourite continental groundbait in any remaining available orifices, we ordered bags of brown and white crumb, gallons of maggots, casters and large packs of worms to be collected at the start of, and during the trip, from the nearest Irish Angling Services outlet. This in itself brings to mind the first anecdote from my visits, which gives an indication of the famed, laid-back attitude I and my fellow anglers, grew to know and love.

My father-in-law, John accompanied me on my first trip and we'd taken the ferry crossing from Holyhead to Dun Laoghaire and booked to stay in Mullingar, County Westmeath. Sometime before, I'd purchased and read Hugh Gough's book, *Coarse Fishing in Ireland* and the plan was to try our luck on the River Inny, Lough Ramor and other venues within a comfortable drive of our guest house. Prior to fishing on the first day, we pulled up outside the fishing tackle shop in Mullingar in anticipation of collecting a copious supply of the aforementioned selection of baits. John and I parked the car in town and walked the short distance to the shop, only to find that it wasn't open, even though it well past nine o'clock. After a look in the window and establishing that we'd got the right place, we noticed the sign which read: 'Open 9 a.m. until 5 p.m., or ring bell.' We did as requested, but even this didn't bring about an immediate response. We weren't though, in any hurry and some minutes later, a gentleman opened the shop door and promptly announced, 'You'll be Mr. Brewster... Come in!' The welcome we received that first day was one I would become accustomed to and sometime later, our bait appeared!

Finally armed with a large quantity of bait, John and I began our first fishing holiday in Ireland with a session on the River Inny and enjoyed consistent sport from roach, occasional perch and larger roach/bream hybrids. On that first day, we were also introduced to Irish weather. I'd been told that in Ireland, it was either raining, had just stopped raining or it was about to rain! I remember John pouring a drink from his flask just before a shower and it lasting about three hours (the shower that is, not John's drink). Nonetheless, the fishing was everything I'd been led to expect. John trotted a stick float and I alternated between the same method and the pole. Feeding heavily with groundbait and caster and holding a pole rig back hard over the top and with a worm on the hook helped me pick out the hybrids and their fight in the strong flow didn't disappoint. Whilst we were more than happy with the sport we enjoyed that day, we were keen to explore other venues.

We took a drive to the famous stretch of the Shannon at Lanesborough, just north of Lough Ree. Lanesborough's claim to fame is that it was the site of Ireland's first turf-fired electricity generator. The warming effect of the plant on the river results in prolific fishing as bream, tench and roach congregate there between May and September. On arrival however, John and I were disappointed, or more disgusted to see the amount of litter on the bank left, quite obviously, by anglers. We didn't hang about and decided instead, to fish the first appealing stretch of water we happened upon. We ended up spending a quiet day on the River Feorish, a tributary of the Shannon. The fishing wasn't exactly spectacular, but it was rewarding and enjoyable nonetheless. We didn't see another soul all day, apart from the local postman who, on seeing us fishing, parked his van and wandered down for a chat. In consequence, his letters and parcels reached their destinations a little later than usual; not that it seemed to bother him, or I'm sure, the eventual recipients.

The advice given to English anglers fishing Ireland for the first time is to pre-bait if possible and revisit venues, giving the fish time to find the bait. The fishing should then improve, which is what we found at the last of the three venues we fished on that first trip.

Travelling north from Dublin on the N3 road, Lough Ramor can be seen on the left as one approaches the town of Virginia. Following Hugh Gough's advice, we chose to fish the Knocknagarten bank. On arrival, I mixed up a large amount of brown crumb with some Van den Eynde Expo groundbait and a little Brasem. I added casters to the mix and after setting up a light waggler rig and plumbing up; I was ready to 'ball it'. I believe I under-armed around 20 'jaffas' to this waggler line and to John's amazement, the float didn't settle after my side-cast over the top. After it slid away, I connected with my first Lough Ramor fish. I have to say, that John's more refined approach also drew a similar response. That day, we banked a steady stream of modest-sized bream and found that larger and larger hookbaits brought bigger and bigger fish. With around a mile of water in front of us and the lough some two or three miles long, we were enjoying brilliant sport on simple waggler tactics reasonably close in. We returned for a second day there and the fishing did indeed get better.

We agreed that, as we were on holiday, we'd always get a good night's sleep and enjoy a cooked breakfast back at the guesthouse before departing for our day's fishing. We usually managed to fish for a comfortable five hours or so and whilst we didn't record nets of a 100lb-plus like some of the early-risers, we were more than happy with our catches. A year or so later, I returned with club colleagues to fish the same stretch of bank, but we didn't enjoy the level of success we'd experienced on that first visit. Ireland's freshwater fish often move around a great deal, as dictated by season and spawning habits, but in 1990, John and I struck lucky and enjoyed great sport from both lake and river.

At the time, vehicles returning from Ireland were often stopped and searched as the Troubles continued. As John and I left the ferry at Holyhead, we were directed by a female police officer into an enclosed area where presumably, such vehicle searches would be conducted. She gestured for me to wind down the window as a couple of armed, male colleagues with weapons at the ready, looked on. As she then leant closer to the car I noticed her expression change as she caught the unmistakeable odour of wet keepnets, landing nets, damp fishing clothing and stale bait through my partially opened window. She took a step back and, with eyes half closed and head turned slightly away, she waved us through with no further delay. She'd quickly realised and was in no doubt that we were, without question, coarse anglers!

Pickled in Portumna!

On subsequent visits to Ireland, I stayed with GVAC colleagues at Mullingar once again, but also at Ballyshrule Lodge a few miles outside the town of Portumna. Initially we travelled in convoy in our cars, but later hired a mini-bus with seats removed to make more room for our fishing tackle. As before, we sampled the fishing on several venues. We didn't, as mentioned, see the consistent sport at Lough Ramor repeated, although we did bank a small number of larger bream.

Returning to the Kocknagarten stretch, we were greeted by heavy and driving rain and strong winds. As a consequence, we disregarded float fishing and set up feeder rods. Having watched an almost motionless tip for some time during one session, I picked up the rod as, without warning and still in the rests, it took on a savage and dramatic bend. This was no specimen bream or rogue pike however, and I found myself playing a rather modest-sized brown trout! On our return to the guesthouse in Mullingar, it didn't go down well with the proprietor that I'd returned the fish alive and hadn't brought it home for his supper!

When staying at Mullingar we also fished Slevin's Lake nearby, taking skimmers and good bream and tangling with pike that chased our feeders as we retrieved them from the deep, clear water. During our trips we ventured further afield too, spending time on Silvergrove Lake, close to the town of Tulla, and Lough Graney, where we once again, feeder-fished for bream. On the Shannon, we had sessions on the Shebeen stretch, north of Portumna. Possibly the best sport came when we tried the pegs cut into the reeds as the river enters Lough Derg, the last of waterway's big lakes, south of the town. Back at the guesthouse we were subjected to severe ribbing, as we returned each day and gave details of only modest catches. Finally though, when fishing sliding and fixed wagglers where advised and after heavy pre-baiting, we managed several very good mixed nets and had seemingly made the grade as far as our host, Ray Bowes back at Ballyshrule Lodge was concerned.

Our struggle to find fish though, didn't stop us enjoying ourselves in the evenings and we'd usually manage to pop out and pre-bait before heading into town for a drink or two. On occasion, those in our party that chose to have a few more drinks than the rest were able to hitch a lift before more than two or three vehicles passed them as they began walking back to the guesthouse; everyone knew Ray, it seemed.

One evening, we entered what would have been one of a succession of pubs that we visited over the course of the stay and the landlord proceeded to pour me a Guinness (the others tended to drink lager over there, would you believe!). Rather than the customary shamrock pattern in the frothy head, he made the outline of a fish and let the tap drip to form its eye. 'How did you know we were anglers?' I asked. 'Ah...' he replied in his broad Irish accent, 'the fishermen... they have a certain smell about them!'

The conversation developed as we explained where we'd fished and how well, or how not so well, we'd done. A lull in the conversation saw him disappear for a few moments and return with a very large, glass jar. He promptly announced that if we could tell him what was in the jar, he'd let us all have a drink on the house when we came back the following night. He'd also then, tell us the story behind the contents. Without hesitation, I told him that what was in the jar was a lamprey. When he asked how I knew, I explained that I'd recognised immediately, the unmistakeable gill pattern and funnel-like, toothed mouth, clearly visible, through the glass. The lamprey had been pickled and we did indeed return the following night to hear of how he'd had come about this animal – and of course, for our free drinks!

We were recognised on arrival the next evening and with Guinness (and lagers) poured, the landlord began to recount the story of the lamprey.

It transpired that a game angler fishing the Shannon from a boat on the town stretch one evening had hooked a large fish, close to the bank. As the battle with the unseen adversary developed, the angler followed the running fish in his boat and eventually came to net it, in darkness and on the opposite side of the river. The fish he'd hooked was a large brown trout and attached to its flank was the lamprey. Both fish were brought to the pub and as the landlord finished telling the story, he unfurled several large black and white photographs which showed both specimens laid out on his tables as the locals looked on. The trout was later eaten and the lamprey pickled and retained in the large glass jar. That wasn't the creature I saw pickled in Portumna however...

The night before we left for home on that particular trip, two of our party signed in as guests at one of the local hotels for (several) late drinks. They returned during the early hours, courtesy of an obliging and obviously rather tolerant motorist. The following morning, one of the two seemingly suffered no ill-effects. It was a different story however, for his late-night drinking buddy and so as not to embarrass him further, I'll not name him. I will though, add that this acquaintance had brought with him on the trip, a couple of very large groundbait buckets that were most awkward to accommodate with everything else we'd loaded in the mini-bus. On the drive back to Dun Laoghaire however, the buckets weren't stuffed alongside protruding rod holdalls or down between seats with carryalls; rather, they remained close to their owner and he cuddled one all the way to a service station close to the ferry terminal. Here, our somewhat green-around-the-gills passenger took the opportunity to both get some fresh air and wash his groundbait bucket out in the toilets on site.

The fishing we enjoyed in Ireland was varied to say the least. I recall us on one trip finding a clear, but quite weedy stretch of canal close to the guesthouse where we could touch the far bank with just seven or eight metres of pole. We caught beautifully coloured roach and rudd on and off throughout the day. In contrast, the Shebeen stretch of the Shannon, despite being a backwater of the main river, is around 80 yards wide, has depths of up to 25 feet and here we fished heavy groundbait feeders. On Lough Graney we waded out 10 to 15 yards and a decent cast with a small or medium-sized open-end feeder saw us still fishing in depths of no more than a few feet. And at the mouth of Lough Derg, we cast our fixed wagglers and sliders to take good nets of roach, rudd, bream and hybrids. One day when fishing these pegs, standing in our thigh waders with platforms beside us and keepnets in front, we became aware of the noises from large animals in the woods on the far bank. Later, we realised the animals were red deer and I also remember seeing a salmon jump as we fished, looking across the

Shannon with the sun shining and as we listened to the deer.

That same day I had a short, but nonetheless intriguing conversation with some German pike anglers who were fishing from a boat. They'd chosen to fish, albeit temporarily, right on top of where my slider was running through and close to where I was throwing my balls of groundbait. This I found most puzzling, given how wide the river is on the stretch and how much water was available. I kicked off with 'Morning!' and, no longer being able to fish my swim, I continued, shouting to them and explaining that they'd chosen to site their boat right where I'd been fishing, and indeed catching. After a somewhat laboured and rather lengthy explanation of my frustration as I stood in the water with rod in one hand and baited hook in the other waiting to re-cast, all I received in reply and after a moment's pause was, 'Morning!' The brief exchange however, was good-humoured and very soon after their departure, the resident roach, rudd, bream and hybrids were coming to my landing net once again and a diplomatic incident between two prominent EU member states had been avoided.

Back at Ballyshrule Lodge, on the days we returned with wet coats and leggings – and there were many – we'd hang these up in the vast tackle shed. This 'shed', was actually another building, next-door to the six-bedroom bungalow that we stayed in. We stored a lot of our kit there and it also housed spacious bait fridges. The building was never locked, yet there was no doubting Ray's assurance that our belongings and bait would be safe and always there when we went to load up the next day.

Coaching commitments and other priorities seem to have prevented me from getting back to Ireland in recent years, but like Cransley, I have many fond memories of my visits there. The sport wasn't always brilliant and neither was the weather. These days, I no longer have a desire to go back for a week's fishing… it would have to be at least a fortnight!

RADIO AND TV TIMES

A good few years ago, I found myself standing with other club members at Needham Lake after a match and chatting with Alan Fuller. Alan, a boat-builder and keen angler, had been asked to cover fishing in a weekly roundup of sport on Radio Suffolk. He'd sat in for Bill Smith, the sailing correspondent and had seemingly made an impression. As a consequence, when Bill returned to pick up his sailing reports, Alan agreed to visit the studios each Friday, when he'd interview guests and cover different aspects of fishing. After another local club turned down an invitation to go into the studios and chat with Alan, GVAC's Steve Gilbert duly obliged.

A week or two later, Steve was asked about further potential guests and in particular, who might be suitable to go in and talk about pike fishing. One young man who, whilst accomplished in Alan's subject matter, wasn't, it transpired, totally reliable and after failing to turn up, missed out on his 15 minutes of fame.

Alan and Steve's consensus was that I was the man for the job. Apparently, whilst I wasn't exactly Suffolk's answer to Neville Fickling, I could, and had, caught a good few pike and, more importantly it seemed, wouldn't need too much encouragement when it came to talking about the species – or any other for that matter! The fact that I hadn't a long string of specimens to my name didn't seem to be an issue and the following Friday I climbed the steps of the relatively new BBC studios of Radio Suffolk in St. Matthews Street, Ipswich.

I met up with Alan and he explained studio protocol before introducing me to the BBC presenter and the other programme contributors. Having discussed what I'd prepared and our proposed running order, it wasn't long before we were chatting about legered mackerel tails and popped up sprats live on air. Everything went, we felt, rather well that first week, so well in fact, that I went back again to chat about other species, as well as doing regular freshwater match fishing roundups. I was working for Prudential at the time and having to take time off from my evening work. This became an issue, not only because my sales figures didn't justify the time off, but also because several of my colleagues would pull over in plenty of time each Friday to listen to the broadcast, even though most of them didn't actually fish!

After a number of rather enjoyable programmes together, my time as a guest presenter with Radio Suffolk came to an end. Alan and I however, became good friends and we still keep in contact. No slouch off the boat or beach, these days he also does rather well as a session carp angler and my Christmases aren't complete unless Alan calls in for cup of tea and a mince pie.

Just before we leave radio for television though, I'll share with you, the most memorable of our programme slots. That particular evening, we'd presumed that as it was *Children in Need* Friday, we'd have our time on air cut and that the sports roundup would be reduced to accommodate coverage of local fundraising efforts or location reports from presenters. When we arrived at the studios however, it seemed we were quite wrong. Others that also had weekly spots in the roundup hadn't come in and angling had centre stage. Alan and I were allocated more than 20 minutes' air time and I remember the presenter explaining this quite casually. I also remember telling Alan not to worry as the prospect of filling that amount of programme time was sinking in, as evidenced by the expression on his face! I believe we were to talk about small river chub fishing and I explained to Alan (still quite casually), that we'd be fine and that I could talk for as long as necessary. We even had the luxury of a bit of music played half-way through our slot, giving us time to compose ourselves before finishing. The memory I'll keep of my time with Alan on Radio Suffolk, is that of just the two of us, left by the presenter for quite some time, alone in the studio, in complete control and broadcasting to tens of thousands of listeners - well, my family and a few Pru blokes anyway.

Hello Nigel!

Having attained my angling coaching qualification, I had opportunity to receive reimbursement for my services - though any worthy coach will tell you that's not why we do what we do.

I was asked to attend the King's Lynn Angling Association Open Day at Tottenhill Lakes in Norfolk. The day would be part of National Fishing Week and Sky was going to cover it for their weekly angling programme, *Tight Lines*. On arrival, the half-a-dozen or so licensed coaches were briefed and I was fortunate in securing the job of demonstrating rig-tying. I say fortunate, as it was a very warm day and being on rig-tying duties meant I was stationed in shade under a gazebo. It came though, at a price. As a procession of groups of youngsters came and went, moving from groundbait mixing to me and then on to casting and pond dipping, I soon realised the enormity of the task in hand. Each youngster was to leave the gazebo with a complete rig, ready for the afternoon's fishing - and there were an awful lot of youngsters! I did though, go prepared, was well organised and managed to deliver.

My brief for the afternoon was to assist with the youngsters as they caught, or attempted to catch, fish on the rigs that I'd tied with them in the morning. There were though, plenty of pairs of hands available bankside and as more than one tangled, I never found the opportunity to leave that welcome shade of the gazebo; I was far too busy untangling and retying rigs.

Abi and Cameron came along for the day and looking at the video tape of that particular edition of *Tight Lines*, they may have been on screen longer than me. I was kitted out with a small microphone and battery pack and spoke of placing a small shot underneath the pole float to help it cut through the surface tension of the water. During the programme, I can be heard likening the water surface to the skin on a bowl of custard. I also remember going to great lengths to explain very basic groundbait techniques to Sky presenter Nigel Botherway. Nigel was far too polite to stop me whilst I was in full flow and explain that he was a more-than-accomplished angler himself!

The day was a great success and the clip of youngsters, coaches and organisers cheering at the end of the footage aired took, should anyone be interested, just the three takes.

The following year some of our junior members attended the same event and the Environment Agency were there once again with their fish tank and crayfish tray. As visitors left late in the day, the EA prepared to depart also and their officers started to drain their tank and gather up the crayfish for transportation. Remaining visitors stepped back as the officers began picking up the crayfish that were splaying their claws characteristically. Youngsters especially, stood well away from the tray and the vicious looking pincers. Not so those from GVAC however. I remember smiling as they dived in and grabbed the crayfish, watched by the EA officers and other, slightly concerned onlookers. Unfortunately, GVAC's Manor Farm Lakes have, to this day, a resident population of the North American signal crayfish and the native white-clawed examples in the EA tray held no fears for Ashley Miller in particular, who'd become more than used to dealing with the former, when helping his dad empty traps at Battisford.

HOLME PIERREPONT HISTORY

The National Water Sports Centre close at Holme Pierrepont, Nottingham was the venue for the 1994 World Championships. Very early one Saturday morning I set off from home and headed north to watch the first day's action. After England's disappointing results in Ireland in 1992 and Portugal in 1993, a change in fortune was anticipated as the crowd gathered at Pierrepont that morning. I was nearing the end of my spell with Prudential and made a point of ensuring that I was free that particular weekend, not wanting to pass up an opportunity of seeing the world's best coarse anglers in action. Bob Nudd was among those I went to watch and he'd already won an individual world title in the former Yugoslavia and another in Hungary.

Arriving at the match venue, I found a burger van and overcame the language barrier to order my breakfast. I realised eventually, that I should've asked for a bacon cob, rather than bacon roll; after all, I'd come a reasonable way up the A1! With breakfast downed I made my way to the furthest section of the match length and found myself chatting to Steve Gardner as he waited behind his peg. Double-decker buses were used to transport anglers to their taped off fishing zones and Steve was one of the first on the bank. We discussed the less-than-ideal bright conditions and clear water, before he made his way to his fishing platform and started to assemble his kit. I also spoke to the late David Bird, former president of the National Federation of Anglers. I remember he asked where I'd travelled from and we chatted about Suffolk, a county he wasn't overly familiar with.

As well as the unfavourable weather conditions, cormorants had evidently ravaged fish stocks and pre-match practice sessions had seen weights rarely exceed a couple of pounds; a far cry from those taken by the likes of Alan Scotthorne and Jan Van Schendel in the 1990 European

Supercup event on the same water just four years before. Alan was on the banks of Pierrepont again in 1994, alongside his Barnsley teammate, Dennis White. With Bob and Steve, Kim Milsom completed the home team line-up on peg 18.

Around 90 minutes' setting-up time was followed by the groundbaiting period before eventually, the match got underway. I remained behind Steve Gardener until he landed his first fish. The crowd was, by then, several deep and I fought my way out to make my along the match length. As I'd anticipated, I couldn't get very close to the other England anglers and as the first day's action drew to a close, I stood in the world's longest queue for doughnuts behind Alan Scotthorne on C18. (I should make myself clear, Alan wasn't serving doughnuts, the van just happened to be behind his peg!)

Steve Gardener's efforts saw him eventually finish 12th in E section, having seemingly been on the wrong end of an area that had produced reasonably well. Bob Nudd took the day's lowest section-winning weight of 550gm in D section, but Alan Scotthorne failed to catch. In A section, Kim Milsom returned a very respectable four points on his championships debut. Dennis White's sixth place in B, from an otherwise barren area saw England's total of 53 points put them in third place behind France on 43 and Sweden on 41. The Swedes had caught several gudgeon and with no blanks, were surprise leaders after the first day of competition.

That evening I drove home before returning the next day with a couple of friends for company. With over 60 dry nets on the first day and the French, like England, carrying just one blank, there was all to play for. Surely, Alan Scotthorne, apparently England's best angler in practice, would catch? Could Bob Nudd build on his first day section win and make it a hat-trick of individual crowns? I, along with an estimated 30,000 others, would know by Sunday teatime.

18 Again!

As we arrived on the Sunday morning, it was clearly evident that the size of the crowd would increase way beyond Saturday's – as would the queue for doughnuts! Before the second day's action commenced however, further drama unfolded at the draw. Having pulled out peg 18 on the first day of the World Championships in Ireland in 1992, England manager, Dick Clegg had also drawn it two days running in Coruche, Portugal the following year. With the England team having worn the number 18 tabards yet again the day before at Pierrepont, the Hungarian team manager promised a prize for Dick, should he draw the same number again (and from draw position 18 would you believe), on the second day. He did just that, and duly accepted a bottle of wine from his generous counterpart.

Although 18 certainly hadn't been England's lucky number in Ireland or Portugal, being placed on the same peg two days running on this occasion meant that the whole team knew exactly where their swims had been fed the day before. This was to prove vitally important in a contest where the fishing was so hard. Part of England's team plan was to fish sliding floats at distance and video footage of the competition clearly shows thick rubber bands trapping the mainline on their anglers' reel spools. This technique enabled them to cast and then stop their float tackle at the same distance each time in a similar fashion to when using a line clip when feeder fishing.

Dennis White was in A section on the second day; Steve Gardener in D and Kim Milsom in E. Alan Scotthorne in B section therefore, knew where Dennis White had caught the day before and Bob Nudd in C, could also place his bait accurately in the hope of a fish or two. Unfortunately, Alan had connected with one of his couple of bites on the first day, only for the fish to slip the hook shortly after.

The second day's fishing got underway and predictably fish showed most in A and B sections. Being on the bank that day, I remember that we almost expected Bob to win his section; our anticipation only heightened by the fact that he was, once again, in an incredibly hard area. After almost an hour, the crowd's faith in Bob was rewarded, as he landed the first of a run of fish and a welcome 7oz roach saw him take the lead in his section, before sport died a short while later.

Whilst it was Kim Milsom's turn to struggle, David Hall's commentary confirmed that Alan Scotthorne had caught and that he was continuing to take fish. Steve Gardener was also doing well in his section, as was Dennis White. Generally however, very few fish were being taken and stewards on every peg noted the exact number on large, post-mounted scorecards. The accuracy and availability of this information meant that spectators were kept up-to-date as the drama unfolded. The anglers also knew what was going on, with the commentary backed up by information passed to them via bank-runners. Virtually everybody therefore, was acutely aware that Mario Barros, the previous year's champion and section winner on the Saturday, was doing well in A section. So too though, was Dennis White…

Although we could hear the commentary, my friends and I couldn't really see any of the action. The anglers were all seated on Octoplus platforms, supplied specifically to ensure that all competitors fished from the same distance out into the water. There was a taped off area for the anglers and the tarmac roadway behind was restricted for use by official members of the press, team managers and bank-runners. We were all beyond the next line of tape and whilst the crowds behind English anglers were several deep on the Saturday, they were even larger on the Sunday and the galleries spread to the sides, well beyond their neighbours. Nonetheless, it was a fantastic experience to be there and to be part of history in the making.

The final scorecards reveal that Bob Nudd did indeed win his section. Kim Milsom didn't catch, but the

French also, had an angler that blanked on the second day. The Swedes faltered and Steve Gardener and Alan Scotthorne returned four and three points respectively. Dennis White managed to hold off 'Super Mario' and top-scored in A section. England's two-day tally was good enough to see them overhaul their deficit and take the match as they finished four points ahead of the French. The Italians too, had improved overnight and collected team bronze.

Rain fell late that Sunday afternoon, but it seemed that few spectators were leaving. Dennis White's performance had effectively secured Bob Nudd's third individual world gold. He was to go on to collect a fourth in Spain in 1999, but he explained afterwards, 'Winning on home soil was something very special.'

Soon after the weigh-in was completed and with thousands of others, we clambered for a half-decent vantage point overlooking where the presentations would take place. Eventually, with the rain still falling, the section winners were announced before England and Bob Nudd were crowned World Champions. The cheers were loud and there were many of them, but the loudest was reserved for Bob.

I read recently, that Bob gave his individual medal to Mark Addy, later having a copy made for himself. Mark was one of England's bank-runners that weekend and had sat with Bob, advising him to twitch his hookbait half a reel turn at a time, to induce bites from the perch… It worked!

Bob's Rod

Soon after that weekend, I entered a competition in, what was then, *Match Angling Plus*, the magazine that became *Angling Times Advanced* in 2003. I can't recall the exact format or full details of the competition, other than a question being posed regarding which team was leading the World Championships at the half-way stage. I used to enter many competitions and won several prizes, ranging from thermal boots to poles - three of the latter in fact. First prize in this particular competition however was, to quote Bob, something very special. I remember being at home a week or two later when a parcel arrived. When I unwrapped it, I found a protective tube and bag inside housing the rod that Bob had used on the Sunday a couple of weeks before.

I remember taking the three sections out in the kitchen and the rod bag was damp and the cork handle stained with groundbait and leam. At Pierrepont, there was the customary heavy groundbaiting on the pole line followed by lighter feeding at 35 metres with smaller balls of leam and joker. Other than during the groundbaiting period before fishing begins, rules dictate that balls of feed have to be formed with one hand only. Neat joker was required for topping up, whilst bunches of bloodworm were fished on the hook. Joker, after initially being separated with damp leam, then had grey leam added in order that balls of feed could be formed for catapulting. As mentioned above, it had rained as the competition finished and packing kit away obviously hadn't been a five-minute job!

Along with the rod, I received a letter of authenticity and have taken both to open days and coaching sessions. A year later I raffled a day's fishing with it at a presentation evening and a young James Oxborrow later landed over 50lb of carp on it. It's a lovely, well balanced rod and when once explaining to someone that I'd won it, I was asked whether I'd actually fish with such a sacred item of tackle. 'Well,' I replied, '…you wouldn't have a Ferrari and just leave it in the garage would you?'

CLUB CATCHES AND MEMORABLE MATCHES

As hinted at earlier, if the reader is looking for a recounting of historic captures of monster fish, then he or she will be disappointed. I've fished for over 40 years and there were periods of time when other interests have taken my attention. Playing football every Saturday and Sunday through the autumn, winter and spring for many years, along with midweek training and five-a-side games certainly reduced the number of rod hours I put in when I was younger. I don't regret that time away from the bank at all and it's a pleasure these days to hear youngsters I coach, tell me that they have other sporting commitments to their school or play for their local, football, rugby or cricket team. It's satisfying to know that many youngsters, despite distractions, have the opportunity, and choose to take part in team sports in addition to going fishing. As I said early on in the book, there's nothing like winning as a team. Because of my own involvement when I was younger (and somewhat slimmer and fitter!), I wasn't perhaps, as dedicated-an-angler as some.

Also, whilst some species of fish have flourished, particularly in stillwaters, and the specimen size of these has therefore, increased over the last three or four decades, others haven't. I believe the best roach fishing on the Gipping for instance, has long since been and gone. Those much better qualified than me to comment, will tell you how the inland influx of cormorants has resulted in the decimation of roach stocks and the golden era that saw the capture of so many specimens of this, one of my favourite species, will I'm sure, never be repeated.

Abstraction too, may be one of a few reasons why the average water level and flow rates on the Gipping have fallen since I was a teenager. In consequence - or at least in part perhaps - whilst there certainly may be the odd very good roach along the watercourse that could fall upon an angler's bait; I would say it would do so, more by luck than by design.

I will also say though, that water quality is possibly better than ever and whilst the low, clear conditions of summer and early autumn may make, for instance, catching large chub on my local sections a little difficult on occasion; sport remains good and this species in particular, obliges all year round. In summary, I don't believe that there is anywhere near the number of specimen fish in the Gipping that there once was, and I may have missed the best chances of catching many, if any, from its middle reaches that are particularly noteworthy. I do though, think the river is in very good health and as a possible indicator, I've seen more kingfishers recently than ever before.

Another reason I'd cite for landing very few large fish, is that I haven't fished for them. I can't recall ever travelling to a specific venue anywhere, let alone a local one, just to catch a fish of specimen size. Most of the creditable fish I've taken, I'm quite happy to admit, have been by good fortune – I hesitate to say by accident, because at the very least, I usually know what species I'm trying to catch, even if I'm unsure how big they're going to be! I'll qualify what I've said though, by adding that I have, on occasion, set out deliberately to catch sizeable fish of a certain species. For instance, I have taken Abi pike fishing and have been out with her after chub. I have also taken small groups of school pupils along the Gipping, targeting perch with the aim of catching one or two of reasonable size, but not specifically fish that anyone would regard as specimens.

Coaching, and my love of it, has seen me spend an awful lot of time on the bank, without wetting a line myself; again, no regrets here. Only months before I started writing this chapter I was coaching with Colin Booker and a youngster, fishing for the very first time landed, with our help, a double figure common carp in immaculate condition on freelined crust. The fish succumbed to the simplest of baits, the cheapest of tackle and the most basic of tactics. The excitement of the lad who caught the fish was possibly matched only, by his mother's joy and the coaches' sense of achievement. Ivan Marks used to say that knowing you'd put a sparkle in a youngster's eyes was the best feeling in the world. He wasn't wrong, and Colin and I can recount many similar experiences. So, whilst coaching with GVAC's Junior Academy or working with Suffolk County youngsters for instance has meant missing opportunities to fish myself; experiences like the one mentioned above, are more than adequate compensation.

Another, and perhaps rather contentious reason I'd give for my not catching more notable fish, is that I carry, and use, accurate scales; I'm certain a lot of anglers don't. A one-pound roach in my mind, is a big roach and a fish an ounce or two under, doesn't weigh a pound. A local, respected Chub Study Group member regards a four-pound 'chevin' from the Gipping as 'big'. Chub of five pounds or more on the waterway are scarce and as such, he sees them as 'specimens'; I'd agree completely with his perspectives. On several occasions I've weighed fish for other anglers that, were it not for my scales (and, on occasion, my scepticism at their own initial estimate), would certainly have grown by the time they met with their mates in the pub next!

Whilst match fishing provided me with an opportunity to arrive at a venue at a civilised hour with a peg available; another reason for me going down that particular route was that there were no arguments about weights of fish caught. Fishing matches for many years, rather than deliberately targeting certain species of fish of noteworthy size, and at times when the quarry might be more obliging, has been another factor in my not having caught any number of very large fish. I always say that match anglers rarely catch fish of specimen size, but they do catch a lot of very good ones.

Of course, lack of opportunity - by choice or otherwise - may be a reason why I've not racked up an enviable list of specimens for the reader to wonder at, but I should also consider whether it's 'cos I'm just rubbish!

I'm not though, completely cynical. In match fishing especially, although there are usually no arguments regarding the weights and one soon gets to know who tells the truth during competition and who doesn't. When practising or pleasure fishing too, I've met many anglers that have caught noteworthy fish and whose word I would never doubt. Over the years I've even fished with several friends and club colleagues that have taken very good fish that I've then photographed for them; in fact thinking about how many, perhaps I really am rubbish!

So, off my soap box and with tongue out of cheek, I've penned details of some of the personally memorable, rather than notable fish that I've taken from GVAC waters, local stretches of the Gipping and a little further afield.

Roach

Nothing to write home about here; to this day my biggest roach remains the Boxing Day fish I landed from the Gipping at Bramford. That fish weighed 1lb 13oz and although I've taken several more weighing over a pound, I've not landed any that go close to my best. I have though, taken several good nets of the species.

A good few years ago I had a pleasure net of roach from Maypole Farm Lake that weighed 19lb 10oz, having packed up two fish early, it seemed afterwards! The day though, remains a memorable one as I fished with Abi and our combined nets of mostly roach, but with a few rudd, easily exceeded 30lb. We'd watched a small deer approach the treeline on the other bank mid-session; experienced a rain shower that was followed by a vivid rainbow and, to round off the day, we watched a kingfisher fly down the lake. Most of the fish were taken on caster and the largest fish weighed no more than 12oz or so. Maypole is an intimate club fishery of only around half-an-acre in size, located very close to my home and for these reasons, along with those mentioned above, that day was a special one.

I'm sure there are good roach in Needham Lake, but not enough to make fishing for them exclusively worthwhile. When I started my club work as treasurer, and having agreed to restock Needham Lake, part of the consignment we introduced were supposedly, very large roach. I say supposedly, because I was told later that many of these fish were probably hybrids, given their prevalence in the trout venue they came from. Unfortunately, many of these fish were found dead soon after, having apparently succumbed to stress. I have caught several fish at Needham Lake that, on first impression, were true roach, but on closer examination, proved not to be. Most of the genuine pound-plus roach that I've taken have been in matches and have picked up worm baits intended for bream.

In the early days of fishing at Needham Lake, there was a bank of weed a couple of rod lengths out that roach in particular used to frequent. The weed provided both food and shelter and at dusk especially, good bags of fish could be taken, with better ones coming to bread flake.

There was a time when good bags of sizeable roach could also be taken fishing up in the water on caster. I remember a midweek evening session with Gary Abbott and the late Terry Keymer. We'd enjoyed catching a few fish, but knew we could do better. We were fishing caster, but as is often the case when fishing shallow, we were missing a lot of bites. Many anglers choose to bury their hook in a caster yet even when we hooked our baits like a maggot we still missed bites. Eventually though, we figured it out; we should have been fishing much larger hooks as the fish were competing for the bait and weren't taking time to inspect it. This was a lesson learned well and one that was to put club pools money in my pocket on several occasions after. The technique was developed: feed caster regularly and watch for swirls just under the surface. Then fish the long pole with a short line, soft elastic, a lightly shotted float and a caster on a large hook. Fishing like this with the roach competing and swimming very fast to intercept loose feed; I found the elastic often pulled from the pole tip before a strike was made. This has been one of my favourite methods in matches on venues where the roach population, overall conditions and target weight deem it appropriate. Most of the better nets of roach I've taken at Maypole or on other venues in matches – Melton for instance - have come using this technique, even if for only part of the session and when the opportunity arose.

I remember being involved with running the junior events on Needham Lake soon after my session with Gary and Terry and passing on what we'd learned - although word soon got around and before long, other members fishing in similar fashion were also taking good match and pleasure nets. We weighed a few good roach bags and these occasionally included pound-plus fish. Needham Lake is my favourite GVAC stillwater venue, but it's deep in comparison to most and certainly not overstocked, but that's part of the reason I like it. The fishing here has changed and whilst roach are still the main target for points-conscious club match anglers, bream will usually put you in the money these days.

The simple pleasure of arriving at a venue, picking a sprig or three of elderberries for the hook and then taking a good bag of roach in late summer or early autumn is one not lost on me. I always keep a good stock of cooked hempseed at home for feeding and try to ensure that each year, whilst living close to Maypole, I catch a net of roach with berries picked either on the way to, or at the venue (there's a bush close to the car park). The first time I fished elderberries there, I used them exclusively on the hook, over cupped-in hemp and ended the session with over 11lb of fish. Many school pupils – and teachers for that matter – have taken carp from Middle Farm Lakes on elderberries picked just feet from their pegs after I've introduced them to the bait.

As for that roach PB; personally I can't see it improving, not unless I find the time and inclination to target capture of such a specimen, and perhaps consider travelling to do so. However, I recently had a conversation with a very competent match angler, now in his seventies, who'd fished in some very good company. The discussion turned to roach and it was reassuring to hear him tell me that he'd love to catch one of 2lb or more; the best roach he'd taken in all his years of fishing, he advised, was 1lb 13oz!

Chub

A chub weighing five pounds or more from the Gipping is, as I alluded to earlier in the chapter, an exceptional fish; as I write, I've yet to see one personally. Having been present at a recent Environment Agency survey on the river at Needham however, and having caught a lot of chub from both the free, and the GVAC controlled stretches of the Gipping, I believe the species is thriving. Until 2011 though, my efforts to catch chub from the river had only been very occasional.

That year, with school and local authority coaching sessions keeping me busy most weekdays between Easter and October half-term and with both Junior Academy and Suffolk County coaching taking up time at weekends, I made a conscious decision to make early morning, or late evening excursions during the warmer months, with chub my quarry. My efforts though, coincided with East Anglia's driest summer for 100 years. With water levels so low, I employed stalking tactics from opening day through to October and after returning from the autumn half term break, a pupil under my tuition managed to catch a reasonable fish during an hour-long session with Stowmarket High School. Almost a dozen trips between June 16th and Halloween were rewarded with 40 chub and although most appeared to be long for their weight, a good number were over three pounds and a few were over four. One, at just over four, I took from the free stretch at Needham on crust. Another of four pounds exactly engulfed a large piece of flake dropped beneath the branches of an overhanging willow tree where the Gipping runs close to Needham Lake. My best fish during that period though, came from the river at Great Blakenham. It weighed 4lb 7oz and again took a piece of crust from the surface. Good chub inhabit this particular stretch, but I took only one fish there in the early months of the 2011 season.

In the following few years however, I banked several more fish of similar size on both link-legered cheese paste and artificial maggots fished close to a heavy, in-line feeder. I did bump into a photographer after one early session as I walked back to my car and he explained that he'd been trying to get shots of the otters that frequent the pool upstream from where I took my first 'four' from the stretch. Whether the presence of otters has affected chub sport there I don't know; what I do know is, that the fish there can be extremely wary, more so than the resident rat that dropped into the river on more than one occasion and swum to intercept my free offerings as I trotted another piece of crust close by with my hook in it.

I haven't witnessed first-hand, any exceptional chub catches from the Gipping, but fishing for the species on such a small river is something that's done most effectively alone. I'm aware though, of genuine captures of larger fish further down the watercourse to the stretches I choose to fish regularly and I hope in the future, to be able to give these areas some time and attention.

The region's driest year on record was followed by the country's wettest in 2012. I'd envisaged that the long, lean fish might put on weight with increased flow levels and with them possibly feeding more avidly. On the opening day of the new season I took a modest sized fish at Blakenham soon after dawn and then headed back to Needham. Late morning, I bumped into young Sam Kennard and, after he'd pinched my rod, he promptly landed two fish in successive casts on freelined meat. We then moved upstream and in the town, we fed a few halibut pellets in a shallow run, observing the fish first back off, before they returned soon after to hoover up the free offerings. With Sam just feet away and watching the fishes' movements from behind thick nettles, I under-armed a hair-rigged halibut pellet and PVA bag rig into the swim. A short while later, Sam's running commentary confirmed that the largest fish of the small shoal was approaching my bait and within seconds and after a very positive bite, my 12' Fox Barbel Special was bent double. A few moments later and without hesitation, Sam jumped into the shallows after the fish made for the sanctuary of the near bank reeds. After he scooped up the fish unceremoniously in my landing net, I helped him out of the river. The scales confirmed that I'd banked a fish of over 4lb on opening day in 2012, just as I'd done in 2011 and Sam, it seemed, was as pleased as I was!

    Coaching commitments throughout the summer saw me grab just a few opportunities to get out with my own rods. I did though, venture a little further afield and get around to banking my first chub from the Waveney. Early one morning mid-week, I took a brace of fish on crust, before heading across Bungay Common to target perch with a float rod and centre pin. Also, accepting an invitation from fellow Norfolk Anglers' Conservation Association member, Martin Burgess; I managed a couple of trips to the Wensum either side of Christmas. On our second trip and in mild, and much more favourable conditions than we'd endured on our first, we shared a nine-fish haul, both banking fish of over 4lb. Again, no monsters and nothing to shout about; but the fishing was enjoyable and I was in excellent company.

    A five pound Gipping chub, modest as it may seem to some, for me, remains a fish of considerable merit. Rather than get preoccupied by the size of fish banked, I do tend to regard sizeable chub as a pleasant surprise whilst enjoying whatever sport my local river throws up by way of the species. Size, for me anyway, isn't always everything and as a consequence, I still find myself some early summer mornings, kneeling among stinging nettles, trying my hardest to outwit and bank, fish that weigh no more than a couple of pounds. I take great pleasure in catching them on all manner of baits from big, juicy slugs to marshmallows and given my tendency to eat more of the latter than the chub get a chance to, I endeavour to remember which of these I'm using!

Pike

I remember as a young GAPS member, landing a pike of over 13lb on the Gipping at Sharmford Lock. Since landing that, my first double figure fish, my relationship with the species has been flirtatious, rather than anything approaching obsessive. I enjoyed fishing the Pike Cup matches with GVAC and with club colleagues, once logged and monitored the size and growth rates of individual fish that we identified by various scars, tail and fin markings. I've landed several double figure pike from Needham Lake, including one on the same day that I had the privilege of witnessing Jim Last's 19lb fish.

Before Braham's A, B and C pit were dug into one, I landed double figure pike from what was BSP's water. In more recent years however, I've rarely fished for pike. In 2011 I did take a 'low double' from the Old Nene at Benwick on my first visit after Rob Lincoln suggested I stick a pike rod in the car with some sprats ahead of a winter roach session. I've been back with Abi and plan to return again.

One of my more memorable sessions – though not entirely perhaps, for the right reasons – was the first match of one of the aforementioned GVAC Pike Cup series. During the course of the match I had three 'takes'. I started the day on a spinner and a short while into the match, landed a foul-hooked bream - and there's me saying that the venue's not overstocked! Soon after, I landed a shoe (that's right, a shoe!), although once again, it was foul-hooked. I did though, go on to land a pike as well, after changing to deadbait. In the remaining two matches, I managed to avoid the attention of 'nuisance' bream (and indeed shoes!) and landed pike in all three legs, eventually winning the competition.

So, once again, no monster fish landed, but plenty of good ones and plenty of fond memories. The GVAC pike matches did perhaps, tend to be more social occasions than competitions, but we did catch several good fish. There was also added incentive to catch the largest pike of the series. Alan Parsons, proprietor of the food stores in the High Street at the time and a long-time club supporter, donated a bottle of whisky each year to its captor. I recall this competition within a competition fuelling the event's intensity a little. I've never been a big whisky drinker (by that I mean I've not drank whisky regularly, but readily admit to being rather large and having sampled it on occasion, if you get my drift); but we all wanted to receive Alan's prize come presentation night, along with the cheers that went with it.

Perch

Sitting on one of the early pegs at Needham Lake on 1st November 1990, I'd been enjoying some good sport on the waggler. With the water temperature dropping however and with it losing colour as a consequence, I'd changed down to a size 23 Mustad 90340 barbless hook (for those that remember the pattern) and a 12oz hooklength – line diameter to breaking strain ratios weren't as good then. Late on, I hooked a fish that took off on a powerful run. The run however, came to a fairly abrupt end and after a short episode of nothing much more than head-shaking, a large perch came across the top of the water to my landing net. I'd been fishing some way out, but in the deep, snag-free peg, the fish didn't give me too much trouble, even on a fine set-up. I rang Hazel and she drove to the lake with my camera; the fish weighed 2lb 5oz.

As with pike and indeed most species, I've not deliberately targeted perch with any real conviction. In 2011 however, I came within an ounce of banking a river 'two' when float fishing on the Waveney at Bungay Common. One of several good fish I took from the GVAC stretch of the Gipping late in 2013 also took the scales round to close to two pounds. All fought like demons on a centre pin and float rod, but whatever their size, I'd challenge anyone to show me a fish that looks more striking than an autumn perch landed from a river and I certainly intend to give this species much more attention in the future.

Dace

I'm sure dace are a species that many anglers don't give a second thought to. I remember as a teenager though, catching good bags of these fish from shallow stretches of the Gipping alongside Barham Pits. Fishing a short, buoyant stick float in the fast flows, with a maggot or pinkie on the hook whilst loose-feeding the same, the fish were often very obliging, even on very warm, bright summer days. These fish weren't very big, but as fast biters and being as prolific as they were, they provided great sport during a few hours' fishing.

Roach sessions with friends on the river at Great Blakenham were punctuated occasionally by the appearance of large dace. We caught them to around 12oz; a very good size for the watercourse. Returning to Blakenham one Friday in November 2012, I took a bag of fish on caster with the river rising. At the tail end of the weir pool, I moved my seat-box up the bank twice during the session as the water rose. With an increasing amount water coming through the pool after heavy rain, I fished a slack that had formed and where the resident dace were shoaling up. My net of 63 fish included over 40 dace, most of which were of a consistently good size. It was an unexpected pleasure to be reunited with the species; I was after roach and had been told that dace were no longer present in the stretch. The session was even more pleasurable, given that once again, I'd partnered my float rod with my beloved centre pin reel.

As far as other species go, I have caught some good fish, but most, if not all of the tench and bream for instance, I've landed in matches. I've looked to catch what I felt I needed to on match day to win or do well or have, more often than not, been happy to accept what came along during a few interim pleasure sessions. I've been fortunate enough to win a good number of matches on Needham Lake and with what I feel were occasionally, very good bags of fish. I've also won matches at both Manor Farm and Middle Farm Lakes, including the very first competitive event at the former. I recall fishing only around a couple of dozen open matches however, with successes limited to section wins at Alton Water and Kettlebaston for instance, framing at Suffolk Water Park in the odd silver fish event and occasionally doing well in the British Sugar opens at Bury St Edmunds.

    As the title suggests, I've devoted the second half of this chapter to sharing some of my experiences from club matches, along with accounts of one or two other competitions. The following pages won't, I'm sure, impart a wealth of knowledge of devastating techniques or baits, and no revolutionary new methods will be discussed; I hope however, that they bring back a few fond memories to those that were with me on the bank at the time. Whilst fishing may seem an incredibly dull and boring pastime to many, I hope, above everything else, that the following accounts and anecdotes put an occasional smile on the reader's face. When taking part in matches, like all the other branches of the sport I've sampled, the fishing, for me anyway, was never just about catching fish.

Kettlebaston

I remember the Kettlebaston open I alluded to earlier reasonably clearly. I'd travelled with Craig Fulcher who'd previously attended club junior events, and who, like several others, later joined his former tutors in senior competition. I'd never seen the match venue before. This was a rectangular-shaped pit with a stock of carp, bream, roach and a few very large rudd. Tackling up, I perched my seat-box on the loose bricks at the end of the lake where I'd drawn and noticed small shoals of roach and rudd around old tree roots close in. Whilst setting up more appropriate kit for larger fish, I also set up a light whip rig for the roach and rudd. With the sun shining and carp showing, I asked anglers nearby whether surface baits were permitted, given I had a box of Chum Mixers with me. I remember not getting a straight answer; for whatever reason, I received more of a mocking. Mind you, it did seem that of the 33 competitors, 31 that knew each other and then there was Craig and me!

It's not permitted, in most matches, to introduce bait before the whistle, so I'll say no more than I was extremely confident that the roach shoaling by the tree roots close to my peg would take a maggot. However, before the match started, one of the locals came over and brazenly explained that he'd fed a few pinkies and the fish were taking them! One thing I did notice though, was that the rudd that mingled with the roach, were slightly smaller and the roach would be the 'weighers'. I knew that once fishing, I'd aim to catch the roach, by picking them off and watching the hookbait rather than the float; the water was very clear and this may have accounted for the presence of the big rudd.

As the match unfolded, some sections started to produce big fish, but not mine. A guy in the next section was losing them with alarming regularity and he eventually ended the match with just two fish for 11lb. My area was quiet and after an unsuccessful dabble for larger fish, and having noticed my new friend along the bank catching only small rudd; I set about trying to win the section. I finished with around 5lb of roach, beating Rudd Man comfortably.

Craig, it seemed, hadn't drawn well and therefore spent part of the match sitting behind me offering encouragement. After we'd packed away and loaded up the car, we waited for the results. Now, given that everyone seemed to be someone else's brother-in-law (although Craig and I were just good friends), the presentation was a kind of mutual back-slapping affair, with the two of us spectating. That changed however, when my section win was announced; I can't recall anyone clapping me! I was though, still happy to take the cash and after someone asked how I'd fished, I couldn't resist telling them how I'd caught all of my roach on Chum Mixer... shortly before being bustled into the car by Craig and leaving in a bit of a hurry!

Alton Water

The Alton Water open matches attracted some well-known anglers and I remember drawing Alton Hall Lane on one occasion, but still being able to hear Dickie Carr on the opposite bank!

The venue fished very well in those days, possibly because the water level was low and the bream, the target species in most matches, were shoaled much more tightly as a consequence. I believe my best pleasure net there was 21 good fish. I also remember another pleasure session for reasons other than the obliging bream. It was a long walk from where anglers parked to the bank, and in broad daylight, my car was broken into as I fished. A window had been smashed and my stereo had been taken, along with several cassette tapes. Apart from everything else though, I was disgusted that my Thompson Twins cassette had been left on the passenger seat; the thieving scumbags obviously had no taste!

GVAC held regular club matches on the reservoir and to this day, award the Alton Cup annually, albeit that the competition is now fished on other venues. Over time, the Alton bream became finicky and I decided therefore, to try hair-rigging baits. We had no knowledge then, of the knotless knot and so tying a hair to accommodate a couple of bits of corn on to the shank of a size 14 Drennan Carbon Chub (my hook size and pattern of choice for the Alton bream then) was a fiddly affair. It transpired though, that my efforts would be worth the time and trouble.

In those days, I wasn't the most accomplished bream angler in the club by a long chalk (not that I am nowadays either, I should add) and I was fairly rubbish with a groundbait catapult. I'd discarded use of a depth marker for initial feeding and resorted to using a large feeder for baiting up. I felt I'd always play catch-up to the guys that had proven track records with bream, but wondered if hair-rigging - a technique that match anglers regularly employ nowadays - might just improve my odds a little.

For one particular club match, I hadn't drawn that well and was pegged just on the inside of a large bay. The anglers with more water in front of them would undoubtedly take more fish. As the match progressed though, I picked up odd bream and was ahead of one or two of the better anglers. As I continued to land occasional large bream, I was asked by one of them what my bites were like. I explained that after a couple of tentative tugs, the quivertip would pull right round and the fish would be on. My response seemed to confuse one or two that weren't able to connect. I fished a Silstar Traverse-X feeder rod at Alton in those days and in that match, picked it up from the rests several times as it formed a semi-circle. I ended the match with over 30lb and made the frame.

I'm always happy to pass on information should anyone ask, but I hadn't then, broadcast my hair-rigging. After the match though, word had been passed along the bank that I'd done okay and, within earshot of some of those that had been experiencing finicky bites, I was asked by someone privy, 'Did you get 'em all on the hair?' With my book having a family target market, I'll not repeat what I was called by the aforementioned club colleague and friend who'd asked mid-match what my bites were like!

First Team Win

Alton wasn't the only venue where I used the hair-rig in club matches. I believe the first team match I fished was the friendly event against Blue Circle, three years after GVAC had been established. A team of 13 had been invited to fish against workers from Claydon's large cement manufacturing facility at their pit at Great Blakenham. I hadn't seen the venue before, but friends of mine, whose parents were employed by Blue Circle, fished there. The water was renowned locally for its numerous small tench. We also knew it held plenty of carp; by all accounts though, these fish rarely showed in matches. Just in case however, I put a carp rod in my holdall and arrived at the match with quite a bit of both six-foot long sections sticking out the top of it. After assembling my float rod, I remember plumbing up and finding that, after shelving off close in, my swim shallowed up again some 20 yards out. I chose to fish the first part of the match at the bottom of this shelf with a waggler and perhaps try the shallower area later in the match, especially as it was warm and as it might attract the odd carp.

After the whistle things went quite well. I had two small perch, followed by a few roach. Within the first hour or so, I'd put almost a couple of pounds of fish in the net whilst many seemed to be struggling. My Blue Circle neighbour had landed a small carp and didn't add to it during the rest of the match. The sun got higher and the sport got even slower; the fish had seemingly shut up shop in the oppressive conditions. I was reasonably pleased with myself as the match was to be decided on weight and it was clear I'd already done okay. However, it was also clear that, to catch anything else, I'd have to do try something different.

I've always had a philosophy of preferring to not catch big fish than not catch small fish, if you follow. So, with nothing doing at all, I baited the carp rod set-up with two bits of sweetcorn on the obligatory hair. I then made a gentle cast with a two-ounce bomb, placing the bait on top of the shallow bar. I didn't need all that weight, but a heavy bolt rig was de rigueur back then. I'd under-armed some groundbait to the area at the start, but added sweetcorn to what was the same mix as I'd used on the waggler line. Having clipped a washing-up liquid bottle top on the line, I pulled some slack off and began to tackle down my float rod, knowing that it was redundant.

I didn't get far with my attempts to pack away as, within minutes and without warning, the indicator slammed against the rod and the reel handle became a blur. To coin a cliché, the rod took on a healthy bend as I lifted into a reasonable carp and, as I stood up to play the fish, it seemed that 25 pairs of eyes were watching me. I landed the fish safely, just as a teammate appeared at my shoulder. 'Do a bit of carp fishing then do you?' he asked. After explaining my tactics, I cast out again and continued with my packing up, before once again, up went the indicator and round went the reel handle. As I played my second carp, I noticed that over to my left, my inquisitive teammate was also into one. I ended the match having had three carp runs. I landed two and pulled out of the third. By today's standards, the carp were small and the tactics employed to catch them a little primitive to say the least. Nonetheless, the brace took my net to 13lb 8oz and I picked up the winner's pools as a result. Ian Craft – the only other angler to land one of the larger carp – returned 7lb 3oz and GVAC won the match comfortably with a total weight of 38lb 11oz. Ian and I had, on our own, almost matched Blue Circle's combined weight of 20lb 13oz. The following year I drew in the corner of a bay and caught virtually nothing; that's match fishing!

Colchester Police

Following that first victory at Great Blakenham, I've been fortunate enough to win several GVAC team matches, including a few against Colchester Police. Historically, these events have also been decided on weight rather than points and many years ago, our opponents used to take us to various venues that held good sized carp. One lake we fished was extremely deep, but the stocking level meant those who knew what they were doing, could still put a good weight together. The first year I fished that particular venue though, I didn't – know what I was doing, that is.

Having mostly been a spectator the first year there, I vowed to do better next time. I read up on the 'wag and mag' technique and arrived on match day with a gallon of bait and a packet of powdered strawberry carp flavouring. I tackled up my float rod with a waggler and 3lb line straight through to a small, forged hook. As the match started, I cast out and got busy with my catapult, waiting for the rod to pull round and ignoring indications on the float.

With such a large quantity of bait, I'd sieve the maize meal from my maggots every now and again before tipping them from the large container into my bait box. Partway through the match though, I mislaid my sieve. This didn't affect my fishing; I just got covered in maize and strawberry flavouring every time I loose-fed! From memory, I hooked five carp and pulled out of two, eventually landing three for over 17lb. This was top weight by a mile and GVAC won the day comfortably. I'd fished, standing in the margins, unaware of how steeply the bottom dropped away and on advice, didn't go looking for my sieve. When I pulled my keepnet out at the end though, it was laying in the bottom with the three carp. A year later the lake was drained and we all got to see exactly how deep it was, dropping off sharply just beyond where I'd stood in the water fishing 12 months before.

With that lake drained, the following year we fished another carp venue not far away. Once again I arrived with a gallon of maggots and fished the match in similar fashion. I took a bit of stick for my choice of hook size - a forged 22 - but won the day with two large carp; these were the only decent fish landed by anyone. Steve Gilbert was second with, if I remember rightly, a pound or so and GVAC had won away from home again. We didn't always get our own way though, and the large, doorstop-like team trophy has crossed the Essex border more than once.

Coaching commitments and personal preference see me fishing few, if any team matches these days, but I have managed to fit in a number over the years and another that I took top spot in was the very first match at Manor Farm Lakes, Battisford. I drew peg 16 in the near corner of the far bank of the top lake and returned over 8lb. My weight comprised mainly small fish with three tench of a pound or so that I took after scaling down my hook size late on. With my head down and with my neighbour catching odd fish too; I was unaware of how difficult things were for everyone else. I knew that I'd done okay, but was surprised to learn afterwards, that some had struggled for ounces. Peg 15 returned a little over 3lb and that was about it. I've won matches on both lakes at Battisford, but have also had the experience of being the only GVAC angler not to win his (or her) two-peg mini-section in an otherwise whitewash. Mind you, on that particular occasion, I'd had a reasonable match - or so I thought – but was beaten narrowly by three carp on cat meat next-door!

Abi too, has done well at Battisford and we've had a one-two there in a team event when I topped the returns on the small lake and she won on the top and where more anglers were pegged. On that occasion, small fish nets won the day and I pipped her by only an ounce or two. It was usually a different story in the Mixed Pairs' Cup matches we fished on the venue though, where she usually carried me to the silverware… she says!

Melton

The lakes at Melton, near Woodbridge became famous for their very large bream. I understand that these fish reached specimen size by feeding on the freshwater shrimp in the slightly brackish water; the venue being in close proximity to the River Deben. During my visits with GVAC, most winning nets were made up of carp, bream and skimmers. But after a couple of matches spent finding my feet, I realised that there were plenty of roach to be caught. Given I'd always been better at catching roach than carp, I decided to give the former priority in competition. I've always said that if you want to compete with roach when there are carp or other large fish in a water, as well as ensuring the target weights are achievable with the smaller species, you have to get your head down for the duration of the match and focus purely on the job in hand. I don't think I've fished more than seven or eight club matches at Melton, but have been fortunate enough to pick up cash in all but two or three.

    The first time I tried an all-out roach approach, I drew close to the car park and on plumbing up, found no discernible shelf. I settled on starting long on the pole, but plumbed up with consecutive sections removed, almost back to my footplate. This resulted in me having an evenly spaced line of Tipp-ex marks up my top kit. If everything went well and I could feed the fish in closer during the match, it would be a simple matter of removing a section and adjusting my depth slightly, as I coaxed the feeding roach in. I also fed groundbait and hemp with a few casters on my top kit lines either side of the peg right at the start, just in case the roach were already in close, albeit that the relatively still and bright conditions told me they wouldn't be.

    Having also fed long at the start, I was soon taking roach at regular intervals once the match got underway. Not too long into the five-hour contest, I started to remove sections and the fish obliged by following my casters, which by then, I was loose-feeding, as I looked to catch on-the-drop. I also picked up a small tench which gave my no. 4 elastic a decent stretching.

I knew several anglers were catching carp on the feeder, but had vowed to keep my head down for those roach. I could see club skipper, Bob Gunn landing good fish every now and again on the opposite bank, but carried on taking roach. With the fish feeding just a couple of sections out as we went into the last two hours, I switched to a lighter float. I continued to loose-feed caster by hand, most of the time after I'd unhooked a fish and before I put my rig back in. Dropping a rig over a handful of loose-fed casters usually results in a very confident take, with the float sliding under almost horizontally. I picked this tip up from an old video featuring Roy Marlow and have never been frightened to delay getting my bait back in the water by a second or two, feeding beforehand and knowing the potential of the tactic. Catching roach up in the water can be frustrating, but when the fish are confident, it's also very enjoyable and a great way to get several pounds of fish in your net quite quickly.

With around 40 minutes to go, my catch rate and stamp of fish improved as patchy cloud began to obscure the sun. With reduced light levels, I began laying my rig in very close to where I sat and much larger roach were taking both single and double caster. I'd switched to a blue Hydrolastic (5 to 8), yet still had to add my fourth section a couple of times as the larger fish ran after taking the bait. I even had a couple of holidaymakers stop beside me and say that they'd never seen anyone catch fish so quickly - I explained that not all days were like the one I was enjoying! Occasionally the sun would reappear from the patchy cloud and my catch rate would stutter as a result. When the final whistle went though, I was still catching well.

Afterwards, I knew I'd done okay and checking the clicker on the side of my seat-box, was sure I'd had more than 20lb. Bob eventually weighed in somewhere around 25lb and I took second spot with 22lb-plus. It wasn't a huge return, but when most fish are around an ounce or two, that weight of roach takes a lot of catching. Bob even apologised for beating me, saying that he'd watched me most of the match and would rather have been doing what I was.

In another match soon after, I drew a deeper peg on the opposite bank and with the stiff breeze blowing straight into my face as I tackled up, I knew I'd do well with the roach. I was conscious though, that the roach weights I thought were achievable could be beaten easily by carp nets, but not from pegs everywhere on the lake and not by every angler. Once again, and to hedge my bets, I fed long at the start of the match, as well as close in. My instincts regarding the wind and depth of the swim proved correct though, as I began catching on my inside lines as soon as I dropped my rig in.

Bizarrely, in all the matches I've fished for roach at Melton, I've only ever been broken by carp once or twice. I always cup my groundbait in for roach when I know carp are in a venue in any numbers; knowing also that the roach are widespread and not therefore, ever far away from where I feed. I believe that the noise of balls of groundbait thrown in will only attract the carp, which I often see as a nuisance. This match was no exception to what I'd experienced; I wasn't bothered by carp as I put together a personal best match-roach bag. To my left however, and slightly obscured by trees, Colin Provins was hooking, and landing carp of various sizes. At the weigh-in, I was pleased to take over 30lb of roach and a few rudd to the scales, but Colin, having taken a good fish in the last 20 minutes, had pipped me. Once again though, I'd had a thoroughly enjoyable five hours' fishing, finished second in the match and was going home with pools money. I'll admit that my net did include one carp; it weighed about two ounces! It's also worth noting that Colin, whom I've known since very soon after GVAC was established, has lined up in England's beach fishing team on more than one occasion, so I wasn't too disappointed to be beaten by him.

I believe I won my section in the next match, even though some large bream had shown and the carp were feeding well. The matches I fished at Melton though, were memorable not for the results, but for the quality of the roach fishing. Those nets may seem modest to some, but they were good bags for the venue and when fishing GVAC matches, one is in the company of some very competent anglers.

I was fortunate enough win with roach at Yaxley, fishing similar tactics at the Quiet Sports venue off the Ipswich-Norwich road. Bob Gunn and Phil Slee had advised me beforehand, that roach could be worth targeting, although odd carp were showing. I started fishing 'to hand' at around five metres, near the edge of the reeds that flanked my peg. I became frustrated however, by missed bites and so reduced the length of my rig substantially and resorted to fishing 'long pole, short line'. Fishing with little line between the tip of the pole and the float had the desired effect and I started to connect with around four out of five bites, rather than one in five or six as I had been. To save time, I chose not to break down when swinging in fish, but lifted the pole up above my right shoulder as it slid it back on the roller behind. The momentum of the fish as they left the water brought them to my left hand for unhooking, as I then dropped the front part of the pole on to its rest beside my right hip. With each fish in the keepnet, I'd throw out some more loose feed before re-baiting the hook. The pole was then shipped out again without having to put sections together. The technique looks clumsy when not executed correctly, but with practice, can save valuable time in matches. I'd advocate breaking down however, for 'net' fish on most occasions. Oh, and I should add that, to show my gratitude for the information they shared with me; I passed a bottle of beer each to Bob and Phil at the next match.

Returning to Melton; as for actually winning a match there, I managed this eventually with bream, rather than roach. On a mild March day, I drew a peg at the top end of the lake and having 'bombed up', spent 10 to 15 minutes feeding groundbait with chopped worm and caster via a feeder. My neighbour and I began taking odd skimmers before he hooked and a little later, landed a very large fish about an hour into the match. I knew that I was catching quicker and so wasn't overly concerned; but any thoughts I had regarding what I needed to do to catch up disappeared when I too, landed a rather large bream a short while later.

From what I could see, sport appeared patchy, although Phil Slee had also landed a big bream and Bob Gunn appeared to be catching well. At the end of the match, we'd enjoyed a steady day's fishing and the three of us made up the frame. My one large bream weighed 6lb 13oz and I was fortunate enough to take top spot, but Phil's fish, at 7lb 3oz was the largest of the day. What I remember from the match is that Phil, Bob and I all fished the feeder, but with a variation on a theme. Bob had used a swingtip; Phil, a quivertip, but with direct monofilament on his reel, rather than standard line and I'd used braid. Those anglers that had targeted bream without the additional refinements had seemingly missed out. It could have been though, that Bob, Phil and I are just lucky and drew the best pegs…

Ardleigh Reservoir

I've included a short passage on Ardleigh as it was in a match there, that I realised the potential of braid. I'd travelled to the reservoir to fish a three-way team event between GVAC, British Sugar and Eastern Electricity. On the day I was fishing for British Sugar, having been a regular at their charity open matches at Bury St Edmunds.

I'd read that braid was being used as a mainline by a few match anglers and purchased a spool of Feeder Tension from Vale Royal Angling Centre for the princely sum of £19.99. Word was, that the match at Ardleigh would be a feeder affair and my new line would therefore, be put to the test.

We fished in mini sections of three, comprising one angler from each team. To cut a long story short, one of my neighbours struggled and ended fishless and one small perch was all the other could muster in five hours' fishing. Whilst I didn't do any good overall, I did at least, win my section. I took around 30 small perch and, in the last 20 minutes, also banked a bream of around five pounds. I put the resounding section win, at least in part, down to the effectiveness of the braid.

Over time, I found the positives easily outweighed the negatives regarding the use of braid as a mainline. I went on to use it exclusively when fishing for bream on GVAC's original home venue and it effectively paid for itself several times over.

Needham Lake

I won my first match on Needham Lake with 2lb 12oz of roach and perch and I don't recall doing anything special (probably a lucky peg!). More recently, because of coaching commitments, I fished just four matches on Needham Lake in 2011. The last of these on 6th November was a bit of a non-event for half of the 10 anglers taking part in the sweep, as we seemingly drew the wrong end and could do nothing to bring fish to our baits. With higher water temperatures however, and with the bream more widespread, I managed two wins and a second in the three matches held on the venue between 31st July and 28th August. In the final match I took five bream from peg 4, for 17lb 5oz.

GVAC introduced small bream to the water in the eighties and the species have, it seems, always thrived. As alluded too however, the changing nature of the venue has also seen a variation in approach and techniques employed, if not by all pleasure fishermen, then certainly by match anglers.

Years ago, the peripheral weed was sanctuary for the resident roach. The lake's water level fluctuated and anglers placed their seat-boxes on the shingle below the grass bank or stood in the water catching roach and rudd to hand. Nowadays, a revetment and purpose-designed metal platforms round the permitted fishing area of the lake provide comfortable fishing for all.

One evening though, before the bream began to feature heavily in results, I found myself sat on my box in the water, with my pole tucked into my wader top, as was the fashion then (this was before the advent of the pole sock) waiting for the start of the match. This particular Thursday evening fixture was designated as the East Anglian Daily Times Angler of the Year qualifier, with the final scheduled for Alton Reservoir sometime after. With the match underway I fished the long pole and took small roach steadily throughout the first couple of hours. In an effort to secure a top three place, I'd patiently fed casters, one pole section beyond my main maggot line and in the closing stages, slipped two casters on to a larger hook before I shipped out and waited patiently...

As the float slid under slowly, I began to count: 'One-one thousand, two-one thousand, three-one thousand...' I lifted the pole sharply and deliberately and connected with something. The fish responsible however, wasn't the first of a run of large roach, nor was it a bonus tench; it was an eel, and those that know me, know how much I dislike eels. Still, on that occasion, I gritted my teeth, landed the fish and it saw me into the final. Unfortunately, my luck didn't hold at Alton and for me anyway, the final was a bit of an anti-climax.

The Needham Lake bream grew, and later became a worthwhile target for match anglers. Initially, short evening and five-hour matches alike were won with roach or odd bonus tench. As the bream reached a few pounds in weight however, they became the preferred quarry for those after an outright win, rather than league points. In the early days of GVAC, anglers could groundbait via a feeder only and, with better bream beginning to show more frequently, this was the method employed by some. I wasn't as proficient with the feeder then as I am now and preferred to use the waggler, often fixed at depths of 10 feet or more. I'll admit to practising for club matches in those days and found that heavy feeding with casters initially, then fishing red maggot over loose-fed samples of the same paid dividends and I can recall feeding six to eight pints of bait on occasion.

A couple of us also used Sticky-Mag in an effort to get the bait down quicker and attract match-winning skimmers. One match I remember doing well in was the annual team contest against Eastern Electricity Board (as they were then). I took nine bream for around 11lb on the fixed waggler, having fed as described above, and won the match easily. One of my neighbours blanked and the other weighed in just over a pound. The bream continued to grow and one autumn match saw me take over 40lb from peg 25. That net, made up of mostly bream, but which included one large roach, remains my best match weight from the venue. As for the anglers each side; one blanked and one returned 8lb-plus. By that time, feeding groundbait via a catapult was permitted, but as I still do now, I'd put my faith in feeding accurately via a (clipped up) feeder at the start of the match and then waiting for the fish to move in.

I remember having a good run on Needham Lake when, from the five Evening Series matches I fished, I drew the coveted river bank four times. In the final leg though, I drew peg 1. Then, peg 1 was one of the better railway bank draws, so I wasn't too disappointed. Casting diagonally to my right, I spent a good 15 minutes baiting up as usual. With around two hours' fishing time remaining, I took half-a-dozen bream for around 22lb. Second weight on the night was Steve Barnes on the river bank with 4lb of roach. Steve had utilized his famous pole-feeding tray, which enabled him to get several balls of groundbait into his swim in one go before he started fishing. In the two-and-a-half hour event, the tactic was one that saved valuable time and Steve and I returned top weights on our respective banks, but fishing different methods for different species. As for the series, young Greg Hammond pushed me into second spot and my mistake - apart from not fishing all six matches, that is - was, we agreed after, my use of a sweet groundbait mix, instead of fishmeal.

From what I'd learned in that particular competition, I switched to fishmeal when looking to catch Needham Lake bream. Given the occasional lack of colour at the venue, I settled on a green mix, feeling that fish would feel confident moving over it. I'd also found that, despite using relatively small hooks and fishing with braid, the fish remained seemingly very finicky. Over the years, I'd won matches from most areas of the lake. I'd also won with bream more than other species, but I wasn't 100% confident with my approach. I'd found that, although bream appeared to move on to my bait and were apparently happy to feed – the small movements on the sensitive glass quivertip always announced their presence – it took some time for bites to develop... or not, shall we say.

With the water well coloured after rain, I remember winning a February match from peg 5 with seven bream for over 30lb. Given the time of year and low water temperature I used pieces of worm no bigger than the maggot I tipped them with. A small hookbait on match days seemed to be what was needed to keep odd fish coming, once they were in the swim. The tactic though, was just as effective come the summer, but it took time before I realised that fishing with such finesse – size 18 hooks or smaller, to 0.11mm or even 0.10mm line – was what was often required.

I regard worm as the best hookbait for bream and I usually tip a worm segment with a red maggot or a caster. I often also, use a floating maggot to tip the worm; my theory being that its buoyancy will slow the rate of fall and make the bait more attractive to any passing fish. In the first year or so of my bream fishing at Needham and as a matter of course though; I'd scaled up my hook size when reaching for the worm pot and shortened my hooklength. I'd found over time however, that for the old, large and very often finicky bream of Needham Lake, these tactics didn't always result in the 'rap rounds' that we may have experienced previously. I'd played around with terminal set-ups and lengthening my paternoster that the feeder was attached to resulted in less resistance to taking fish and better indication on the tip. I believe the breakthrough however, came during a long conversation with former world match record-holder and fellow coach, Dennis Willis. Whilst these fish may, on occasion, take large pieces of worm, double sweetcorn etc. confidently; match days often saw them seemingly eager to feed, but wary of hookbaits. I'd caught several good-sized bream and noted that even with small hookbaits, they'd often be hooked lightly, just on the edge of their mouths.

Dennis's suggestion was to increase the hooklength to a couple of feet or more. I then figured that the fish would take the worm bait gently in their protrusive lips, manipulating it carefully, rather than sucking it up in one go. I believed that with reduced resistance and with no large hook catching on their lips as they gingerly accepted the offering; the fish would eventually take the worm into their mouths.

Following our discussion, I entered the 2009 Evening Series on Needham Lake as confident on a method as I'd ever been. The two and a half hours' fishing didn't leave much room for error, but one bream usually meant a section win at least. Five hours was plenty of time though, to feed accurately, having bombed up to locate any slight variation in depth that might prove attractive to any feeding bream.

I'd practised my casting and looked at small differences in technique. I'd also looked at colour of groundbait and presentation. I examined how I fed too. I had no hesitation in spending as long as 20 minutes at the start of matches feeding my swim or swims, accurately with a feeder. On no occasion, did I see anyone that used the same tactic, feed for longer. After being criticized by one fellow competitor for feeding a lot of bait, I challenged them to see how little was actually used in the process (I'd already carried out such an exercise myself). Towards the end of this initial feeding, I added only crushed casters to my groundbait. Having counted how long it took for my (full) feeder to reach the bottom; on the last four or five casts when feeding, I made a point of yanking the rod back hard before the feeder reached the bed of the lake. The idea behind this particular tactic was to deposit a cloud of groundbait above my initial feed that might encourage fish to feed in it. The fragments of caster that would take a while to sink or that would even, be suspended in the last few feet of water for some time; would perhaps attract smaller fish. This activity I felt, could bring in the larger bream.

After casting to the clip when initially feeding, I dropped the rod on to its rest, looking to ensure that I was replicating as accurately as possible, my casting when I'd be fishing with a bait on the hook later. My aim was to ensure that I reduced any variation in rod position that might increase the area over which my feed was spread. Accuracy for me was absolutely everything and I wanted to ensure that any bream that wandered across my feed and that chose to get its head down had no difficulty in finding my hookbait.

After my first 'payload', I had no hesitation in spending five minutes or more re-feeding during a match in an effort to get the bream feeding again in earnest. This particular tactic often brought me additional fish, particularly late on in matches.

I used a varied selection of feeders in different sizes and taped up the holes on open-ended models to ensure that all my feed was deposited where I wanted it and that none was lost on descent, unless that's what I intended. I also ensured that I had feeders of the same capacity, but with varying weights. I looked to be able to reach the same distance by increasing the weight of my feeder if, for instance, the wind increased during a match; it often does on Needham Lake! I also wanted to ensure that I could reduce the weight of a feeder if I felt resistance was preventing bites developing.

Admittedly, I made odd mistakes over the next couple of years and still found that, on occasion, the bream just wouldn't play ball. I also made an error of fishing the pole and looking for points on a couple of occasions, rather than having the courage of my convictions and sticking with the feeder. Nonetheless I was to enjoy considerable and consistent success in subsequent matches on the venue after examining my whole approach.

Between 4th June and 4th October 2009, I fished seven matches on Needham Lake for four outright wins (from pegs 9, 10, 15 and 17) and a first in section (peg 9) and my results seemingly warranted publication of a four-page article in the June 2010 edition of *Match Fishing*.

The magazine's editor at that time, Dave Harrell, had invited submissions from match anglers earlier that year and on receipt of mine, he made contact, requesting I post some suitable photographs on disc. I duly obliged and the article appeared just before the start of the 2010 Evening Series. As Murphy's Law dictates however, I blanked in the first match! Having taken quite a bit of stick, I did redeem myself though, with a section pick-up, a third and a win from the remaining five matches (from pegs 8, 16 and 10 respectively). Bizarrely, I blanked in the final match, having drawn peg 10 for the second week running and having left my reels clipped up from the week before when I'd won. Once again, that's match fishing.

Prior to completion of that series, I fished a team event against Diss AC and won that match with a net of skimmers for 17lb 3oz, taken at a distance of 55 reel turns from peg 19, but only after I'd got things completely wrong on the same peg in a previous evening match. Phil Slee had told me exactly where to fish when I drew the peg a second time… I should have spoken to him sooner!

Then followed the four matches in 2011 mentioned earlier in the chapter. Looking back at all my results in the three-year spell spanning 2009 to 2011; I'd won eight of the eighteen matches I'd fished. As many as 23 anglers fished these events, with 10 being the fewest and the average attendance being approximately 16. Along with the outright victories, I had one second place, a third and won my section twice. That gave me 12 pick-ups from the 18 matches.

I hadn't broken any records, but all things being equal, I could have expected to win a couple of matches at the most from the 18. The results were extremely pleasing, but I'd also learned a lot through questioning and analysing my approach and discussing my experiences with others. I accepted though, that coaching commitments restricted opportunities for me to tackle other venues so thoroughly. I also realised how professional and dedicated our top match anglers must be, given that they're able to produce and replicate even more impressively consistent results on different venues and with many more anglers on the bank. But what I also realised, was how I could take what I'd learned regarding analysis of approach and use it in my coaching.

The three-year spell of matches at Needham detailed coincided with the beginning of my professional coaching career and that in itself was a particularly steep learning curve. It would however, be the voluntary work with Suffolk County youngsters, where attention to detail and thorough preparation would prove to be so important, in the quest for success that started back in 2007.

WHOLE LOTTA ROSIE

One morning when Abi and Cameron weren't yet a year old, I went into their bedroom having heard from downstairs, the noises that children of that age make when they've just woken up and need changing, feeding or both. 'Hello Rosie!' I said, noting Abi's bright red cheeks as she sat bolt upright smiling at me. The nickname stuck, and from that day, Abi's been known as such by several family members and a few close friends. I have, therefore, borrowed this chapter's title from a 1978 single by one of my favourite rock bands.

Given that their parents both fished, it wasn't too long before Abi and Cameron were on the bank. They'd often sit on my lap having a dabble with a top kit after a match and one August Bank Holiday, we took them to their first Evesham Festival. They were just a few years old and were both asleep in the back of the car by late afternoon. With accommodation booked nearby, Hazel driving and the event in those days, being sponsored by John Smith's, I'm sure I wasn't far behind them!

As they got older, it was only natural that I'd encourage them to come fishing. I took Cameron along to a few junior events with GVAC, but as with most young boys, he also had other interests. He was in the cub scouts by then and when, on one occasion, I mentioned a forthcoming junior match, he advised that he would be camping that weekend. 'I'll go, Dad!' Abi exclaimed, and she did.

We took a trip to Thornham Lakes, the venue of the match in question and she soon got to grips with hanging on to a few metres of pole as small, but hard fighting carp tried to pull her in the opposite direction. Having arrived for her practice, I had Abi sit on my platform, with its legs lowered. I placed a seat-box cushion on one side with room for bait boxes and a landing net on the other. We pegged the keepnet (we were obviously hopeful!), out in front, along with a bank-stick and v-roller. The next step was to show her how to feed by hand or with a catapult, to attract those carp. As is usually the case, it's easier to coach someone when they're catching fish and before long, Abi was doing just that. We kept things simple and experimented with baits and, come match day, she was ready to approach the competition just a little differently to the other youngsters.

Our junior events then, saw us incorporate two age categories and Abi was in the under-12s. The match was spread over three small lakes and she'd drawn one of two that held the carp of a size usually required to win. Keeping things simple and noting how adept the carp were at knocking the bait from the hook, I'd bought a small pack of steak and had cut this up into small pieces the night before. The rig was just 18 inches of line to a strong, barbless hook. I instructed Abi to bait the hook with a piece of steak, feed the pole out to 'top kit plus two', lay it on her v-roller and start feeding pellets. When the elastic pulled from the pole, it was a simple matter of her stopping feeding, shipping back and netting the carp, just as in practice.

The steak worked a treat. It was tough enough not to be knocked off the hook and Abi soon got into a rhythm as I divided my time between keeping an eye on her and helping with the supervision of the other competitors. I remember, with several parents on the bank, I was able to spend a good deal of time on both the other lakes. By the end of the match, she'd done rather well, taking almost 21lb of small carp. It was the summer of 2001 and Abi had won her first match aged just nine. The second placed angler returned an ounce under 6lb and in the older age group, 15lb 9oz was top weight - not a bad start to her match fishing career!

Very occasionally, Abi and Cameron were on the bank together. In one junior event at Creeting Lakes, Cameron even pushed his sister out of the frame, but modestly, he's never made much of it. As he got older, he became more and more interested in computers, and gaming with his mates was obviously more appealing than getting up early for a match or spending time riddling maggots and mixing groundbait the night before.

Abi's enthusiasm gathered momentum after her first match. After her impressive start she began to frame regularly at GVAC junior events and made her mark early in the annual Mid Suffolk District Council-sponsored events.

Later in 2001, with a dozen or more youngsters divided into the obligatory two age groups and spread along the railway bank at Needham Lake, I remember her setting her stall out for roach, as others looked to the feeder for an outright win. She fished maggot and pinkie over Van den Eynde Supermatch groundbait and caught reasonable roach throughout the short contest; she'd been warned though, that her peg could throw up a surprise late on.

In the closing stages, I was away from her peg when she hooked something that definitely wasn't a roach. It led her a merry dance on her number 4 elastic, but under the watchful eye of club colleagues, she managed to net the fish and with it, the winner's trophy for her age group. The 'surprise' was a modest-sized, but very lively tench. To this day, Supermatch remains her first choice roach groundbait - and her father usually gets the job of mixing it for her even now!

The following year, and with the fishing a little harder, she retained her title, taking a couple of pounds of small roach on pinkie fished on a size 22 hook at eight metres. In 2003 though, the hat-trick eluded her as a young James Head pushed her into second place from the next peg.

Nene National

As a junior angler with GVAC, it was only a matter of time before Abi was called upon to travel with Andy Wilson-Sutter's young Suffolk County squad. Andy was good enough to channel a lot of effort into putting representative teams on the bank and he was ably supported by GVAC parents. It helped that very competent junior match anglers at GVAC seemed to come along in pairs: Adam and Joe Slee, Daniel and James Oxborrow, Mark and Greg Hammond and Luke and Ashley Miller for example; throw in the three Benningtons and GVAC could have entered football tournaments too!

It was in 2003 that Abi reached the next milestone in her match angling career with a request for her to join the NFA Junior National squad on the North Bank of the Nene. At the time however, I wanted to ensure that she'd continue to enjoy her fishing and not be put under any unnecessary pressure, so we chose to go along to the event as assistants and spectators. Looking back, I feel that she'd have had nothing to fear. Whilst Suffolk's youngsters may have been competing against the best in the country, it didn't seem that high level competition fazed either the management team or the competitors.

Early on the morning of the match, we met up with Andy in the Tesco car park just off the A14 at Bury St Edmunds. Before heading on our way however, we helped him dismantle most of his van's broken exhaust pipe and load it inside the vehicle with the fishing tackle. He also explained how he'd prepared the squad's groundbait the day before using a cement mixer!

On a blisteringly hot day, Abi and I spent most of the match watching Ashley Miller pick off small perch from the shade of his umbrella. Despite the lack of silverware, Suffolk's contingent of anglers, parents and siblings seemed to get a great deal of enjoyment from the day. In addition, those fishing gained valuable experience ahead of future events. The squad's enthusiasm rubbed off on both of us and Abi made her county debut in the National Junior Angling Association Challenge on the Bridgewater Canal soon after. It wasn't all plain sailing, but Abi went on to be one of the most consistent members of the squad, returning several high section placings and picking up team silverware along the way.

Having sampled the national circuit, Abi began to work hard on various aspects of her pole fishing. She was getting to grips with carp and I remember the fun and games she had netting a seven-pound fish that she'd hooked on cat meat near the end of a club match at Creeting. Fish of that size were rare on that lake then and her white Hydro elastic was stretched to its limit.

Despite the distractions of carp, we continued to work on Abi's roach fishing and with Maypole Farm Lake not a mile from our house in Great Finborough, we made a point of having a few early season sessions on the water. I remember the first time she fished with hemp and tares there and with her set up and ready to go I looked to get my own gear sorted on the next peg. As I finally baited up, having fed a large pot of hemp, I asked Abi how many fish she'd had… 'Fifteen,' she replied. I then asked how many she'd had on tares… 'All of 'em!' she shouted back.

Abi had several double figure roach nets at Maypole and she familiarized herself with the light line tactics often required for the species. She learned to appreciate how effective casters could be and her ability to catch mixed nets of fish stood us both in good stead. In 2004 we won the GVAC Mixed Pairs' Cup together for the first time. In the 2006 event at Manor Farm Lakes, Battisford, she topped the returns with 8-12-4, her maximum points score carrying my paltry 4-13-8!

I was even more outclassed in the same event five years later when her net of carp at Barking took the scales round to 156lb 9oz. I returned 106lb 12oz and Reece Page's 118lb 9oz splitting us in the frame. Her catch was all the more remarkable given that the fish then, weren't very big and all of four ounces or over had to be netted under club rules. I remember having one eye on her on the opposite bank as she landed almost 300 fish on paste. In the five-hour match, she'd averaged almost a fish-a-minute.

Looking back, it was around 2005/2006 that something seemed to click with Abi. It was evident from her results that she'd suddenly found another gear. We talked through approaches to matches, but it became clear that she was adapting during competitions and thinking for herself much more. It was also clear that she was often able to put me right afterwards!

On a Mission!

In 2005, Abi was pictured in the *Angling Times* with one of her roach nets. She had a proper seat-box by then and had claimed one of my long poles. We travelled to the 'Women in Angling' conference at Holme Pierrepont and shortly after, she won a Fox Sideliner margin pole for having a letter that championed the cause to get more ladies on the bank published in *Advanced Pole Fishing*. Further letters to various publications saw her pick up a rod, supplies of hooks and a second Fox Sideliner. Inspired by Wendy Lythgoe and Lucy Bowden, whom she'd met at Pierrepont, she sent her catch details to *Improve Your Coarse Fishing*, collecting several of their 'Mission' badges. Also in 2005, she won her first Ladies' Seymo Shield with GVAC and before her 18th birthday, won it three times more.

    A visit to *Go Fishing* in 2006 saw Abi return with a brand new Garbolino G796 - and me with a reduced bank balance! She parted with her own hard earned cash a year or two later as she added a G-Force Power to her armoury.

'Pink Wellies Step Forward'

Former world match record-holder, Dennis Willis had been an assessor when I took my coaching qualification. Shortly after the course, he invited me, along with other GVAC coaches to the Norfolk Anglers' Conservation Association Open Day. Abi came along to assist, as we coached a procession of participants that booked half-hour slots at Bawburgh Lakes. On arrival, we'd pick up our bait, head for our allotted pegs and set up before finding time for the customary pre-session bacon roll from the barbecue. As well as guided bird watching walks, pond dipping with the Environment Agency, tackle and bait demonstrations etc. there were often famous angling personalities in attendance. We met Bob Nudd and I also remember Matt Hayes laughing and joking with Abi and Ashley one year, tipping the morning's rain water off the top of a tent on to their heads!

It was evident that Abi enjoyed helping out and this wasn't lost on Dennis. He and NACA colleague and fellow coach, Dave Nelson sourced funding for her to attend a Level 1 coaching course shortly after her 16th birthday. On GCSE results day in 2008, Hazel and I went to the school with Abi and Cameron where they received confirmation of passes in all subjects. Abi achieved 11 A* grades and when we returned home later that morning, a letter was waiting on the doormat confirming that she'd also passed her coaching course. With the above headline, a full page article in the *Angler's Mail* proclaimed Abi as the country's youngest ever Level 1 angling coach and it was befitting that Dennis presented her with her licence at GVAC's presentation evening the following January.

With the support of the Angling Development Board's Jonathan Wilson, Abi later took her Level 2 course and became the country's youngest, fully licensed female angling coach and Lucy Bowden, previous recipient of this accolade, was one of the first to offer her congratulations.

With their GCSEs out of the way, Abi and Cameron began studying for their A levels. Whilst Cameron kept himself amused – and earned a little bit of pocket money – as an Apple developer, Abi took a part-time job with Sainsbury's.

In 2009, Abi and I travelled to Heronbrook Fisheries in Staffordshire. Heronbrook was to be the venue for that year's Ladies' National and we enjoyed a couple of days' practice on the lakes catching carp and occasional barbel. Shortly after however, the fishery was closed temporarily and the scheduled match was moved to Baden Hall. As a result, Abi put back her Ladies' National debut until the following year.

In practice for the 2010 event, the Specimen Lake at Larford threw up plenty of large carp and a good few bream for Abi and her Suffolk County teammate, Abbi Kendall. Come match day, a reasonable draw saw Abi hook a dozen good carp during the competition. Unfortunately, hook-pulls resulted in her taking only six of these fish to the scales. She returned 10kg 780gm for 16th place in the 61-peg match, one place and just 20gm behind Sandra Scotthorne. One very large common that Abi played for some 20 minutes before the hook-hold gave, would have both won her the section and given her Ladies' Fish O'Mania qualification. Hazel had travelled with us for the match as Cameron stayed at home looking after our flat-coated retriever, Raps. Whilst we were all a little disappointed, Abi had not disgraced herself by any means and she was to get a second bite of the Larford cherry before too long…

Supermarket Sweep

Abi had established that Sainsbury's held annual fishing competitions for their employees. Rather than being laid-back affairs for pleasure and occasional match anglers, I found out later that these were once big money contests and competent matchmen had even resorted to taking part-time driving jobs with the company just so they were eligible to enter. Nonetheless, and despite Abi not having fished the Match Lake before, we arrived back at Larford on 24th July with her well prepared and seemingly quietly confident, having sourced information from Steve Ringer and Rob Lincoln.

The 50-plus peg match comprised four sections and Abi was the only female angler taking part - something not lost on one 'gentleman', given his sexist jibe as we passed him on the way to her peg with her kit and bait.

As Abi set up her four pole rigs, feeder and bomb rods, I took a walk along the bank to eye up the competition in her section. To her left she had a Level 2 coach and on her right, was a rather professional looking match angler with a White Acres regular beyond him. It was evident that this wasn't going to be the walk in the park we expected before we arrived.

The match got underway and with Abi taking odd fish, I headed back to the café for a cappuccino. As I returned to her peg with over an hour of the match gone, I could see that she was catching sporadically, but hadn't as yet, got a run of fish going. The smaller carp and F1s of the Match Lake though, were of much more manageable size than the fish she'd tussled with six weeks before. As she continued to take odd fish, I could see an angler on the early pegs catching up in the water and he was surely to be Abi's main threat. Whilst she was clearly opening up a gap on her fellow coach to the left, the angler on her right then took four good fish in quick succession on the Method, as she looked to continue to catch on her long pole line. I remember her swivelling round on her seat-box and looking me in the eye as he landed yet another fish; nothing needed to be said…

After taking a couple of fish on the Method herself early on, Abi had tried the pole and landed a few more. However, as her neighbour took his run of fish on the Method, she then followed suit. She had however, been advised to fish at a distance of no more than 25 yards and it was evident that her neighbour was casting much further. She stuck to what she'd been told, casting to this distance repeatedly. From that moment on, everything seemed to go like clockwork and she picked up reasonable F1s, small carp and odd better fish; a light shower in the closing stages of the match didn't upset her rhythm.

The coach on her left then followed Abi out. From where I stood along the bank however, I could see that, like her other neighbour, he was casting beyond her catching line. Periodically, I chatted to Rob Lincoln on my mobile phone, updating him with her progress. His repeated advice, which I passed on, was for her was to squeeze her feed over her hookbait hard so that the resident small bream wouldn't be able to get to it and to ensure that each fish she brought in would be a carp. With the match drawing to a close, I stood some 50 yards up the bank, advising him that she'd had around 35 fish. As the match ended though, I was convinced that the angler on the early pegs had beaten her and was hoping that he'd perhaps frame, thus giving her a default section pick-up. I shouldn't have been concerned; he was top weight, but only until the scalesman reached Abi. Her nets totalled around 77lb and she'd beaten the previous top weight with a couple of fish to spare. She'd also almost doubled the weight of the coach on her left and had beaten convincingly, the two anglers to her right. All were gracious after, congratulating her either directly or through me. We cleared her kit and loaded it into the car, before heading back to the café.

A junior competition had been held on the opposite bank and after the results had been read out, the winner of the first of the four sections of the main competition was announced. In her trademark pink Hunter wellies, Abi walked up to claim her £40 section prize and was later confirmed as sixth place overall. The match was won from the area way down to her right and close to the island by a local angler and regular open winner at the venue. Evidently, he'd fed several mashed loaves and fished bread on the pole over the top. As for the chauvinist we encountered on the way to Abi's peg, well he appeared to be in a minority of one and wasn't as vocal after the match!

Water Park Wins

Abi was a regular visitor to Suffolk Water Park and developed an affiliation with the venue. She and other juniors from GVAC took part in our club events there, as well as the occasional open match. Her first senior club match wins there were notched up before she relinquished her junior permit and included three in a row on Match Lake 2.

The 21-peg Matchman League event in September 2009 saw Abi return 44-12-8 of carp for first place from peg 64; despite her texting advice to me during the match, I could only muster just under 17lb for seventh.

In the corresponding match on the same lake the following year, she drew peg 44. This was admittedly, a good peg, and definitely better than 52 where I was. Once again I finished in seventh, perhaps a reasonable result in a 23-peg match, but not up to the standards of some! If I remember rightly, she started off by taking fish on the Method, before switching to the long pole for several more up in the water on hair-rigged, banded pellet. After popping along the bank to give me both advice and a few of her Hobnobs, she netted her final couple of fish on the bomb. She returned 62lb 12oz as her neighbours managed just over 10lb between them (sorry guys) and won the match with over 20lb to spare.

The last of her hat-trick of M2 club wins came on 4th September 2011 in the third and final match of the Alton Cup series. I sat at the top of the bank on this occasion, writing a press release for the county youth squad after their successes on the Grand Union Canal the day before. Abi was on peg 55 and was advised to fish the Method with polony, targeting the bream. We'd been keeping an eye on results ahead of the forthcoming NJAA Challenge match scheduled for the venue and had noted that carp weren't coming from M2 in any numbers. With the match underway, skimmers came steadily, with the occasional larger fish. The information Abi had obtained proved accurate and her choice of tactics correct. Her net of 24-8-0 was just good enough to beat a couple of carp weights and win the 19-peg event to make it three in a row on that lake.

In July the same year, she'd fished the second of the three Alton Cup matches on M1, finishing fourth and winning her section. She had however, missed the first of the series on June 12th, given that we'd travelled back late from the Ladies' National on the Kennet and Avon Canal in Wiltshire the day before. Nonetheless, Abi's two results were good enough to give her third place overall from 28 anglers.

Over the years, Abi and I have had the privilege to meet several high profile and very successful match anglers who have been only too willing to pass on information. This has helped her on occasions such as the Sainsbury's match at Larford. The joy and disappointment we've experienced however, have been at their most extreme when we've been on the bank with the young Suffolk County anglers. As I said near the start of the book, I don't think there's anything quite like the feeling of elation when winning as a team. Conversely, there can't be many worse feelings than having to return to match headquarters at an important event to face your teammates after coming last in your section. Abi suffered this ignominy in her 12-peg section on the Kennet and Avon Canal in September 2008 when Suffolk fielded two teams in the National Junior Angling Association National. Just nine months later she finished second in section at Lindholme in the NJAA Under-18s' Championships. In July 2011, on the third day of the Wall's Solero Ladies' Festival at White Acres in Cornwall, she won her four-peg section on Twin Oaks with 58lb of carp and F1s, narrowly beating England's Wendy Locker for maximum points. Former Ladies' World Champion Wendy was the first to congratulate her. Abi recovered quickly from the Kennet and Avon match and, as mentioned, went on to become one of the county's most consistent performers.

For the second part of book, I'll move from catching to coaching and take a look in more detail at those highs and lows on canals, rivers and stillwaters that we've visited up and down the country with the Suffolk teams.

FROM WILLOW PARK TO WARRINGTON

After the children were born I fished far fewer club matches and prior to 2003 I had no direct involvement with the Suffolk County squad. I also attended fewer committee meetings when Abi and Cameron were very young as these, held on a Monday, coincided with my busiest day's (and evening's) work with Co-op Insurance Society. Whilst I lost contact a little with club matters, I remained GVAC's treasurer and continued to organize the trophy order ahead of the annual presentation evenings, as well as attending on the night. I remember meeting new club members at these prize-givings, whose sons and daughters travelled with the county squad. Not having been part of the early youth development at county level however, I had to do an amount of research before I was able to put this particular chapter together.

In my quest to piece together a history of the squad prior to my own involvement I sent emails and texts to possible sources of information and made follow-up phone calls; I thank the anglers that were in the squad at the time who responded via social media. I also thank various parents, particularly Phil Slee and Stuart Oxborrow who came back to me with accounts of some of the matches. John and Julie Hammond - parents of Mark and Greg – were also extremely helpful. Julie furnished me with her collection of newspaper cuttings, old photographs, match programmes and other information that referred to events in which Suffolk had competed.

After hearing about Suffolk County winning the All England Junior Pole Championships at Willow Park and given that the squad went on to win the same competition many years later when I was part of the coaching set-up; I was keen to find out more about their earlier success. After contacting some of those that were on the bank on match day, I managed to piece together details of who fished and how the match was won. I also understand that following the Willow Park event, the competition wasn't fished for quite a number of years until a new event organizer stepped forward.

I managed to establish that there used to be more than one national pole competition for youngsters. Whilst I'm unsure of all the exact details and I'm not completely familiar with the politics, I understand that there later followed an amalgamation of events and a change of format. This might explain why these days, the team winners of the All England Junior Pole Championships are presented with a large and rather splendid hand-carved wooden perch with the inscription, 'British Youth Team Pole Championship'. As far as I'm aware, this was Suffolk County's first national team trophy.

Searching further in an effort to piece together information, I confirmed Ian Reynolds as individual winner of the 2003 National Junior Angling Association Challenge, on the day Abi made her county debut. Unfortunately, I could find no historical records online that detailed results from NFA (National Federation of Anglers) competitions prior to that year and searches on the Angling Trust website produced very recent event results only.

Delving through Julie's information, it struck me that the young Suffolk County squad entered far more events than I'd realised. During what I believe was their most committed period in the late nineties, I was, as mentioned, GVAC's treasurer and involved in organising the annual presentation evenings. These days, club and county achievements at junior and youth level are celebrated together and with digital technology and the internet at our disposal, it's much easier, I'm sure, to record and access results. During the period I researched, Suffolk teams were competing in several matches most years, on various types of venue up and down the country. In the information handed to me by Julie, I found details of matches at Willow Park, the Worcester and Birmingham Canal, the

Bridgewater Canal, the Grand Union Canal, the Stainforth and Keadby Canal and, more locally, the River Cam, River Waveney and River Yare.

Most communication between team managers and parents before these events was obviously by phone, rather than email or text. Match information was typed, photocopied and posted or distributed by hand. I find it hard to imagine how we'd organise entry for a similar event these days without use of a computer or mobile phone!

An Audience with Tony

In addition to those already mentioned, I contacted Tony and Bev Bennington whose three children: Terry, Tracy and Gary fished for Suffolk. GVAC youngsters still compete today, for the Ivan Goymer Memorial shield, a trophy in memory of Bev's late father who'd always encouraged and supported the children with their fishing. One afternoon between Christmas and New Year, I sat with Tony and Bev, enjoying a beer as the anecdotes and short stories flowed.

As I sat chatting with Tony, he first recounted how he, John Hammond, Andy Wilson-Sutter, Phil Slee and Stuart Oxborrow were with Suffolk's youngsters practising on the Coventry Canal ahead of a big match. With nothing much doing, John agreed to stay with the anglers whilst the others went for a walk. Before long, they came across a gentleman fishing with his elderly father from a narrow boat and they were both doing rather well. On seeing how well, Andy evidently, with a view to projecting a persona of complete innocence, put on his best West Midlands accent and extracted full details of how these two gentlemen were, as they say, baggin' up. Their secret, and one which Suffolk would use more than once in years to come also, was bread. Apparently the anglers even advised Andy that the local Coventry youngsters had been practising the previous weekend and were all catching on it. Returning to the squad with the news, Andy gave instructions regarding hookbait and also ensured that all were supplied with copious amounts of bread feed on the day of the event. I understand that on this particular occasion, bread wouldn't see Suffolk County sweep the board in the match, but I believe they caught many more fish than they would have done, were it not for Andy's subterfuge.

I was fortunate to work alongside Andy as Abi began to figure in the young Suffolk County squad's campaigns. Before our trip to the North Bank of the Nene and Abi's debut on the Bridgewater Canal, Andy's dedication to his squad was clearly evident. Tony explained to me how Andy, on more than one occasion slept in his van overnight before a match. One time that Tony recalled however, wasn't just a case of 'no room at the inn'. Tony explained that Andy had, as he'd done repeatedly, obtained a large supply of maggots for the competition concerned. It was unseasonably warm and with night-time temperatures not falling sufficiently for his liking, Andy chose to sleep with the maggots, turning them periodically during the night to keep them sufficiently aerated.

One story that I've heard more than once, refers to Tony himself and how he crossed swords with a certain England international. Barnsley were often regarded as the team to beat and with many matches being held on canals, the cards were usually stacked in the northern outfit's favour. I'll not name the England angler, but can say that at this particular event Tony took exception to how much help he was giving his squad and told him so. A response of 'Do you know who I am?' fell on deaf ears as Tony advised that he didn't particularly care, given that he was breaking the rules. Tony was threatened with being reported and he in turn countered by making it perfectly clear that he'd do his best to see the team punished and if necessary disqualified if said England angler didn't desist. Having watched from a safe distance, Stuart Oxborrow advised Tony of the identity of said England angler and also broke the bad news after a somewhat heated exchange; 'You'll never fish for England now Tony!' warned Stuart... I understand Tony took this devastating revelation quite well! I have to say, I found it quite reassuring that long before I chose to do my best to bring forth impromptu rearrangement of my facial features by other team managers and coaches in my efforts to see fair play, Tony had paved the way.

Tony continued recounting stories, advising that on another occasion, Suffolk's youngsters had arrived for a competition and were a little awestruck by Barnsley's team clothing. He told me also, that Stuart, once again, took control with another incisive statement. 'Jackets don't win matches,' he told the squad. They duly regained their focus and went about their business.

We carried on chatting and Tony explained to me how some squads chose to hold inquests on the bank soon after events and how team managers appeared to openly chastise their anglers for below par performances – something that Suffolk County coaches would never do. Whilst debriefings are vitally important, ours in recent years tended to be informal and held in fast food outlets on the journey home. The tradition of stopping at McDonald's and Burger King is nothing new, I found out from Tony and he also told me about how one Suffolk County intermediate, believed to be Andy's son Glen, took the Fatty Arbuckle Challenge at Warrington. A substantial menu was laid out and he managed to consume all before him. Joe Slee sat on the next table and watched him finish off with a litre of ice cream. His time of around twenty-nine minutes was well within the one-hour limit and all the more impressive given that he'd had a Big Mac shortly before!

My afternoon with Tony and Bev enabled me to paint a clearer picture of some of the events that I'd been told about and there were also little snippets of information that he shared that, whilst not apparently crucial to the county squad's performances, demonstrated nonetheless, the camaraderie of all involved. For instance, Tony advised, when the youngsters were fishing autumn and winter venues such as the River Waveney at Beccles, Julie Hammond would provide hot teas and sausage rolls for everyone. Husband John would often see that a mini-bus or van was provided for events, just as his brother-in-law, Ian Head has done in more recent years.

Chatting to Tony though, it was evident that possibly his proudest moment during his and his children's time with Suffolk was nothing to do with any squad result, net of fish or specimen landed. No, he told me how for several years Phil Slee often practised with his boys and the rest of the anglers at venues up and down the country. Having admired Phil's technique and prowess on the bank for quite some time, Tony was finally bestowed the privilege and great honour of sitting on Phil's Milo Tardis seat-box!

Julie's documentation included a number of NFA National programmes. Looking through the programme for the event on the Grand Union Canal on 11th July 1998, I noted that over ninety competing teams of six anglers were listed in full, in the three categories of Cadet, Junior and Intermediate. The match headquarters were at Tring Football Club and the map on the middle pages of the document shows locations of the sections between Leighton Buzzard and Berkhamsted. For the record, Mark and Greg weighed in 480gm and 370gm on peg 25 in E and F sections respectively, as confirmed by the draw cards stapled to the programme. With Julie also having kept the *Angling Times* pages that detailed full results, I was able to confirm the team positions. One of the two Suffolk junior teams was placed seventh, with the best intermediate team achieving the same placing. Top performer for Suffolk County was Danny Bradford who returned 4kg 540gm for a win in C section.

In the same event one year later, county teams were in action again, this time on the Bridgewater Canal. Mark and Greg were on the bank again and there was a similarly impressive entry with a total of more than eighty teams competing in the three age groups. I was able to refer to the following Wednesday's *Angling Times* and confirm that the best placed of the Suffolk teams was the intermediate Red line-up that also included GVAC's Dan and James Oxborrow. Suffolk County were placed a creditable 18th in a field of 43 teams. A photograph also included in the full page coverage of the match shows just some of the 400-plus youngsters that fished; little wonder then, that these events were, more often than not, held on canals.

The *Angling Times* report of the 2000 match on the Stainforth and Keadby Canal detailed 'plummeting temperatures and clear water' and it seems the three Suffolk County teams found the going tough. Joe Slee was forced to fish the event with a broken arm and father Phil, having obtained appropriate permission, accompanied him on the double-decker bus to his section before helping him to his peg with his kit and with tackling up. Joint top scorers in the junior team though, were Adam's brother, Joe and Greg Hammond with 24 points. Greg also took the best weight for the squad on the day, returning 850gm. Looking through the results, I noted a certain Emma Pickering as a section winner with 2kg 900gm.

Tracy Bennington threw herself into practice for the 2001 event on the Sibsey Trader Drain and Hobhole Drain, or should I say threw herself in *at* practice! Tony recounted that Ashley Miller also took a dunking, but in much less dramatic circumstances. Whilst Ashley was fishing again soon after clambering out of the water, Tracy, I was told, did a proper 'Tom Daley'! After leaning forward to pick up a plummet that she'd dropped in front of her seat-box, she then over-balanced and fell headlong into the drain. I understand James Oxborrow next-door raised the alarm and shouted to his dad. Stuart then ran down the bank and hauled Tracy out. This wouldn't be the last time that one or more of Suffolk's contingent fell foul of the steep banks and difficult pegs on this type of venue; but it was usually the coaches that took the unplanned dips – as I'll testify personally a little later in the book!

In the match itself, Ian Reynolds top scored for Suffolk taking 1kg 570gm to the scales in the intermediates' event for 22 points. As they had done the year before, Greg and Adam were Suffolk's best performers in the juniors, with 20 and 19 points respectively. Evidently Tracy's brother Terry was pegged next to the individual winner. I was advised by Phil that Terry's heavy and, shall we say perhaps, less-than-always-completely-accurate feeding of caster late on as he acted on Andy's instructions; may have curtailed his neighbour's catch rate a little, but the damage had already been done.

After I'd practised with the squad on the North Bank of the Nene for the 2003 National, landing a solitary (and modest sized by Norfolk standards, Andy advised me) bream on the feeder; Abi and I travelled to the match to watch the squad in action as mentioned in the previous chapter. Phil's younger son Joe sat the match out for bream and with just thirty minutes of the competition remaining they arrived in his peg. Joe evidently missed a bite right on the whistle, just as his swim was coming alive.

Other than the NFA National matches, a couple of events to note included the 'Anglennium' event on the River Cam. The information detailing this event confirmed that the late Percy Anderson and his stewards were on hand to give assistance. The Cambridge Fish Preservation and Angling Society website report later announced Greg Hammond as overall winner of the tournament with 4lb 3oz 8dr. Greg also topped the returns in the 14- and 15-year-old age group. In the 16- to 18-year-olds' category, brother Mark was confirmed as top weight with 3lb 2oz.

I've no date for the event, but one cutting confirmed Suffolk as runners-up in the National Junior Anglers' Anglo-Welsh Leisure Knockout match on the Great Ouse Cut-Off Channel. This may have been the match that Greg recalled when he said, 'It was especially sweet beating Dennis White's Barnsley that day... they usually destroyed us!'

As alluded to earlier in the chapter, junior competitions a decade or two ago saw many more young anglers competing than nowadays. As an example, whilst fifteen teams competed in the intermediates' category of the NJAA National in 2011, there were only six junior teams entered that day and the debate regarding age limits and how competitor numbers could be increased was reignited at NJAA meetings soon after the event. Declining match attendances however, hasn't been an issue confined to junior events, as we all know.

One thing that hasn't changed and something I've appreciated fully, is the amount of work involved in just getting a team of youngsters to a competition, let alone on to the podium. Hats off then, to Andy (Wilson-Sutter), the clubs and officials that supported him and particularly to those devoted parents that travelled with the squad. Who's to say, without all their groundwork, enthusiasm and commitment, whether GVAC would have been involved at the level it is nowadays and whether the county would have been represented at all at junior and youth level in national team events.

As far as the Willow Park win is concerned, I thank Phil Slee, whose sons, Adam and Joe were on the bank that day, for providing me with details of the match itself. Suffolk had two teams fishing and Phil explained to me that his main memory was of bank-running.

On a very warm day, Phil had spotted an angler spraying loose feed and catching carp half-deep. Believing it was hemp that the angler was feeding, he found Andy, who then went for a closer look. On his return, Andy explained, 'That's not hemp, Phil... they're casters!' Andy and Phil then split up and set about getting word to all Suffolk's anglers. 'That was the best bit of bank-running ever!' exclaimed one of the squad as they spun round on their box to speak to Phil after the final whistle sounded.

Some of the types of venues the squad visited weren't those that youngsters from Suffolk would have been overly familiar with, namely canals and drains. Looking back, it's surprising how well our anglers did, especially considering the strength and experience of some of the opposition.

The Bridgewater Canal, Warrington was an example of what the Suffolk County squad members faced when it came to tackling waterways that were somewhat different to those back home. I have a cutting from the Evening Star dated 14th October 2003 confirming that James Brinkley, Karl Westlake, Luke and Ashley Miller, and Abi were GVAC's junior representatives in that year's NJAA Challenge match on the venue. It seems therefore, that Suffolk were one short in the under-16s' category and balancing having an adequate number of anglers for competition against not disappointing those that don't, for one reason or another fish, remains a headache today. I know too, that Suffolk had only two anglers in the four-man intermediates' event and this was to prove a decisive factor come match day.

One of the intermediates was Ian Reynolds and I spoke to him on the River Nene in September 2010. He was packing his kit away after the Winter League final, his Browning Hotrods team having finished runners-up. I caught up with Ian again recently, when he was good enough to give me a run-down of how his match went, back in 2003.

Ian told me that he remembered the match quite well. 'We had a fairly simple team plan, "Pile it in; you've got nothing to lose!"' Ian's lone teammate on the day was Tom Porter, whose swim was seemingly devoid of anything except small perch. Having drawn opposite some rugby pitches at the beginning of a slight bend in the canal, Ian told me how he fed round his keepnet and on the near shelf. Despite not planning to give these lines much attention, he explained, 'I wasn't going all that way and blanking! I also got my posh roach rigs out... just in case someone important walked past!'

Having fed some groundbait, squatts and a pinch of chopped worm with casters at the bottom of the far shelf, he also fed 20 chopped dendrobaena with around 40 casters up it. Half an hour in, Ian wasn't, he said, going anywhere with only a gudgeon and a modest-sized perch in his net. He was then faced with the simple choice of rotating his swims or reverting to the aforementioned, slightly less subtle plan.

'I fed a few more worms and casters down the shelf, then dumped in two big, 250ml pots of chopped worm and another of casters up the shelf and my plan was to leave it and then plug away down it and try and catch a few perch. The next couple of hours were pretty boring... watching the rugby match on the far bank and trying to look like I was busy when people walked past. Then, out of the blue I caught a 10oz skimmer down the shelf, just over halfway through the match, then another two in successive casts as soon as the rig settled.'

With no more bites materialising, Ian then tried up the shelf. 'The bigger skimmers had luckily settled on my '"dump" line and I caught three two-pounders and a couple of smaller skimmers during the next 30 minutes. The bites then totally dried up, so I fed the swim again and rested it, but I never had another fish. The last hour I just watched them swimming around in my keepnet.'

Having told all those that had asked how he was doing, that he'd caught only a few skimmers, Ian remembered with amusement, the look on their faces when he weighed in. In Ian's defence, a two-pound bream is regarded as a skimmer on his local River Yare (as Andy had made quite clear when I caught one of similar size on the Nene earlier in the year). Ian returned 9lb 7oz and won the match easily, with the runner-up weighing in 7lb exactly and the third place angler just 5lb 6oz. One thing I remember vividly was the excitement before the presentation, with the squad knowing that a Suffolk angler would be receiving silverware. It was very apparent that the younger squad members were taking a lot from Ian's achievement

Ensuring that the whole squad benefited collectively from an individual's success, or the success of one of the squad's teams when we had a large number of anglers on the bank, was something that we, as coaches, would be very keen to continue with in the years to come.

As far as I'm aware, the 2003 Challenge was the last event for some considerable time for Suffolk County and it would be another four years before GVAC's youngsters would represent their county in national competition.

BACK ON THE BANK

With the Suffolk squad not having fished together in competition since 2003, I found myself a few years later talking on the phone to Barry Reid, who was then a committee member of the Suffolk County Amalgamated Angling Association. I recall I was in my garage sorting out groundbait when I took the call and remember that I'd attended one or two of the SCAAA meetings shortly before he phoned. Given GVAC's venues and facilities, I'd advised that club coaches would be prepared to manage the Suffolk youngsters, as well as us running our own Junior Academy. Following that telephone conversation, I advised my fellow coaches of the situation and we began making plans to put a representative team into national competition and indeed, rebuild the squad. At the time, Steve Barnes, Barry Miller and I ran the GVAC Junior Academy and consequently, we were charged with managing and coaching the county squad.

  At that juncture, I'll admit that I wasn't prepared for what lay ahead. Probably the most apt quote that illustrates my experiences as a county coach reads, 'Nobody said it would be easy, just that it'd be worth it.' Unlike bestselling authors that have an agent, a publisher and perhaps a team of experienced (and expensive) lawyers behind them; I'm without such luxuries. Consequently, I'll not recount some of the many incidents that have made me question both my sanity and why on earth I chose to put myself forward as a county coach in the first place. Even at club level, there has been more than one occasion when I thought that enough was enough and considered packing it all in. It's at these times though, that I've looked for, and usually found, support from fellow coaches. One thing I know is that I've experienced a lot more aggravation and hassle from voluntary work than from paid 'gigs'. I'll also say that I've never had a youngster that I couldn't cope with, at club or county level... it's always been adults that have caused major problems!

I was naïve, I feel, in believing that all coaches have the same principals and aspirations when it comes to angling development; this isn't, it seems, the case. I'll admit happily, that I'm not perfect and that, looking back, I'd have tackled some issues slightly differently. It seems also, that you can't reason with some people and no matter how noble your intentions, with certain individuals, you'll never get through. I remember taking a week's holiday one summer and giving over most of that time to getting the squad ready and organizing bait for a national competition, only to hear afterwards that we'd been criticized for our lack of preparation! When stewarding, I have been sworn at and threatened on more than one occasion and have been left totally dumbfounded by how some adults have behaved, particularly in the competitive angling arena and in the presence of youngsters. The reader may now appreciate how I came about the somewhat cryptic title of the book.

The appreciation however, shown by hundreds of young people I've coached, the gratitude of their parents and guardians and the progression of GVAC and the success of the Suffolk County squad; more than outweigh what I, and my colleagues have endured over the years.

Coping with Canals

Early in 2007, Steve, Barry and I looked ahead to the NJAA National on the Grand Union Canal and we got together a small squad. Rob Foulger from Diss and District Angling Club lined up for practice at Manor Farm Lakes, Battisford alongside Gipping Valley's youngsters a little over a week before match day. The session saw them fishing the narrowest bank at Battisford, ensuring they became accustomed to fishing with long poles in the narrow confines they could expect on canal towpaths. We also instructed them on how to peg their keepnets out so that they weren't affected by the wash from boats. Obviously all this was new to our anglers and whilst we stopped short of actually taking to the water in GVAC's inflatable dinghy; we did shout 'Boat!' periodically during the fishing, instructing our squad to lift their poles and, when necessary, to re-feed. Two days later we travelled to Milton Keynes and practised on the match venue itself. August Bank Holiday weekend is not the quietest time on a canal, but we figured if our anglers could cope with the boats then, match day would be a doddle by comparison.

  I'd been given details of a plan by an England international following his own team's triumph on the same venue some years before, but I was sworn to secrecy! I'll say no more, other than the plan involved looking for early skimmers before building a weight with small roach and bonus perch. The practice went rather well, although a large barge with some 50 passengers aboard passed through very late in the session and completely killed sport. Some squad members caught skimmers as per the plan, but we soon realised that these were usually no more than a couple of ounces in weight; Abi also had a bonus perch. Rob though, did particularly well and by placing squatt in a small pole cup with dampened groundbait and holding it upside down over his float, feed trickled out very slowly; the tactic brought him bites whilst those around him struggled in the hot conditions.

  With weights recorded and a few photos taken, we headed back to Suffolk. One thing we established during the practice was that we needed to downgrade our elastics from 3s and 4s to 2s and 3s. We also came to the conclusion that uncoloured latex was softer than a dyed brand of the same grade. I spent time at Maypole Farm Lake the following week with Abi, ensuring that her elastics were tensioned correctly; we had great fun with roach that were substantially bigger than were expected back at Milton Keynes!

  Two days before the National though, I took Abi and three of her Suffolk County teammates to the River Yare.

Dennis Willis had been good enough to arrange for Nick Larkin to run one of his teach-ins for us and a couple of youngsters from Norfolk. Nick's a class act and the first fish he caught was a roach of around a pound. The photograph Dennis then took is the one that appeared on Nick's Nisa brochures soon after. With Nick having run through groundbait mixes and terminal rigs, we spread ourselves along the bank close to the Beauchamp Arms and a few fish were had by all. Dennis and I had been liaising regarding Nick's availability and we managed to fit the day in finally, just 48 hours before our trip to Milton Keynes. Those team members that travelled to the Yare were throwing out 1.5oz feeders and fishing two maggots on a size 14 hook, two days before scaling down to size 22s and 24s and with 4 x 12 and 4 x 10 pole floats. I remember reflecting on these extremes at the time and our anglers were (as I was too) learning a lot in a short space of time.

Very early on Saturday 1st September we all arrived at the Peartree Bridge Inn at Milton Keynes for the draw and other formalities. In addition to our full complement of six junior anglers, Robert Murphy and Reece Page were with us as they'd agreed to fish the intermediates' match for King's Lynn. Shortly after and with bait distributed, we had the joys of getting all our anglers to their different sections. We'd get used to these logistics in the coming years and become familiar with many of the local roads, footways and bridges.

As for the match, on a canal that fished hard, our squad put on a good show, beating the likes of Barnsley and District and both Leeds teams to name but three. Top scorer for Suffolk was Alice Bullock, who finished third in section. Abi drew next to Worksop's Marc Playforth, a previous individual winner of the competition in 2005 and later an England trialist. On this occasion however, Abi came out on top, but only just. Bites were few and far between in their area of canal and I chatted to Marc's parents before leaving them to it and going for a long walk. When I returned an hour and a half later, I was somewhat relieved to be told by

Marc's mother, that Abi had finally netted a very small skimmer. Managing then put the odd run of fish together, she claimed a top-half finish in section as a result.

Fishing with older anglers, Robert and Reece both topped a kilo and were rewarded with top 30 placings in the 56-peg intermediates' match. My other recollections include how long it took to put several kilos of Supermatch groundbait through a pinkie riddle the day before the competition and the cold and very welcome pint of lager shandy Ian Head bought me as we all waited for the presentations after the match.

Ten Mile Bank

Traditionally, the NJAA National was always held on the first Saturday in September, with the same organization's Challenge event the corresponding day in October. In 2007 the Challenge was scheduled to be held on Ten Mile Bank in Norfolk. With just four anglers required for a team of intermediates, we sent off the entry forms, having picked members from our then, small squad, that were familiar with both long pole and feeder tactics and who would, we felt, be able to adapt these methods for the Great Ouse. I remember we agreed to attack the venue with a somewhat 'death or glory' approach and with just one Suffolk team on the bank, we were prepared to gamble a little in an effort to bring home some silverware.

Dennis Willis and Judy Ford had made the journey from Norfolk and were with us on match day; Abi was also present to lend support. Before the whistle we all busied ourselves helping our team at their pegs. Barry had brought along some soft-actioned feeder rods which were set up for our anglers to use and we worked our way along the match length, spending time with each of our youngsters. We listened to Dennis' advice and assisted with clipping up their feeder and bomb rods, swapping some over to more appropriate hooklengths and placing rod rests etc. As the match got underway, we stepped back and watched the drama unfold.

Rob Foulger seemed as relaxed as ever, as his dad sat in his van at the top of the bank and before too long, he had two very large bream in his keepnet. It was evident though, that it was going to be tough going on the earlier pegs for Reece Page (A section), and Ashley Miller (B section). Ashley had the pleasure of one Oliver Scotthorne for company next-door and Ollie showed his pedigree with a comfortable section win. I remember he explained to me that he'd practised on the venue a week or two before and that the fish had responded somewhat better than they were doing on match day.

In D section, just before midday, Robert Murphy landed a large bream; another followed 20 minutes later. Despite re-feeding, these were the only fish that graced Robert's net that day, but they were enough to see him finish fifth overall.

During the match, those of us not fishing were distracted frequently by the goings-on in Marseilles where England were playing in the Rugby World Cup. Along the road beside the river, many of us crowded in groups around car radios, listening to the commentary of a narrow quarter-final victory over Australia.

Back in Norfolk and specifically in C section, Rob Foulger's third and final bream came shortly before 4 o'clock and we knew then that he'd secured a top three individual place as a result. With peg D6 empty and being on the end of the match length also; James Jackson of Leeds on D7 made no mistake, taking almost 30lb to the scales for an easy individual win. Rob's three fish gave him close to 17lb which was good enough for a runner-up spot. As Suffolk County's first trophy recipient since Ian Reynolds in 2003, Rob's name appeared in the results along with that of Alex Clements, who finished third in the junior event the same day. Alex went on to win the bronze medal in the Under-18s' World Championships in Italy in September in 2011, shortly after Abi and I had met him at White Acres where he worked during the summer. Team winners of the junior event on Ten Mile Bank were Farnborough, who fed joker in groundbait at 13 metres, as well as fishing a feeder line. Clearly, we had a lot to learn and were going to have to look to familiarize ourselves with baits that we'd not fished with before and get to grips with alien venues when continuing to compete in events around the country.

A YEAR OF MIXED FORTUNES

At the start of 2008, Steve, Barry and I were looking to enter teams in all the NJAA events, in addition to hosting our usual Junior Academy days. After some considerable debate, the NJAA had replaced their annual knockout competition with a June event for under-18s. This new competition would traditionally be fished on commercial venues with eight anglers in each team, four of which would be under-16. The inaugural contest was scheduled for Decoy Lakes, near Whittlesey in Cambridgeshire. The venue includes four 'strip' lakes named Damsel, Elm, Cedar, Oak and Yew and the perceptive reader will have noticed that their initials spell the word 'Decoy'. Abi and I had a recce and caught a few fish on different baits, shortly before another trip was arranged for the whole squad.
  At the time, Tom Pickering was the England Ladies' manager and he'd arranged a day's coaching at Decoy that was aimed specifically at aspiring female match anglers and this coincided with our preparations for the match. Given that Decoy wasn't a million miles from home; I travelled to the venue again, with Abi and her teammate, Alice Bullock, for Tom's session. As one would expect, we learned an awful lot on the day and I sat and observed as he went through seat-box placement, positioning of rollers, plumbing up, groundbait mixes, feeding techniques etc. for three hours or so, before the girls got to wet a line. Once they were fishing, Tom made every effort to spend some time with each angler at their peg.
  The rules at Decoy required anglers to fish with a minimum of 12 inches of line above, and the same below their pole float and as part of preparation for the match, I bought a supply of plastic rulers for the team. I also remember carrying one as a steward and recall the look on the face of one young man who, let's just say, was rather sure of himself when he told me, 'No-one's going to be

coming round with a ruler!' only for me to produce one from my pocket and then challenge him regarding his short rig, mid-match.

As is often the case, match day didn't pan out as expected. A cold easterly wind cut across the venue and heavy rain showers the evening before had obviously affected sport. Modest weights below ten kilos were good enough to win five of the eight sections. Suffolk County finished a disappointing 7th from 11 teams on the bank, with the boys in the team struggling on a venue that we thought would be suited to their attacking style of fishing. The fact that the teams on our neighbouring pegs had finished 8th (Barnsley) and 11th (Milton Keynes) was little consolation on the day. However, Alex Gissing, who'd travelled with us as a reserve, picked up a third-place team trophy after guesting for Leigh Ospreys with Tameside Fox Match's total of 26 points good enough for a comfortable win.

As for Abi and Alice, they drew almost back-to-back in what proved to be the two worst sections of the match. The girls' session with Tom Pickering had paid dividends as Alice finished fifth in her section and higher than any of our boys. Abi returned Suffolk's best score, after taking 5kg 400gm to the scales for fourth in a close section where just over a pound of fish more would have given her second. The respective fortunes of the girls and boys in the team however, would be completely reversed three months later.

Kelly's Heroes

Prior to the NJAA National, Steve and I took a small group for a practice session on the Kennet and Avon Canal in Wiltshire. With no overnight stop, this was easily the longest roundtrip I've ever undertaken for a day's fishing and one that I couldn't contemplate now. It seemed like a good idea at the time however and Steve spent some time planning the excursion. As a result, we fished a very picturesque length of the waterway and enjoyed a good day's fishing, catching mainly roach and perch whilst all learning a great deal in the process.

In the lead-up to the event, Suffolk County colleague, Dave Gladwell introduced us to his young protégé, Chris Kelly. In turn, Chris introduced us to the Tubertini Concord - in my humble opinion, one of the best and most versatile canal floats on the market. At a Suffolk County meeting before the match, Chris met Abi and Ashley and we left them in the Apollo Rooms bar at Harleston to get to know each other and discuss tactics whilst we went through the formal stuff next-door. Dave and Chris also travelled down from Bungay to attend a squad get-together at Barking before match day. By this time, the young Suffolk County squad had swelled sufficiently for us to enter a team in both the intermediate and junior age groups.

We all set off very early from Suffolk on the Saturday morning of the match, having planned to stay over after the event, rather than the night before. This made it a little easier when it came to storing the large supply of bait, particularly the squatt and my feelings were that we'd be able to relax on the Saturday night. So at just after 6.30 a.m. we gathered for a short breakfast at a motorway service station just off the M4. We arrived in good time for registration and the draw at match headquarters in Marlborough and set about distributing bait and giving last minute instructions. The Suffolk captains delivered the goods, drawing peg 1 in both competitions and our anglers headed off to their respective sections.

I helped Abi to C section and on arrival at her peg, she was faced with a large overhanging branch on the opposite bank that extended quite a way across the water and which, in the wind, moved around so much that it would be impossible for her to present a bait towards the far shelf where the majority of the fish would be. Elsewhere, Steve Barnes walked the bank and noticed anglers on the high numbers in A section bringing back slime on their hooklengths as they plumbed up! Once the match was underway, it became clear that it was going to be the boys' turn to shine, whilst the girls were going to struggle for any kind of weight.

In the junior match, Ashley Miller took 1kg 640gm to the scales for second in section. Robert Murphy's superb 2kg 790gm saw him not only win his section, but finish overall runner-up; he was just 10gm short of the winner's weight - a difference of just one small gudgeon!

Ash, Robert and their teammates made their way back to match HQ as the intermediates' competition reached its conclusion; the latter running for an hour longer. I remember visiting a Portaloo sited at one of the designated car parks just as the heavens opened and but for a delayed start due to late arrivals, we may have escaped a drenching. Earlier, I'd watched Chris land a couple of reasonable bream, but Abi and Reece were still struggling when I left the towpath. Whilst I was in the Portaloo however, I received a text from Reece's mum, Debbie, advising that he'd also managed a couple of late bream. These fish were to push him up the section to fourth. Lady Luck though, was to desert Abi completely that day. She too, managed to hook a couple of bream very late on, but she pulled out of one and the other broke her hooklength. She'd seemingly done nothing wrong and I took responsibility for the breakage, having advised her on what line diameters to use on match day; although this was of little consolation to her.

Drawn in B section with the likes of Oliver Scotthorne (Barnsley), England trialist, James Drakulic (Milton Keynes) and double individual NFA National winner, Joel Whitely (Wakefield); Chris Kelly had risen to the occasion. During the torrential downpour Chris remained unfazed - even though he'd left his waterproofs in Steve's car and got completely soaked towards the end of the match. He beat the anglers either side of him comfortably with a second-in-section weight of 3kg 360gm. A few pegs further along, James had shown his class, finishing overall winner with 5kg 630gm and Ollie took the section by (double) default with

2kg 830gm as Chris finished third individually. In the photographs taken post-match, Chris can be seen wearing a GVAC and Suffolk County coaches' shirt after I leant him mine given that he was wet through after the heavy rain.

The only silverware that was to head back to Suffolk that day were Robert and Chris's individual trophies, as the two teams both finished in eighth place. We'd booked accommodation close to the M4 and that night, along with our (not so) waterproof clothing, Abi's pole sections were spread around our room to dry out and the components of my mobile phone and camera were laid out on a bedside table. As far as the latter were concerned though, all efforts to dry them out were fruitless. In the weeks after the National, several buttons ceased to function on my phone and my camera gave up the ghost soon after. Those that see me on the bank nowadays may be familiar with my bright blue Panasonic Lumix digital camera; it's a waterproof and shockproof model!

Barnsley Bloodworm

Following the considerable effort put in at Decoy and again for the National, Barry and I agreed to travel to the Chesterfield Canal near Retford for the NJAA Challenge in October with just a team of intermediates. The match itself was a bit of a non-event for Suffolk as we finished eighth yet again, in a field of ten teams. I recall scraping a thick layer of ice from the car windscreen before setting off early that Saturday morning - a far cry from the record high temperatures we would experience years later at Suffolk Water Park for the same event. Shortly after arriving at Retford and as the teams gathered outside the competition HQ, one of the team managers wandered down the car park offering a match-pack of bloodworm and joker to the first taker and I was quickest to produce a £10 note. We'd arrived with squatt and pinkie, but were very grateful to Barnsley's Alan Davis who was good enough to give us a demonstration there and then, on how to separate the joker with damp leam. He then gave our young team a few guidelines on how we could both fish and feed these baits. We were then able to adapt, if not perhaps, overcome!

Our line-up (in section order) was Reece Page, Ashley Miller, Robert Murphy and Abi. Despite having bloodworm and joker at our disposal, the low overnight temperatures and cold, clear conditions saw few anglers break a kilo, with the junior match length fishing much better than the intermediates'. Abi was pegged two away from Worksop's Danny Huxley, a team bronze medallist at the World Junior Championships in Portugal in 2006, and his sixth-in-section 510gm was an indication of just how hard the fishing was. Abi battled the cold that we both struggle with and was grateful to return just 150gm. Reece and Ashley both finished seventh in section as Robert top-scored with a fourth.

Despite our disappointing team placing, we'd learned a lot from our trip. Gavin Liversidge had also been in Abi's section and he went on to finish third in the following year's Angling Trust event at Cudmore. I watched him and Danny 'double leam' their joker just before the match started and on my return to Suffolk, made a point of researching suitable groundbait mixes. I then obtained a supply of both damp and grey leam to experiment with and for possible future use. I'd received conflicting advice regarding suitable hooks for fishing bloodworm and a couple of years later I was grateful to three times World Youth Champion, Matt Godfrey who, at the Evesham Festival, took time to produce some examples of appropriate patterns from his seat-box and also answer my numerous questions on the subject. Whilst we weren't called upon to fish bloodworm and joker in the next few years, Abi and I did use damp leam regularly in our roach mixes. She would also put her roach fishing skills to good use before the year was out.

Following their efforts on the Chesterfield Canal, our Challenge squad received an unexpected, but welcome invitation from Dave Gladwell, Nigel Poll and Mal Runacres to fish the Nisa Club Angler of the Year final at Weybread Pits two weekends later. Come Sunday 19th October, we'd had little time to prepare, but I'd gleaned some information of how the pit to be used might fish. Carp would make up the winning weight, but these wouldn't be caught from every peg it seemed and silver fish could play a part, especially as far as section prizes were concerned.

    Before the match started, Dave advised that he'd put up a cash prize for the best weight from our four youngsters and soon after the whistle, Ashley netted a good bream on the pole. He then followed up with several skimmers, before building his net on the feeder. He had his work cut out though, as the eventual winner was to come from a few pegs along in his section. Ash did however, take the best weight of our four with a net of 23lb 4oz, gratefully accepting Dave's tenner as a result. Robert had the draw bag to thank for a tight and seemingly sparse peg, but persevered nonetheless. Mal was good enough to give me some information on Reece's peg which I passed on, helping him to put a roach weight together to back-up his early carp and he wasn't far off the section winner's weight come the end of the match.

    With a few expander-caught skimmers in her net, Abi was unlucky to pull out of a carp early on and she made her mind up then, to get her head down for silver fish. A large roach-bream hybrid taken on double caster boosted her weight and with her immediate neighbours both tipping back shortly after the final whistle, I knew then that she was in with a shout. Dave himself had taken the only carp I'd seen landed in her section and there were no other decent silver fish nets. Abi returned 13lb exactly for an outright section win and at the presentation, she collected a brown envelope from match sponsor, Nick Larkin. Mal had also won his section and generously shared his winnings between the Suffolk teammates at the end of long, but enjoyable day.

LINDHOLME LESSONS

In May 2009 I enjoyed two days' fishing at the Garbolino-backed Lindholme Lakes complex accompanied by Reece Page. Following a double booking elsewhere, Neil and Bev Grantham had agreed to host both the NJAA Under-18s' Championships in June and the National in September.

In a hectic half-term week, I'd already spent two days at Heronbrook Fisheries in Staffordshire with Abi before my Lindholme recce with Reece. The plan was to practise for the Ladies' National on Monday and Tuesday, before spending Thursday and Friday at Lindholme. As mentioned a few chapters ago, the Ladies' National was subsequently switched to Baden Hall close by after Heronbrook closed temporarily, whilst an investigation into a possible outbreak of Koi Herpes Virus (KHV) was carried out. Abi then postponed her Ladies' National debut until the following year and Heronbrook was given the all clear and reopened a fortnight after it was closed. Early on the Thursday morning, Reece and I headed up the A1 on a journey to Lindholme punctuated only by my usual road-trip breakfast of a bacon roll and a cappuccino (from memory, Reece preferred Coke to a cappuccino).

We arrived at Lindholme in good time for a few hours' fishing and took in the view across the famous Bonsai Lake before parking the car. Having introduced ourselves and purchased our day tickets, Bev took time to give us directions around the 90-acre complex. Before long, we were both set up and catching fish on Oasis: a canal-type lake that formed a rectangle around a large field and parking area. The fishing was exceptional; we took sizeable ide up in the water and I netted good roach and rudd, as well as tench and bream. Most of the session, I was fishing caster no more than a couple of pole sections out. Reece also enjoyed himself and included a barbel and a golden tench in his first day's catch. The highlight of Reece's day however, was probably the ride with Bev in her golf buggy, when they popped back to the shop mid-session for some pole sections that he'd ordered.

That evening we took the short journey to Doncaster airport and found the Ramada Encore. For the first time, we took in the ambience of the modern, open plan bar and reception area of the hotel and after checking in, we took our gear to the room. That night, we took advantage of the air-conditioning, ensuring our worm and caster stayed cool in the wet room. The weather was pleasantly warm and I remember enjoying a pint of Guinness in the outside dining area as we watched the planes take off and land not too far away. It struck me that whilst we were staying at an airport, we weren't disturbed by the noise of the planes. I was told later that the whole design and construction of the airport was based on that of molehills so that noise was reduced.

The second and final day of our visit saw us on Beeches and again we enjoyed good sport. I caught several species close in on worm over micro-pellet, whilst also feeding my long pole line. I watched Reece take chub, carp and F1s up in the water as he experimented with a double elastic set-up in his top kit. As I too, switched to the long pole, we were enjoying ourselves so much, that I didn't notice a dark grey people carrier pull up behind us shortly after midday. There was a rover match scheduled for that afternoon and a couple of anglers watched us for a short while before continuing round the lakes; Reece told me later that it was Alan and Sandra Scotthorne.

Having caught around a dozen species of fish over the two days and familiarized ourselves somewhat with the fishing and the facilities available, we packed our kit away before stopping at the shop to purchase a supply of fishery pellets and thank Bev and Neil, before heading back to Suffolk.

Three weeks later and with me having taken more time off work to help with Suffolk County's match preparations, I was back on the banks of Oasis with Abi, looking forward to another couple of days' fishing ahead of the Under-18s' Championships on the Saturday. We picked up where I'd left off with Reece and after another enjoyable session, once again it was back to the hotel where I'd blagged a room very close to the foyer and reception area. Carrying our kit to the room wasn't too onerous-a-task therefore - and it wasn't too far to the bar either!

As Abi and I tucked into our breakfast at Lindholme on the Friday morning, Tom Pickering walked in and, remembering us from Decoy, shook hands as we explained that we were there for the NJAA match. He sat at the end of our table and went on to chat about the fishing on the lakes being used on the Saturday. Given what we'd already found from experience, it was interesting to hear Tom tell us that fish tended to come off the far bank during matches on Oasis and whilst many fished tight across, loose-feeding caster down the track and fishing the same bait either up in the water or dead depth, should prove fruitful; as ever, Tom explained that the fish would let us know what they wanted. After a few more words of advice and explaining that he'd see us on the Saturday as he'd be around at presentation time, we let Tom enjoy the rest of his breakfast as we headed off to Beeches.

Sometime before we travelled to Lindholme, I'd driven Abi to Oxfordshire where she'd purchased a 14.5 metre Garbolino G-Force Power pole from a match angler who was upgrading to a Daiwa Spectron. With the G-Force Power's sections being interchangeable with her G-796, she was well prepared for breakages during match situations and had enough top kits to cater for several types of venue and various sizes of fish. It was the G-Force Power that got a good workout at Lindholme that day as, like Reece and I had done, she took several different species, including ide which, she found, became livelier once they were in the landing net! That day we packed up reasonably early to ensure that we had plenty of time to make final preparations before the match. We also wanted to get showered and changed and be ready to greet other members of the squad as they arrived at the hotel.

Gathering up-to-date information is always an important part of the preparation for any team match. As well as what Reece, Abi and I had found out about the fishing at Lindholme; we'd also established that, on a Friday night the Ramada Encore offered two steak meals and a bottle of wine for £20. I'd obviously ensured that this information was available to all the squad and so those parents that arrived in time to eat, had every opportunity to persuade their son or daughter to have steak, whilst they in turn had a bottle of wine all to themselves!

The squad had all checked in on the Friday evening and Saturday's draw saw Suffolk County once again, on peg 1. In NJAA competitions, placing of anglers is not permitted and the pre-match, random section draw by NJAA Results Officer, Roger Drew put Abi in A and at the start of the match length on Oasis. Abi had some clear water to her left, just as the last (Tri-Cast Calder) angler on Oasis had on his right, with the sections running clockwise round the lake.

As expected, northern teams dominated the event, and Tri-Cast Calder took top spot with 19 points, with Barnsley runners-up (30) and Wakefield third (38). Suffolk's anglers gained valuable experience though, on their way to a top-half fifth place and a couple of the squad performed particularly well. In D section, Matt Snowling had attacked his peg and I remember passing more worm to him via a steward mid-match, as he headed for third-in-section with a final weight of 4kg 650gm. Matt also beat both his immediate neighbours by almost two kilos.

Abi pulled out of a very good fish early on, but kept her composure and set about building a team weight with mainly small fish. Many in her section were fishing the Method feeder tight to the far bank and taking occasional carp, but these fish were no more than a couple of pounds each. Mid-match, I'd helped other stewards tape up a broken section for the Worksop angler on peg 2, as Abi

continued to put small, 'cigar' barbel in her net. From a good distance away, I stood with Barry Miller, as she then played a carp, eventually landing it with several sections of pole up in the air. Whilst a couple of passing team managers weren't too complimentary about her set-up, given the amount of elastic she had out, I pointed out to Barry that the next fish would be another small barbel and upping the elastic grade would only result in bumped fish. The end peg advantage was possibly reduced by the number of spectators passing on and off Oasis at the access point close behind where Abi sat. Nonetheless, as the weigh-in began, her 5kg 750gm, made up of over 50 barbel, a couple of F1s and the bonus carp, turned a few heads as she put an unexpectedly high marker down for the rest of the section. It was perhaps fitting that, with Tom having been so generous with his advice at breakfast the day before, it was the Barnsley angler only, that bettered Abi's return with his section-winning 6kg 130gm.
    The top three match weights had all come from Beeches and Abi's 22nd placing overall (88 pegs), and Matt's 26th saw them also finish 9th and 11th respectively on Oasis (55 pegs). Suffolk's top five finish reflected a reasonably consistent performance with no anglers in the bottom three of their section. We'd also had our first experiences of England's largest match fishery and were looking ahead to having another crack at the venue - and to another steak the night at the Ramada!

Coach Trip

June 2009 also saw me attend a meeting at the University Arms Hotel in Cambridge, where a handshake marked the end of my career with CIS. Immediately after the meeting I was debriefed by my union colleague, Steve Whiting. Steve and I continue to meet up occasionally and share the odd fishing trip. Very soon after that debriefing in the cafeteria at John Lewis, I began regular coaching sessions with

Springfield Junior School. Steve Barnes was instrumental in getting that first project up and running following an approach from their head teacher, Michael Lynch. During that first year with Springfield, I also held classroom sessions with pupils through the winter. On occasion, I took live bait into the school, including maggots, casters and lobworms. I talked the pupils through video and DVD footage showing, among other things, bloodworm and joker in a fish tank and also did some work on fish recognition. The most popular sessions though, involved watching PVA bags filled with pellets dissolve underwater and simulating accurate groundbaiting by using a long pole and cupping kit to deposit tennis balls in a bucket in their hall. Possibly the most memorable afternoon though, was when I took in an array of different bait flavourings. Scopex was by far the most popular and at least two pupils went straight to Boys' Brigade absolutely reeking of it!

Having been elected Head Girl at Stowmarket High School, Abi suggested I contact the Gipping Valley and Thurston School Sport Partnership. Based at Stowmarket, they had over 40 schools within their catchment and it wasn't too long before I was running a couple of Sport Unlimited angling projects. I also picked up relief work driving the partnership mini-bus. Qualified coaches that were old enough to have this type of vehicle included on their driving licence and again, because of their age, be an acceptable insurance risk, were few and far between it seemed. When driving pupils from various schools to and from boxing, gymnastics and golf activities, I got to see several coaches from different sports delivering sessions.

As the school summer holidays of 2009 came to a close and with Suffolk County being familiar at least, if not exactly venue experts, with Lindholme Lakes, the decision was taken to enter a team of junior anglers in the NJAA National, along with two teams of intermediates. Ever supportive, Nigel Poll of Harleston, Wortwell and District Angling Club secured for us, the services of four local lads who, as well as being rather useful match anglers, could also get themselves to the venue and therefore not overburden us logistically. Nigel also passed us a welcome and rather generous donation towards their accommodation, entry fees and bait.

I travelled up to Doncaster reasonably early with Abi the day before the match and was on hand to check our party in, as they arrived at various times during the afternoon and evening. I'd booked a total of fourteen rooms at the hotel for our three teams, Jack Damant, our reserve angler and all the coaches and parents in the party. As the different groups arrived, the circle of chairs and stools that we occupied in the bar area got gradually larger. Eventually, with everyone accounted for, we held a pre-match briefing that covered bait and possible tactics before most of us headed for bed, leaving the Harleston boys to it.

I was one of the first up next morning and greeted others from the Suffolk contingent as Abi and I carried rod bags and pole holdalls from our rooms back to the vehicles. Steve Barnes was busy with bait preparation and a mini-bus head count before Ian Head led the way in his Bristo's van laden with squad kit, as we later departed for Lindholme once again.

With many more taking part in the September competition, they were spread over most of the lakes, some of which, we hadn't practised on. Nonetheless, Suffolk's anglers all managed to catch a few fish. Our juniors - most of whom were fishing the venue for the first time - finished 13th from 16 teams and whilst all struggled as far as section positions were concerned, valuable experience was gained as ever and this would stand them in good stead in years to come.

Among our top performers squad-wise, were Ashley and Abi, both of whom finished 8th in their 20-peg sections. Abi, having prepared and set up countless top kits and pole rigs, finally put a run of better fish together on the Method feeder after following Steve's advice and searching the large area of free water to the right of her peg on Laurels. Ash and Abi's performances helped their team to 11th. On a tight peg on the opposite bank of Laurels, Eddie Howman finished one section place above Abi, as Jack Weatherley took fifth spot in D, the Norfolk boys helping their team to eighth.

With 80 anglers on the bank in the intermediates' sections, Abi finished 21st overall with 6kg 750gm. Eddie's 7kg 290gm was good enough for 18th and Jack's 8kg 150gm put him 14th. As the post-match presentations began though, two other Suffolk anglers were called forward. Jack Damant, who'd enjoyed a day's fishing on one of Lindholme's stock lakes was the youngest angler at the event and later received a silver cup in recognition. Alice Bullock then received the award given to the highest placed junior girl. Suffolk County were though, still without team silverware during the time that GVAC had been coaching and managing the squad. I was aware though, that team performances were improving, if only gradually.

TAKE THREE GIRLS...

The keepnets were barely dry after the NJAA National before we had the Challenge to consider. October 2009 would once again see us head for Milton Keynes, so we were thankful for the small mercy of knowing something about the venue. Suffolk County were a long way from being canal experts, but we'd learned a lot since 2007.

With Barry Miller stepping back from coaching and managing the squad, decisions regarding team selection and make-up fell to Steve and me. Barry though, continued to be ever-present at competitions and his son Ashley, was to go on to win both individual and team silverware whilst wearing a Suffolk shirt.

The Challenge fell just four weeks after the National, so with all the associated logistical issues to consider, the decision was made to enter just two teams of four in the intermediates' competition. This would see all the under-20s that were available get to fish, but it also meant us having to decide which juniors would make up the number. After much deliberation, we felt that we were effectively one angler short of being able to put eight anglers on the bank that were able to cope with both the difficulties of fishing a hard canal venue and the pressures of a national competition. A chance email from Steve to an old acquaintance though, saw us achieve a full complement.

I'd met Kye Jerome a few years before when coaching at the King's Lynn AA Open Day where he was, among other things, manning the Environment Agency aquarium. A key member of the successful Browning Hotrods squad it was Kye who, having picked up Steve's email put us in contact with his teammate, Rob Lincoln. Rob's step-daughter, Abbi Kendall, was not only available, but was, from all accounts, rather good. In hindsight, it was hard to see how or why, no other teams had asked her to fish for them. All of this was of no consequence at the time though, as Steve made contact and final arrangements were made to meet Rob & Abbi on match day in the familiar surroundings of the Peartree Bridge Inn.

Whilst we now had eight names for our two team sheets, the deliberations around their make-up continued. For most, if not all, national competitions, entry forms have to be in around a month before match day, so it's rare that all the names remain unchanged. Steve and I have always though, endeavoured to email organisers before en event with details of any changes in an effort to make life just that little bit easier for them on the day of competition. Whilst there's always a strong argument to put the best team out, there are more considerations to take into account when working with young people. In the weeks leading up to the 2009 Challenge, Steve and I were aware that most of our intermediate anglers were fairly evenly matched ability-wise and we also had, in Alice Bullock and Dan Clarke, two under-16s to consider. We were looking for both to feel valued and not part of a second string team.

We debated long and hard as to how Suffolk County's 'Red' and 'Gold' teams (these being the colours of the county's coat of arms) would finally line up. We considered drawing names from a hat, but dismissed this idea given the possibility of ending up with two, rather imbalanced teams and perhaps, some disappointed and demotivated anglers. One thing we've also been aware of is that even if we named our perceived best team, there would always be a chance of a good angler being on a bad peg, or an inexperienced angler 'drawing on fish'. These factors could lead to our teams taking points off each other (although we'd always rather see this happen than have disappointed youngsters not fishing) and end up with two respectable finishes, but no silverware. Who'd be a coach, eh?

Following Steve's 'signing' of Abbi, I then came up with the suggestion to put all three girls in the same team, and for them to be skippered by Jack Weatherley, our top performer at Lindholme. 'Captain Jack', would therefore lead Abi Brewster, Alice Bullock and Abbi Kendall, and Daniel Clarke joined Reece Page and Robert Murphy (who'd both done well on their first visit to the Grand Union two years before), with Matt Snowling completing the line-up.

Using our Loaf!

In the lead-up to the event, we'd been happy with our groundbait mix and standard canal tactics that we'd used two years before and we had the usual array of main baits associated with this type of fishing in squatts, pinkies and maggots. As ever, I'd had very little sleep the night before the match and was up more than once checking the squatt. After speaking to Rob beforehand though, it was clear that we should now consider bread. 'It's a "bread" canal!' is how Rob succinctly put it.

Whilst Steve had done some work at our Junior Academy with punched bread, it's fair to say that our anglers weren't overly familiar with the stuff. Nonetheless, we did our best to make everyone aware of the revised team tactics and ensure none had any reservations regarding how to use a bread punch. Rob had offered to make up enough liquidized crumb for all our anglers and supply hookbait and spare punches where required. We were though, unable to fit in any practice sessions before the match and as a consequence, I'm sure we didn't realise the bait's full potential in the competition. Hindsight's a wonderful thing though and, to be fair to the coaches and anglers alike, we didn't do too badly...

On the morning of the match, the all-important draw saw Suffolk line up on adjacent pegs 11 and 12, with Kings' Lynn (Gold) and Tri-Cast Calder (Silver) on pegs 10 and 13 respectively. Reece was pegged next-door and just below Abbi; Matt next to Alice; Robert next to Jack and young Daniel beside Abi. With Abbi just yards away, Reece was able to see at close quarters, just how effective punched bread could be. Rob's information had been spot on and Reece top-scored for his team with 800gm and finished fourth in A section. Alice could be forgiven for her modest section placing in B, given that she'd spent the evening before in Accident and Emergency and fished the match with her left leg strapped up and resting on her bump bar! In C section, Jack had struggled early on, but a late gamble to chop maggots and feed his swim heavily saw him net valuable bonus fish, including a large perch that helped take his net to 1kg 620gm for fourth in section. Jack also made the top 10 overall.

    I may be biased, but I don't think Abi's always enjoyed the best of luck in big matches. On 3rd October 2009 however, her luck was to hold, possibly thanks to my saluting every magpie on the journey between Finborough and Milton Keynes that morning. An encounter with some dog mess on the tow path that saw us having to clean the butt section of her G796 and her not exactly having 'the Lynx effect' for the duration of the match, could only have helped the cause, I'm sure.

    With the match underway, Abi started to take small fish at regular intervals and later netted the odd one of a few ounces, but not much bigger. At just after midday though, she lifted into a bite that saw an unnerving amount of very light elastic stream from the end of her pole. Calmly and slowly and without ever seemingly being in any danger of losing contact with the fish, she manoeuvred her pole back on to her rollers before finally breaking down to her top kit. I've always referred since, to the fish that then graced her landing net as 'that skimmer'. It wasn't enormous, but it was certainly the largest fish I saw netted that day. I knew immediately, that whilst the angler to Abi's right, close to a bridge, was also doing well; she'd done herself no harm as far as section points were concerned and at the weigh-in, just two anglers in D section bettered her 1kg 690gm.

    Farnborough's Charlotte Gore, whom I'd also seen net a good fish and who would be in Suffolk's line-up two years later on the same venue, returned 1kg 840gm for second (fifth overall). The section was won though, by a young Frankie Gianoncelli who, among other things, went on to finish runner-up in the 2011 Dynamite Baits Festival at White Acres behind one Steve Ringer. Frankie was one of only two anglers on the day to break two kilos, the other being Abbi back in A section. Abbi had taken her section, and indeed the match apart with 2kg 320gm. No-one at her end of the match length got close and less than a kilo was good enough for second in section.

Abbi's overall win also helped her team to a creditable 18 points as they finished comfortably ahead the chasing sides. It didn't go unnoticed that, when the third-placed team was announced, three girls followed Captain Jack to collect their silverware.

The difficulties of getting a full quota to the bank were evidenced by the fact that no fewer than three teams didn't show up on match day. Barnsley took full advantage of this as they won the team event from peg 6, with 7 and 8 spare and, with peg 4 also free; Farnborough on peg 5, took the runners-up spot.

As for Suffolk County, well we'd seen three of our anglers finish in the top ten and return the second-best total team weight. We had finally secured team silverware and, in Abbi Kendall, had a national champion to boot. Rob's up-to-date information had given us an edge on match day and his technical knowledge was something that we would apply and we would, we felt, continue to improve. The sense of achievement and accomplishment wasn't lost on my daughter on the long journey home. When I say 'long', I refer to the fact that temporary roadworks on the A421 saw us diverted. We also then missed the signs to re-join the more direct route home and we eventually picked up the A14 again north of Kimbolton (please don't ask!). There were however, no raised voices or overheated exchanges in my Vectra estate that night. Yes, we'd lost the other vehicles in our convoy and having also recently lost my full-time job; I could ill-afford the extra fuel. None of this mattered, I was told by Abi repeatedly. Suffolk County had made the podium and she had finally added a national trophy to her growing collection of silverware. Those that know me reasonably well, know that I continue to salute magpies!

DENTS DIARY

The All England Junior Pole Championships was a competition that had, since 2007, escaped our attention. With the 2010 NJAA Under-18s' Championships scheduled for Langwith Lakes in Yorkshire requiring, should we enter, a long return journey to an unfamiliar venue; I made a concerted effort to find out more about the Pole Champs. I'd heard reference made to the competition and managed eventually, to track down and contact the organizer, confirming that the next event was due to be held at Dents of Hilgay, not too far away in Norfolk. I also established which lakes were to be used for both the team event (for under-18s) and the individual match (under-21s). At the time, we hadn't a huge number of anglers to choose from and were content with focusing on the team competition.

Entry was limited to twelve teams of four anglers. Two sections of the match would be on Farm Shop Lake and two on Willows. Having gathered all the information on entry and eligibility, Steve and I looked at our options and consulted Rob Lincoln, who immediately proved his credentials. Before we even set foot on the complex we knew that one lake, Farm Shop, was relatively shallow, silty and held a good stock of carp, crucians, bream, skimmers, roach and rudd. Willows on the other hand, was deeper, had a hard bottom, and along with carp and tench, there were good-sized barbel to be caught, along with the ever-present roach and occasional rudd. Rob was also able to confirm that, as is often the case, whilst carp could make up individual winning weights; many anglers would fail to catch them on match day and would also waste valuable time trying to.

Looking at the calendar of national competitions, Steve and I agreed to consider just the Pole Champs and the NJAA Challenge that year, with the latter due to be held on the South Holland Drain in Lincolnshire. These events were, as ever, in addition to our commitments at club level. With our junior prize-giving evening in January out of the way and although we also had an AGM to prepare for; Rob persuaded us to consider several practice sessions in the run-up to match day. I made contact with the staff at the venue and they were extremely helpful, eventually allocating us pegs on either Farm Shop or Willows, for six consecutive weekends leading up to Saturday 22nd May; and so our 2010 Pole Champs campaign began...

11th April

Meeting at Needham Lake for an early start, as well as the fishing on Willows, we also sampled for the first time, the excellent 'grab and go' breakfast facilities of a certain garage en route just outside Ely – more important pre-match information from Rob!

Aware of the danger of our anglers committing to carp on match day, I set out to prove silver fish a worthy target, fishing for them exclusively. Steve didn't fish and divided his time between coaching and observing. Abi had recently turned 18 and was ineligible to fish the team event, but came along to our practices. Whilst working part-time for Sainsbury's and doing A levels, she planned to join us on match day afternoon. James Head, who couldn't make the event, also fished the first session which saw Ashley Miller take top weight with carp on paste. My efforts with roach saw me return over 18lb and whilst young Tommy Cottrell hadn't matched me weight-wise, he'd had larger roach and rudd in his net and had certainly enjoyed his first visit to Dents. Steve and I compared notes before we left and we briefed our anglers ahead of the following week's session.

18th April

With over a dozen in our party and with breakfast purchased and downed, we began getting to grips with Farm Shop

Lake. Jack Damant was as keen as ever and was soon catching good skimmers. Alice Bullock, like James, would be unavailable on match day, but joined us and took skimmers, crucians and tench during another thoroughly enjoyable day's fishing. Rob and Steve were also both fishing and they, along with Reece Page and Robert Murphy led the way, with good mixed nets. Abi also enjoyed herself, taking over 20lb of crucians to the scales and my bag of mainly rudd topped 19lb. On the shallower of the two lakes, I'd had to follow the fish out on occasion and vary between caster and maggot on the hook to keep the fish coming.

25th April

A chilly spring day saw us back on Willows with Steve fishing and me coaching. Barry Miller stole the show after we weighed, photographed and returned his carp of over 18lb and he finished the session with 30lb-plus. Abi also took a good bag of silvers and Tom grabbed our attention with his tench and more quality roach on caster. Ashley and Reece caught odd carp and the danger of sitting out for the species was becoming very apparent. I'd threatened them both with a frontal lobotomy, but chose the less drastic option of getting back on my box the following week to prove a point.

2nd May

The May Day holiday weekend saw Abbi back in the country following an unintentionally long break abroad, courtesy of the ash cloud from an Icelandic volcano. We had another good turnout, with parents and siblings also joining us on the bank and my efforts to show how fruitful targeting roach and rudd could be, were more than worthwhile. Whilst others were catching what I refer to as 'brown silvers' (crucians, bream, skimmers etc.); it was evident that I was on for a very good weight as the practice session progressed. Rob though, reminded me of the technique of leaving the fourth section of my pole on and using the momentum of hooked fish to bring it them to hand when fishing 'top kit plus one'. After sitting on my box for a couple of minutes, he advised me to up my hook size and to, 'Swing everything!' After returning to my box, I was soon in a rhythm again and fishing how I had done when framing in a Suffolk Water Park match a few months before. Whilst the platforms at the Water Park lend themselves to the technique of leaving the additional section on; with a little care, it could be done on Farm Shop also, as Rob had advised.

In-between talking about what ever Abi and Abbi talked about further along the bank, both girls put together good mixed nets. Abbi was particularly impressive on the day, taking large bream and skimmers, as well as roach, rudd and even crucians on the drop. Top weight though, went to yours truly and as Robert Murphy recorded my 30lb-plus bag of roach and rudd; even Reece and Ashley were impressed and the need for major brain surgery was therefore avoided!

With just under three weeks to go until the match, things were looking good. We'd had ever-improving turnouts for practice sessions; so much so in fact, that our garage stop for breakfast saw us blocking the lorry access with our convoy of cars! We'd also got Abbi back from abroad, despite the goings-on with the Eyjafjallajokull volcano (and you're right, my spellchecker didn't recognise it) and we could see that anglers in our squad were enjoying themselves, whilst learning at the same time. As a coach, I saw these two final factors as the most important and in the right order.

9th May

Back on Farm Shop, the squad was joined by Sam Kennard. We had over a dozen fishing again and adults and youngsters alike enjoyed continued good sport. Tom took another impressive net and it was obvious that Dan Clarke was getting to grips with the venue. Abbi and Abi were proving consistent fish-catchers and Steve and I spent our time assisting and coaching.

Before and during the session, we spent time explaining the importance of feeding, fishing and rotating different swims; but also of re-plumbing after a spell of catching, should fish disturb the silt. We were told that depths could vary by as much as four inches during the match and we looked at how swims would 'fizz' as fish fed avidly, whilst seemingly ignoring hookbaits. With the only discernible shelf on most pegs being virtually under the anglers' feet and with contours therefore preventing us from fishing at the bottom of any slopes where silt wouldn't be an issue; the most effective way to combat this phenomenon was to lift one's rig from the bubbling area and fish just outside it, re-feeding via a pole-mounted pot as necessary. These techniques worked reasonably well and I'm sure they helped our anglers put additional fish in their nets in competition. Come match day, I watched one very competent angler from another team sit for several minutes without a bite after fish moved on to his feed and created the proverbial Jacuzzi. Although bank-running and verbal coaching was permitted, on that occasion, I reserved mine for my own team!

After the practice session, Dan's dad, Andy made a point of acknowledging and thanking us for our advice to fish several swims. Andy included a large bream in his net that displayed spawning tubercles and his friend, Paul Moore took a nice chub to add to our extensive species list for the venue. We looked ahead to the final practice session on Willows, quietly confident and we felt, by then, as prepared as any team could be.

16th May

We'd been warned about how large the carp were in Willows and this was confirmed by the specimen taken by Barry three weeks earlier. I'd also heard from other team managers how their anglers had had pole sections broken whilst playing these beasts. Our approach though, was to restrict elastics to no stronger than a soft 12 or 14 and if these large fish were hooked, to allow them to run in open water, finally netting them with several sections of pole in the air. This worked well for those that latched on to these fish - apart from Ashley that is. Having played a fish for quite some time, he had his number 4 section shattered by one that made a dash for freedom to his left after it was seemingly beaten.

As it was our final session, we looked to merely fine-tune what we'd learned. Abi was placed on the end of the practice match length and charged with feeding heavily with chopped worm. This didn't work at all and whilst she was too old to be considered for our teams, she'd done a valuable job for those that would be fishing and worm was discarded on Willows.

With Farm Shop being so silty, softened micro-pellets were the preferred feed, along with chopped worm and caster. Hard 4mm and 6mm pellets were to be used on Willows, but with the consideration that the carp might not feed. With the water temperature rising, meat was also an option for the barbel. Caster loose feed was to be a universal choice on both lakes for the roach and rudd, along with a suitable groundbait.

Despite the mishap with his pole, Ash returned a good mixed bag, whilst Tom took yet another net of very good roach. Jack included a tench in his bag of fish and on a day when Bosmere Tackle's David and Christine Shipp joined us on the bank; it was Abbi who took the honours. Whilst the squad metaphorically let their hair down on our final practice day, Abbi had hers tied back, facilitating convenient storage for her disgorger. Rob, David, Christine and I, along with Reece's mum, Debbie (and, I have to say, one or two others from rival teams), spent a good deal of time watching Abbi as she played large carp and she finished the session with three of them for over 30lb.

After a few shots of individual catches were taken, along with some group photos, we debriefed and made final arrangements for the match six days later.

22nd May

A bright blue sky greeted us as we all pulled in at Dents and it was shirt sleeve order as we grabbed a photo opportunity shortly before the draw which, once again, saw our two teams of anglers pegged side-by-side. With the pre-match formalities over, Rob walked the pegs on Farm Shop and gave Dan, Robert, Ash and Tom final instructions. Bait was then distributed, with bags of worm passed to the above, as Jack, Abbi, Matt and Reece began setting up on Willows.

Now, as if the usual preparations before the all-in weren't enough to contend with, I had another issue to manage. In an effort to save time the night before the match, I'd divided up supplies of home-turned casters for the teams on the Thursday. Unfortunately, they'd turned earlier than expected in the warm weather and my separating them a night early had resulted in a large percentage of them floating when water was added to them in our anglers' bait boxes. With less than half an hour to go before the whistle and armed only with my trusty tea strainer (retained for just such a situation); I set about getting to all our anglers' pegs to separate the floaters and putting them aside for the hook. I believe I managed to visit everyone before the all-in, carefully negotiating their pegs, straddling top kits, landing net handles and pole holdalls and apologising profusely as I, shall we say, strained! As the match got underway, let's just say that I was feeling the pressure a bit.

Usually, when a national match begins, it's time to relax and let the anglers get on with their fishing; but Rob and I had bank-running duties to attend to. I was on Farm Shop where Dan (Gold) and Robert (Red) were taking fish steadily and following our instruction of not to go five minutes without a fish. Dan in particular was doing well and although it was in our team plan to feed for, and then try for larger fish, we also made it clear that our anglers shouldn't give these big fish lines any more than a few minutes before continuing to build their weight with silvers. It appeared somewhat tougher going for Tom (Gold) and Ashley (Red) further round, where pegging was much tighter. Nonetheless they persevered and as the match progressed, Rob's advice was for them was to be aware that the hotter the weather became, the more chance they had of sneaking better fish on worm.

Whilst Robert was clearly doing okay, Dan next-door was fishing like a well-oiled machine and although he was catching only roach and rudd, he was doing so quicker than anyone in his section. Later, Dan was extremely unlucky to pull out of a couple of carp and, just as he was instructed, was straight back in on his silver fish line and catching again soon after continuing to feed. Dan's efforts were rewarded with a third-in-section placing; with Robert fourth, as only local King's Lynn anglers bettered their weights. Ash and Tom, just feet apart where a narrow path also saw the task in hand made even more difficult by bankside footfall, recorded fifth and seventh place in their sections respectively. Noticeably, none of our four anglers on Farm Shop had included any carp in their nets. Those from other teams that did catch carp, had them very late on and as a result, all finished in the top three of their section.

Down on Willows, the carp were spawning and large numbers of them were shoaled up in a shallow area in a corner of the lake that wasn't pegged. Matt Snowling (Gold) managed to latch on to, and land, the only carp taken by any Suffolk County angler on the day. Of modest size, this fish nonetheless helped Matt to a top-half section finish of fifth. In the still, bright conditions, it was hard going and next-door to Matt, Reece plugged away and was eventually rewarded with a better-than-expected sixth place in section.

Given Jack Damant's tender age, I'd contacted the match organizer beforehand for express permission for him to fish. This proved not to be an issue and despite Jack being two years younger than the advertised minimum age; he lined up with his older squad members for the match. I'm sure Jack won't mind me saying that in practice, I'd noticed his head dropping when he lost fish and I spent time reassuring him that this happens to all anglers. We endeavoured to instil in him the merits of fishing to a rhythm and how getting back into the water quickly and without delay would see valuable additional ounces in the net come the weigh-in. In turn, even more valuable section points could be gained as a result. Jack was not only *our* youngest angler; he was the youngest in the field by far, as we found out when competitors were asked to step forward in order of ascending age for sponsors' gifts after the match. Jack's only brief before the match was to do nothing more than enjoy his day's fishing. However, in typically inimitable fashion and riding the luck of having an unused peg to his right, Jack fished an extremely accomplished match, promptly beating four anglers much older than him to finish eighth in section.

Despite the early disappointment and frustration of pulling out of three good carp - one of which, she'd played for some time on her roach rig - Abbi had recovered and the three large barbel taken in the margins on meat, helped her to third in section; she top scored for Suffolk once again, along with Dan. Rob and I had been in contact by mobile phone and as section points were confirmed, we were looking at totals of 18 and 23 points for our two teams. We'd also realised that local anglers had been one step ahead, fishing for, and taking very large fish in the dying stages of the match, with a number being landed (legitimately) after the whistle. In fact I photographed a fish of close to 20lb for its captor, Toby Pepper who went on to win the match overall with 37lb 3oz. We were to see a lot of Toby and his brother, Timmy in the coming years. Anna Blyth (Milton

Keynes), who also landed a huge carp after a prolonged fight which helped her to fourth place individually, would also line up in the squad in the future.

Abi had arrived fresh from her shift at Sainsbury's in plenty of time for the presentations and the Suffolk County contingent were hoping for a podium finish, despite knowing that King's Lynn's late fish had given them two section wins and a second. As ever, results were given in reverse order and with seven teams announced before Suffolk were mentioned, our anglers and supporters grew evermore expectant. A professional and consistent performance that belied their collective age and experience saw our Gold team finish 5th with 23 points. Would 18 points though, be enough for a top three spot? The all-conquering Maver Farnborough were announced fourth, with Waveney Juniors third and the cheers from our anglers were the loudest of the day, as they realised they'd finished runners-up. With both teams in the top five, and despite our eight anglers landing just one carp between them; practice had almost made perfect and I was mentally composing our press release as we pulled back on to the A10 to head home.

My paid work with schools continued and occasionally I took individual bookings. That spring I answered an advertisement from Suffolk Coastal District Council for an angling coach. Having submitted my CV and received a favourable response, I travelled to Woodbridge for my interview - possibly the first I'd attended without wearing a tie! Come July and with the interview having been successful, I attended an induction course before working three full days each week for four weeks in August, at venues in Aldeburgh and Bromeswell.

This work continued in the coming years and I became good friends with fellow coach, Colin Booker, whom I knew from GVAC and the NACA Open Days at Bawburgh. Colin and I ran the popular fishing sessions as part of Suffolk Coastal's programme of summer activities with our young assistant and occasional blame hound, Calum King. I went on to enjoy some of my most memorable and, it would be fair to say challenging coaching experiences with Colin and Calum. On my 51st birthday at Chapel Barn, Aldeburgh, I spent a good deal of the afternoon lying on my stomach, peeping over the edge of a wooden platform until eventually, a reasonably large carp took one of our participants' baits. With half-a-dozen or more floating casters crammed round the bend and up the shank of a size 10 Kamasan B981 hook; we'd dangled it from, shall we say, a less-than-expensive rod and reel combo in the margins. Despite all hell breaking loose very soon after said offering was sucked from the surface by a pair of huge lips; the fish was landed and several day ticket anglers' noses were put firmly out of joint by that, the biggest fish of the day. After receiving presents and cards from participants, a birthday cake on the bank and a supply of free range eggs from the venue's owners; it was home for an evening pint.

Four days later and after considerable downsizing of tackle strength and bait size, I was with the Suffolk squad in Lincolnshire for practice for another national competition...

Fishing wasn't my only interest. I'm seated (above, front left) with Claydon Sunday Morning Football Club and you can just make out my footballer's moustache... 11-a-side!

On a trail riding holiday in Wales (below), with the summit of Mount Snowdon in the background

John and I (left and above) enjoyed good sport on Lough Ramor in Ireland in 1990

Hazel (below) with a carp from Cransley Hall the same year

A perch (above) from Needham Lake in November 1990

Gwen (below) with a carp from Cransley Hall in 1991

Abi gets some tips from former World Champion, Tom Pickering (above) at Decoy Lakes in 2008

On my way to a match win at Needham Lake in August 2009 (below)

The only female entered, Abi (above) prepares for her Sainsbury's match at Larford Lakes in 2010…

…She went on to fish an almost faultless match (left) and was rewarded with a section win and sixth place overall

A near-30lb net of roach and rudd (above left) from Townsend Lakes taken in Rob Lincoln's end-of-season match for Suffolk County's anglers and coaches in 2010

Abi tussles with a pike (above right) on the Old Nene at Benwick in February 2011 and poses (below) with one of a brace she banked that day

Abi enjoyed her evening sessions with Rob Lincoln on opening day on the Old Nene in 2010 and (left) in 2011

Abi with her second-in-section catch from Twin Oaks (below left) at the **2011 White Acres Walls Solero Ladies' Festival** and (right), she casts a Method feeder to the far bank on her way to a section win on day three

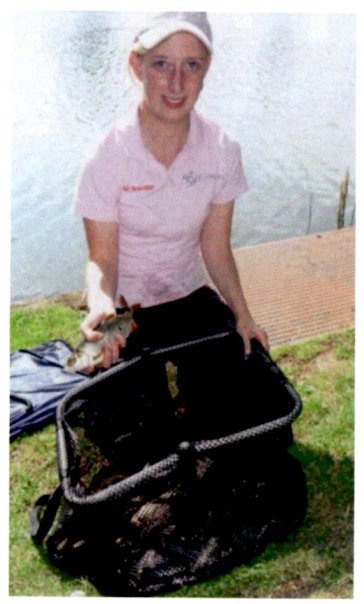 

Abi and me (above left and right): third and first respectively on Needham Lake in July 2011

I was fortunate enough to be named Coach of the Year, Runner-up at the Suffolk Sport Awards in 2011 and again (below left) in 2012

(Below right) Colin with his flies open!

A Marsh Farm perch (above left) taken in 2014 and (right) my first Wensum chub, photographed by Martin Burgess in January 2013

A carp taken whilst fishing for roach with a float rod and centre pin set-up (below) from Horseshoe Lake, Bromeswell in September 2014

Curtis (above left) with a carp caught on a slug. Having listened to my chub fishing stories, he'd collected his bait from the banks of the Gipping before school!

Curtis, Ciaran and Aston (above right) at Barking in May 2012 - amazing how much fun you can have with an ice fishing rod and a bag of pellets!

Ciaran (left) with a carp taken on an elderberry

James (left) took this golden orfe during a session with Castle Hill Junior School

Ethan, Marcus and Patrick (above, left to right) with the best perch taken in an afternoon session on the Gipping

Julie Hammond took this photo of her son, Greg (below) in action for Suffolk County at Willow Park

The Suffolk County squad (above) at the **2003 NJAA Challenge**: (back row, left to right) Luke Miller, Tom Porter, Ian Reynolds, James Brinkley (front row), Ashley Miller, Abi and Karl Westlake

Rob Foulger's net of bream (left) at the **2007 NJAA Challenge** on Ten Mile Bank

Abi (above left) nets 'that skimmer' on her way to third in section & eighth overall at the **2009 NJAA Challenge** and Abbi (right) heads for a clear section win and a first individual crown

Tom (below left) with a net of roach, perch and tench from Willows and (right) my 30lb-plus net of roach and rudd from Farm Shop Lake at Dents of Hilgay, venue for the **2010 All England Junior Pole Championships**

Abbi, Robert, Reece and Ashley (above, left to right) with their runners-up team trophies at Dents

Reece, Abbi, Abi and Ashley (below, left to right) secured third place for Suffolk County in the **2010 NJAA National** on the South Holland Drain. Abbi also won her second individual NJAA title… wearing Abi's spare wellies!

Team champions at the **All England Junior Pole Championships 2011** (above) and Rob and I do our best Sebastian Vettel impression! Robert and Ashley also picked up silverware in the individual, under-21s' competition

A clean sweep of team wins in the **2011 NJAA National** (below) and Jack and Ashley are individual champions!

Abi took this double figure common carp (left), during a practice session ahead of the **2011 NJAA Challenge**

Steve, Rob and I pose proudly with our two junior teams and their silverware (below) at Suffolk Water Park

Our intermediate teams at Suffolk Water Park (above)

Nigel Cottrell took this shot of me (left) with both NJAA Challenge team shields in 2011

Suffolk County were named Junior Team of the Year at the 2011 Suffolk Sport Awards where Reece, Jack, Ashley, Tom, Abbi and James (above, left to right) pose with their certificate, perpetual cup and glass keepsake

Steve and I pose (below) with Suffolk County's 2011 haul of national team trophies at GVAC's presentation evening

We returned to Westwood Lakes for the **2012 All England Junior Pole Championships**, where the squad (above) retained the team trophy and Reece and Abi were also placed in the individual, under-21s' competition

I took one of my favourite photos (below), at the **2012 Angling Trust Cadet/Junior/Intermediate National** at Lindholme Lakes where Ollie, Paul, Jack and Sam sit quietly watching as Abi's match on Bonsai draws to a close

Dick Clegg OBE (left) congratulates young Jamie who left Lindholme with a complete set of medals and Ollie, Jack, Max, Lewis, Paul and Jamie (below, left to right) pose with their silverware as Angling Trust champions 2012!

Another clean sweep of team and individual wins at the **2012 NJAA Challenge** on the South Holland Drain (below)

(Back row) Judy, Jess, Charlotte and Leanne (above, left to right) with (front row) Jeannette, Kayleigh, Abi and Nuala at the **2013 Angling Trust Ladies' National**

(Back row) Callum, George and Ollie (below, left to right) with (front row) Max, Jack and Jamie at **2013 Angling Trust Cadet/Junior/Intermediate National** at Tunnel Barn Farm

I prepare groundbait for Abi (above) during one of her practice sessions at Cudmore

Barry Hearn introduces himself to Abi (below) during **Fish O'Mania XXI** as Les Thompson looks on

SOUTH HOLLAND SUCCESS

Since working with the county squad in 2004, I've become aware of how pre-match hype can affect both team plans and expectations on match days. Although contests are often hosted a considerable distance from home; social media networks and other modern communication methods ensure that much is mooted about how well these venues will fish. Talk too, at national meetings is often, of excellent sport; but those not prepared to accept that some venues will never produce on a match day what they do for pleasure anglers or in practice sessions will often, I've found, come unstuck. I'm no longer surprised that even some local teams often miss out on silverware in national competitions and wonder if there's an argument for some being over-familiar with their own waters and taking them too much for granted as a result.

There's no doubt however, that a strong team that goes to a venue well prepared, with an open mind and a disciplined approach, will usually end up on the podium. Whilst a local angler might make the most of a good peg and be rewarded with a section winner's medal and perhaps even frame; a consistently high spread of section results are required for team trophies.

The 2010 NJAA National on the South Holland Drain near Holbeach, Lincolnshire saw Pride of Derby Juniors clear winners in the under-16s' event, but with just one section win from their six anglers and this with only seven teams on the bank. In the intermediates' competition (twelve teams of four), champions Milton Keynes and runners-up, Tameside Fox Match had no section winners. They did though, produce very consistent performances and all their anglers finished in the top half of their sections.

But what of Suffolk County? Our practice session on the venue a fortnight before the match was reasonably well attended as we prepared to put three teams on the bank for the event, with representation in both age groups. Ten of our squad made the journey to Lincolnshire in August and we were joined on the drain by Browning Hotrods' John Hazelden. Rob Lincoln had invited John along and, not for the last time, our youngsters were able to watch a class angler demonstrate his formidable skills as he went through his rigs and explained the lines he intended to fish. He also explained his groundbait mix and discussed hookbait options before he started putting a net of fish together, as the squad returned to their pegs. Needless to say, at the end of the session, John had top weight. Modestly however, he was quick to point out the substantial advantage of the end peg he'd fished.

All our anglers caught, with Abbi's net including several good roach, but it was evident that it wasn't going to be easy come match day. John had started off on a feeder line close to the far bank, whilst building the main area of his peg with squatt. The idea was to spend five minutes looking for a bonus bream and, on cue, he hooked a large fish shortly after casting out. Unfortunately though, he pulled out of what was probably, a very good bream as we sat and watched. Such fish would be the saviour of a few on match day, but many others would struggle. I sat on Abi's box for well over half an hour in practice without a bite; although she took a reasonable weight to the scales, courtesy of a perch of around a pound. Reece too, found some good fish and if nothing else, we all knew what to expect and had sampled the sport, along with the mood of the venue.

Paper Girl

Around this time, Abi started work at the *Angling Times*. She'd applied to several universities and we'd travelled to Sheffield, Exeter, London, Norwich and Cambridge, as she considered a career in medicine. Cameron settled on Anglia Ruskin University in Cambridge and went on to become a Bachelor of Science with Honours in Computer Science.

Over the first winter of his studies, we developed a fishing app for the iPhone. Whilst weighing up her university options, Abi also had a day at the *Angling Times* offices in Peterborough. One morning in June, I dropped her off at Media House, before driving to Holbeach and visiting tackle shops with a view to glean some information on, and to perhaps get my first look at the South Holland. My exploratory trip however, was curtailed. England were playing Slovenia in the World Cup that particular Wednesday afternoon and I collected Abi somewhat earlier than we both expected. Her prospective employers had, it seemed, seen enough and she was offered the job shortly after. She was also offered two university places and whilst Peninsular University was arguably the more prestigious of the two, the University of East Anglia had its own broad and the prospect of popping up to fish as a guest of one of their medical students was an attractive one.

The deciding factor regarding Abi's career - apart from the daunting prospect of an initial five-year course and any consequent financial encumbrance - was being turned down by Cambridge. With 11 A*s, her GCSE grades were higher than the average of the 200-plus applicants. Knowing that fewer than 20 places were available for medical students at her college of choice was little consolation to us when we received the letter of rejection. Abi achieved straight As in four subjects at A level, but looked to a job connected with her hobby for her first full-time employment - something few school-leavers have the opportunity to do.

Soon after she started work, along with a few other young Suffolk anglers, I joined her on the North Bank of the Nene where she was helping to cover the *Angling Times* Winter League final and where John Hazelden, Kye Jerrom and Ian Reynolds were part of the Hotrods team that finished runners-up, second only on the day to Kamasan Starlets. I spent a large part of the match watching Steve Welford catching roach on hemp and he, along with his Hotrods captain, Tim Nash, went on to win their sections. I chatted to Ian Reynolds as he tackled down after the match and also thanked John quickly, for his help with our Challenge preparations. To quote their local Hunts Post newspaper, it was 'a fantastic result for Hotrods' that saw 'many of the big-name teams of the fishing world trailing behind'.

The weekend before had seen us arrive at match headquarters in Holbeach for the NJAA National with an expectation, rather than a hope, of returning to Suffolk with silverware. Looking back, Suffolk County had clearly made progress and some squad members had acquired that most important of attributes: confidence. We were far from complacent though and were well aware, as mentioned earlier, of how fickle the venue might prove to be.

With pre-match formalities completed, our anglers made their way to their sections. Abbi had an absolutely plum draw: peg A1. Yet again, our teams had drawn side-by-side and our intermediate Gold team were on peg 2. Abi and I arrived at her peg: C1, close to a busy road bridge. Here, it was immediately obvious that negotiating the steep bank and placing her platform would be a somewhat tricky and muddy affair. As Rob slowed his car on his way to Abbi's peg, he commented on the speed of the water; it was hammering through! I remember managing to get Abi's platform placed, only to have her keepnet almost taken from my hands as I tried to attach it to the footplate of her box. Over the next hour however, the flow slowed dramatically. Afterwards we were informed that the gates that control the flow on that stretch had been left open by mistake and a frantic phone call from the match organiser had seen the situation rectified.

Abi was eventually positioned safely on her platform, but only after I'd managed to fill one of my boots with water, drench most of one leg of my trousers and cover both in copious amounts of black mud. As the whistle announced the start of the match, I left Abi to it.

The junior match was pegged in the area where we'd practised and the concrete stagings were suitable for the younger and less experienced anglers. Under the watchful eye of Steve Barnes, our under-16s put in a valiant effort, but it was evident that fish were in pockets and some of the team struggled. Once again we fielded the event's youngest competitor in 10-year-old Jack Damant and his inclusion in the team at the time was perhaps, an illustration of the limited experience and indeed modest size of our junior squad. That situation would soon change and our strength in depth would become a major factor in our successful campaigns. Jack's early experiences would also see him challenge for team selection with anglers much older. The NJAA National team of 2010 all gained valuable experience on their way to an eventual sixth place. There was reason to celebrate in this category however, as James Head and Sam Kennard, like Jack, took home silverware.

On A2, James did well to fend off the challenge from his neighbour on the end peg of the match length and his 1kg 590gm saw him rewarded with a section winner's medal. Sam will hopefully forgive me when I say he's no Mark Pollard when it comes to the tidiness of his kit, but his watercraft is probably better than a lot of adult anglers. If there are fish in front of him, Sam will catch and catch well. His 1kg 670gm net of silver fish beat those of both his immediate neighbours by over a kilo and was good enough for second in section and third overall.

Back in the intermediates' competition, all bar two of Suffolk's eight anglers finished in the top four of their sections, despite some areas fishing very hard. One of the unlucky two was young Dan Clarke who, once again, stepped up to fish in the older age group. He was pegged the other side of the road bridge to Abi in C and, as ever, stuck to the task in hand, taking 130gm to the scales. The two anglers that finished below him in C returned just 80gm between them. Dan's weight came partly courtesy of the smallest pike I've ever seen and whilst he was concerned that it might not count, I reassured him that it was so small the stewards wouldn't notice that it was indeed, a pike!

Robert Murphy (Gold) and Reece Page (Red) also found the going tough in D section. The angler to Reece's left weighed in just 20gm and on part of the match length that saw even England trialists struggle, he put together 230gm. To his right, Robert had mustered only a few sticklebacks with less than half an hour to go. Robert being Robert though, got out of jail well and truly with a bream of over five pounds that shot him from nowhere to second in section. His 2kg 470gm saw him receive a section winner's medal by default, as he also finished fifth overall. Jack Mills showed his class in B, with a third-in-section 2kg 250gm. His Gold team finished a creditable fifth, just one point behind both third and fourth, as the slightly risky strategy of us entering two intermediate teams saw us come very close to getting both on the podium. Sandwiched between the two Suffolk teams on the results sheet was King's Lynn, who boasted two section winners. Revenge for the Pole Championships was sweet however, as our Red team's superior weight pushed them off the podium and into fourth.

Within the first quarter of an hour of the match, Rob had informed me that Ashley had landed a tench. Whilst the fish wasn't, shall we say, of Sywell proportions, it certainly guaranteed him good points. Ashley eventually returned 1kg 360gm for fourth in his section. Abbi wasn't far behind in getting among the better fish and soon after, I received further news that she'd netted two large bream and was continuing to catch. With bream in her net, Abbi then built her weight with skimmers to return 5kg 490gm. She finished two kilos clear of anyone in the match as she added the individual NJAA National trophy to that from the Challenge 11 months before. One more high section score was needed though, to get Abbi's Red team among the trophies and that came courtesy of her namesake in C section.

I'd not seen much of Abi during the match itself, given that I was stewarding in D section. I knew though, that she'd struggled for most of the match. Whilst being pegged next to a bridge is often an advantage, it hadn't seemingly helped Abi. Local youths were apparently attracted by the commotion of a large fishing match and one even chose to pull up and test his car exhaust just yards from where Abi was fishing. She persevered though, and pointing her pole towards the shade of the bridge, she was eventually rewarded with a short run of fish mid-way through the competition. When I managed to grab a quick word soon after however, her frustration and anger was all too apparent, as she explained that several passers-by, including, would you believe, stewards, chose to stop and peer over the railings of the bridge, right above where she was catching. As the end of the match approached I tried to reassure her that most competitors had struggled, but she wasn't convinced.

I completed my steward's duties by recording in D section, working from the high numbers down before meeting up with fellow officials on the end of C. Comparing notes, I had a quick count down the list of results and saw that Abi's hard earned 600gm was good enough for three points. I'll not forget Abi's change of expression as I walked back down the match length, holding up three fingers. 'What's that?' she asked, 'Your section position!' I replied. Needless to say, this was much better than she'd hoped for and Suffolk Red's 18-point tally was just one behind that of runners-up, Tameside Fox Match.

We returned home with a large number of trophies and medals, equalled on the day by just one other team: Worksop. For Steve and me, 2010 had undoubtedly been a success. We'd put an enormous amount of work into preparing for the South Holland match, tying a large number of rigs and spooling spare hooklengths for several of the squad. It became evident though, that we were certainly in a minority with this type and level of assistance. I always took the attitude that I wanted our anglers to have rigs as good as, if not better, than anyone on the bank and if that meant tying them for some of our anglers, we would do so. Steve, Abi, Abbi and Rob would also assist with this preparation and the more I read about coaching, the more important I realised that small improvements and attention to detail could, come the match, make a big difference. It was apparent to me, that no matter what the sport, many coaching principles could be applied in a similar manner and the performances of Suffolk County would continue to improve if some of these practices and philosophies were appreciated and adopted. In September 2010 though, we were still short of a team win and were yet to see our under-16s on the podium.

At Rob's suggestion, we rounded the year off with a trip to Townsend Lakes near Wisbech. My near-30lb bag of roach and rudd was eclipsed by Robert Murphy's large bag of carp. Abbi included a large ghost carp in her net and Sam Kennard enjoyed good sport with skimmers and roach. After several attempts, Abi netted one of the venue's barbel and Tom, as he seemed to, almost everywhere he went, included a nice tench or two in his net. Steve landed a common carp well into double figures right at the end of the session which, looking back, was a befitting way to end a year of competition.

Clubmark

GVAC's 2011 diary of events kicked off with our junior prize-giving evening and in addition to the usual presentation of trophies and certificates, Jonathan Wilson of the Angling Trust presented Steve with our Clubmark certificate. Steve in particular, had worked hard towards this accreditation and we'd taken our time to put together a professional presentation on behalf of GVAC. The high standard of our submission was acknowledged and we were confirmed as only the joint 20th angling club in the country to achieve Clubmark status. Jonathan also presented Steve with a certificate commemorating GVAC's work with young people.

Early on the morning of Sunday 20th February, I arrived at Needham Lake for a sweepstake that Bob Gunn had organized. Bob was the club's match captain at the time and he organized such events on a regular basis, when nothing else was scheduled. The day's contest was to be a 'float only' affair and the day before I'd tackled up a match rod with a large slider float. It was a typically grey, late winter's morning as I pulled into the car park. As I got out of my car however, events took a decidedly untypical turn...

Bob appeared by my car door and advised that I shouldn't go to the trouble of unloading my gear as there was a body in the lake! There were also a few members of the public present as more and more club members arrived for the match. The police had been notified and very soon, an officer was cordoning off the area around the first few pegs where the body lay in the water, close to the bank.

I'll say little more than the story was covered by the *Look East* and *Anglia News* the following day and it also made the early pages of the *Angling Times* – Abi having tapped her father up for a suitable photograph of the venue to accompany the article.

As far as the fishing was concerned, we cooperated fully with the police and the match was moved to Barking. The kit I had with me was completely inappropriate for the alternative venue so I headed home, as did a few others who, given the circumstances, weren't in the mood to fish. On a more pleasant note, I recall that particular day also because having unloaded my gear at home, Hazel called me as she'd spotted a pair of waxwings in our garden. I'd not seen these birds before and I managed to get some reasonably good photographs of the birds perched in a tree close to our bedroom window.

During March, I resumed my coaching work with local schools. A group from Bacton Middle were first up, taking advantage of the Sport Unlimited initiative, shortly before it was superseded by Sportivate that would aimed at older pupils. After Easter, I ran sessions on a similar basis with Chilton Primary School, Ringshall Primary and Springfield.

LINCOLNSHIRE POACHERS

Early in 2011, Steve and I began making preparations for national competition following receipt of details of the All England Junior Pole Championships. The event this time around, was to be staged at Westwood Lakes, near Boston, Lincolnshire and with neither of us having been to the venue before, a practice session was arranged. The team competition for under-18s was to take place on Skylark and Kestrel, with Hawk Lake accommodating the under-21s in the individual event. With Skylark and Kestrel already booked for the days we were available, we settled on Hawk for squad practice. This wasn't an ideal arrangement, but we'd at least get a look at the whole venue and would source information for those that would fish Skylark and Kestrel. A few in the squad also managed to fit in additional sessions before match day and whilst local teams were always going to be a step ahead of us in terms of knowledge of the fishery, we were looking at putting a strong team of four on the bank from our squad ranks.

Josh Balodis travelled up from Bedford to practise with us and stole the show. We'd begun with Rob Lincoln demonstrating and by the end, had gathered all our anglers behind Josh's peg. Rob was more than familiar with Westwood Lakes and a good turnout in practice saw us eventually choose to field two teams of under-18s on match day, with four entered in the individual event.

Nine teams assembled for the draw on May 21st, including Suffolk County Red (Tom Cottrell, James Head, Abbi Kendall and Josh) and Suffolk County Gold (Dan Clarke, Lewis Clouting, Jack Damant, and Ollie Saunders). With the draw complete, Abbi and Tom set up on Skylark with Ollie and Lewis, whilst Josh, James, Jack and Dan prepared on Kestrel. In the individual event, Abi Brewster, Ashley Miller, Jack Mills and Robert Murphy would fly the county flag. Hawk is a rectangular lake with access to pegs via a footbridge at one end. For the duration of the match, all adults were banished from the central island, where competitors fish from and with everyone facing across the water to the 'mainland'. Having helped Abi and her squad-mates to their pegs with their kit, I left them all to it until the final whistle, when I'd agreed to return to assist with the weigh-in.

Back on Kestrel, I helped Dan chop his worm and remember leaving him just as the whistle was blown. During the first hour or so of the match, it was clear that a number of local anglers were doing well; Toby and Timmy Pepper in particular. Fishing for Hunstanton Tackle, the boys looked good for section wins from early on. On Kestrel however, Josh was also doing well, as was James. The team plan on Kestrel was to fish chopped worm and caster, feeding via a small, pole-mounted pot. After a slow start, Dan managed to put a few fish together for an eventual (and creditable) fifth place in section. Top scorer for Gold though, was Lewis. He fished an accomplished match on Skylark, taking a mixed bag of fish from the deep water, needing little or no guidance from me, Steve or Rob as we ran the bank. In the same section as Lewis, but further along the bank, Tom was able to fish tight to the island, thanks to having use for the day, of Rob's top-of-the-range Maver pole. After a sluggish start, he took good fish with increased regularity as the match drew to its conclusion. Abbi meanwhile, who also struggled early on, had clawed her way back up the section by taking good fish from her margin swim. Despite Toby and Timmy's obvious dominance and their teammates being well placed in section too; it was becoming evident that the match was building to an exciting climax.

Whiskers Supermeat!

One of the few regrets I have in respect of my work with Suffolk County was not being on hand to witness one of the most meritorious fish landed in the squad's history. Kestrel is famous for specimen barbel and James Head, fishing the lake for the first time, managed to latch on to one of eight pounds-plus; sometime later, he landed it! This was a pole-only competition and James was enjoying a run of ide when he made contact with something a little bigger. Whilst I wasn't around to see what happened next, I don't tire of listening to Rob Lincoln retelling the story...

Evidently, James soon realised what was responsible for the elastic streaming from the end of his pole and according to Rob, was completely relaxed, taking everything in his stride. Able to control the barbel's initial powerful runs, James eventually broke his pole down and played the fish on his top kit. In fact James was so relaxed, with one hand holding his pole, he half-turned on his box and ran the fingers of the other through his worm and caster, asking Rob's opinion as to how he'd chopped up his bait!

At this moment I understand, the barbel chose to make another powerful lunge for bankside cover and with his top kit assuming a near semi-circular bend; James was unable to add his sections again. No matter; James held firm as Rob eyed the tail of the barbel breaking the surface... with its head some three feet further away!

Minutes later, the splendid fish was netted and with match rules stating that barbel over three pounds had to be weighed immediately and returned to the water, a steward was on hand to do the honours. The drama didn't end there however, as the steward - despite Rob's protests - looked to release the fish in James's swim. Common sense eventually prevailed and the fish was released along the bank in an area not pegged for the match. Rob then headed back to James with the landing net, passing it to him just in time for him to net another ide!

Back on Hawk, I worked my way along the bank, assisting with recording as Jack returned 18lb 2oz and Abi, 27lb 15oz for seventh place. Ashley and Robert fared a bit better though and with nets of 45lb 6oz and 51lb 2oz, they made the podium in third and second respectively, behind local rod, Luke Morley.

From the nine clubs and associations in the team event, our Gold team eventually finished a commendable sixth. Before the presentations however, a drama was being played out on Skylark as the final weights in the last section were noted...

Hunstanton Tackle had recorded a first-in-section, a second and a fourth, against Suffolk's pair of section wins on Kestrel and Abbi's second. Hunstanton however, were obvious winners of the final section to be recorded and with just Tom to weigh, it was calculated that he needed almost 30lb for a top three finish to secure an outright points win for his team. As a large crowd gathered, Tom's bag of fish thumped the scales round, eventually settling at 29lb 8oz and all then, knew the final result. Hunstanton's manager and coach, and Toby and Timmy's dad, Robert 'Pep' Pepper was first to offer his hand to Rob in congratulation. Toby had won the individual event for the second year running with 54lb 2oz and younger brother, Timmy was runner-up with 54lb exactly; Josh completed the frame. For the record, Abbi returned 42lb for her two points and James's 44lb 2oz was over 20lb clear of the rest of the section!

A memorable presentation concluded with Abbi, Tom, Josh and James posing with their squad-mates, the large and impressive wooden team trophy and their individual keepsakes. Toby and Timmy went on to join our squad very soon after.

MILTON KEYNES HAT-TRICK!

I was kept busy during the summer of 2011. After completing my summer term school projects, over 30 youngsters attended our Junior Academy events at Barking. Colin and I, once again, worked for Suffolk Coastal District Council, running three full-day sessions at Aldeburgh, Bromeswell and Swilland. We also had two very wet, but enjoyable days at Barking. The weather didn't stop the carp feeding and the classroom proved a dry haven for us, Calum and all the participants come lunchtime.

Steve Barnes meanwhile, had been on the banks of the Grand Union Canal at Milton Keynes in July with a group of eight youngsters for the GUSAC (Grand Union South Angling Consultative) competition and Olivia Bullock, Lewis Clouting, Tom Cottrell and Sam Kennard all returned home with a trophy. As the school holidays came to an end, Steve arranged a return trip for practice on the same venue, ahead of the NJAA National on 3rd September.

Come 21st August, an impressive turnout saw a long section of the canal taken up by Suffolk County youngsters. Sensas Milton Keynes and former Team Image man, Lee Newson had given us first class information and after Rob Lincoln's demonstration, the squad set about putting some fish in their nets. Once again, Rob's teammate, Jon Hazelden was on the bank fishing and answering questions from our squad members. It's always been a pleasure to watch Jon and in practice sessions; he's a mine of information and a source of inspiration for the youngsters. On the end of the practice stretch, several parents too, looked to catch a few of the venue's small roach and skimmers.

As the session drew to a close, some of the older members of the squad took a break to enjoy their McDonald's take-away meals (a few by now had their own cars), before we assembled for the all-important debriefing.

Final instructions were given and we headed home to make preparations for the competition.

The turnout for practice was matched by the efforts that were being put in as match day approached. With Suffolk having already experienced a degree of success on the venue, Steve in particular, was confident that we'd come away with silverware. Abi was too old to compete, but her preparation as a coach, possibly epitomized best, the attitude of everyone involved.

Having started work with the *Angling Times*, Abi was staying with Rob, Julie and Abbi in Benwick during the week and therefore was able to commute to work in Peterborough. Travelling home for the weekend late one Friday afternoon and armed with a supply of suitable pole floats from Rob; she tied a full tray of 14 rigs that same evening. Steve and I have been criticized by outsiders for the assistance we give to our anglers with tying rigs and preparing hooklengths and Steve Damant recounts a story of how he'd been overheard after a match and was being quizzed regarding our rig-making. After being told by the team manager concerned that this was something that they'd never contemplate; Steve's retort suggested that this may be why Suffolk were on the podium whilst his team wasn't!

This level and degree of assistance however, is completely within all the rules of competition and we feel it's reciprocated with the efforts of the anglers on the bank and much appreciated by their parents. Motivation through preparation of bait and tackle is, I feel, rarely lost on participants in these circumstances and on this particular occasion, we felt our efforts would surely to be rewarded.

As match day approached, it became apparent that no other cadet teams would be competing. This was a disappointment for us, as we had almost enough in the relevant age group to field two teams of three, as well as a team of six juniors and two teams of four intermediates. The NJAA however, allowed Lewis Clouting to make up the second team of cadets, despite his 13th birthday falling 25 days before the match. With two teams from Suffolk then able to compete, this would see a contest take place in the inaugural cadets' competition. (Later, the NJAA would raise the cadets' age limit to under-14, in line with Angling Trust's age categories.)

Match day arrived and after leaving home early, Suffolk's contingent assembled with the other competing squads at the Peartree Bridge Inn. With the draw complete and bait distributed, Suffolk's youngsters headed for their respective sections up and down the waterway. Within walking distance of match HQ, Suffolk coaches, Abi Brewster and Steve Damant oversaw the cadets' match, where Steve's son, Jack took the individual title with 1kg 260gm. Team-wise, Suffolk Red's Paul Christie, Lewis Clouting and Max Rushbrook took the honours. Max also collected the Youngest Competitor salver. There were commendable performances too, from Jamie Marriott and Ollie Saunders as all six anglers weighed in nets of mainly small fish.

With two 'no shows', there were just four teams in the junior competition. In the Milton Keynes line-up, Olivia Bullock was fishing as a guest alongside Anna Blyth. Tom Cottrell was Suffolk's junior skipper for the day and the remainder of his team comprised James Head, Sam Kennard, David Ward, Peter Williams and Charlie Elton. Steve Barnes and I had spent most of Friday first mixing and then dividing up and bagging groundbait. We then made final tackle and bait preparations. After a drive down from Harleston, Charlie had been dropped off at Steve's in the afternoon and as I left, the two of them had headed for Needham Lake. Charlie's size 16 elastic was around 14 grades too heavy and some last minute adjustments were required! With a more suitable grade of latex fitted and with a short session on GVAC's flagship venue under his belt, Charlie looked more the part as he set up on the Grand Union on Saturday morning.

The junior match length was a short drive from the draw and we parked in the residential area nearby. As a roving steward, my time was divided between all three competitions and I recall Anna requiring my services as a first aider just before the all-in. This was in-between my journeys to and from our anglers' pegs as Steve and I ferried hooklength spools, groundbait buckets and other items to those found wanting at the last minute. I also managed to get a photograph of all our anglers before heading back to check on the cadets and to see how the intermediates' match was progressing.

The under-19s were pegged on the stretch that the squad had practised on and in A section and fishing for Suffolk for the first time, I found Bradley Calver. Along the match length also, were Toby and Timmy Pepper, with Adam Skillcorn completing the Gold team line-up. Brad's dad, Brett, informed me that his son was catching and that Ashley Miller was also doing okay next-door; in the 15-peg sections, yet again, the two Suffolk sides had drawn beside each other! Rob advised that Ashley's (Red) teammates, Abbi Kendall, Charlotte Gore and Reece Page, were also doing reasonably well. Word on the bank from another team manager was also that Suffolk's juniors were catching better than anyone.

The juniors were indeed, doing well and early on, Peter Williams had made contact with a small, but typically lively tench that he played with his top kit underwater as a narrow boat passed through his peg. Safely netted, the fish helped him to a second-in-section 1kg 650gm; his catch bettered only in the under-16s' event by Matthew Oliver of Milton Keynes. Sam Kennard fished his usual busy and accomplished match, but he doubted his eventual section win as Olivia netted a large perch at the death. Sam however, returned 1kg 250gm for both the section win and third place overall. Olivia picked up the default section silverware along with the Top Girl trophy. Further section wins from James (who just pipped Anna) and Charlie; a second from Tom and David's third saw Suffolk finish two points clear of Milton Keynes.

With Lee Newson's help, Rob had come up with a precise, but simple plan to fish for mainly small fish. A 200-mile round trip for practice, and rig-making and hooklength tying by Steve, Abi and me proved their worth when we collated results on the bank. Steve and Rob had also put time in with additional practice sessions, bringing individual anglers up to speed before match day and all these factors combined to produce something very special indeed...

After a quiet early spell, Ashley had continued to find bonus perch and skimmers as he rotated his swims as per team instructions. Along the match length, both Red and Gold team members had built their nets steadily, with only Toby Pepper failing to break a kilo with his sixth-in-section 910gm. All eight Suffolk anglers had however, finished in the top six of their sections in the fifteen-peg contest. Toby's brother, Timmy had top-scored for his team with two points with Abbi taking the section next-door. Brad, Adam and Reece all finished fourth in section with Charlotte Gore's three points demonstrating her pedigree and experience on the venue. Given the size of the field however, there were no foregone conclusions as the announcements continued back at the Peartree Bridge Inn where Abbi stepped forward to collect her more-than-deserved section winner's trophy.

After seeing the expensive butt section of her Maver pole roll into the canal, she was threatened with disqualification should she attempt to retrieve it before the match's conclusion and this despite there being nothing prohibiting from her doing so in the rules. Abbi had regained her composure, continued to catch and recorded 1kg 550gm to top her section and finish twelfth overall. Soon after, Ashley, who'd returned 2kg 940gm, was crowned individual champion.

As tradition dictates, the positions of all fifteen competing teams were announced in reverse order and finally, with just the top three remaining, Suffolk still hadn't been mentioned! As the first syllable of 'Wakefield' left the announcer's lips, the Suffolk contingent realised immediately what they'd achieved: a one-two finish! Toby, Timmy, Brad and Adam collected their team runners-up trophies, thanks to their 16-point team tally and shortly after, Reece, Charlotte, Ashley and Abbi stepped forward as 2011 team champions having amassed between them, just 9 penalty points!

With over two years' professional coaching completed, I was reading more and more about team sport and it was becoming clear that principles from outside match angling had an important part to play in what Steve Barnes and I were looking to achieve. The Grand Union, like most canals, had provided a level playing field for participants. Although several teams were much more experienced on this particular type of venue, Lee's information, Rob's high level match experience, the efforts put in by Abi with rig preparation, along with what Steve and I had looked to do, had all combined with the enthusiasm of the anglers, the support of their parents and everyone else involved with the squad to produce what were, looking back, reasonably comfortable victories. I read about 'critical non-essentials' in Sir Clive Woodward's book, *Winning* and application of this concept was clearly apparent in September 2011 when Suffolk County experienced their most successful match day ever. I was keen to put this and other coaching philosophies into practice and to continue to learn from successful and renowned coaches from all sports.

At Milton Keynes, whilst we were perhaps a little stunned, bemused and possibly even embarrassed; we celebrated after the presentations. Coaches congratulated anglers and parents congratulated and thanked coaches. There were handshakes aplenty as we savoured the squad's achievements whilst the teams posed with their silverware by the canal. Later however, there was a word of caution from Charlotte's dad, John. With Charlotte having been a regular member of the sponsored Farnborough outfit and John having noted Suffolk's improving performances; he'd seen such a day coming. He explained that, now we'd become, if not always the team to beat, at least one which was expected to do well at every event, we'd need to look over our shoulders at those that were less than charitable and more than keen to see us knocked off our pedestal.

John's were wise and prophetic words and in competitions following that outstanding day, Steve and I experienced our anglers being accused of various infringements of rules, all of which were completely unfounded. More than once for instance, members of our squad were accused of fishing poles at longer than the permitted length. I would receive verbal abuse when endeavouring to enforce match rules at the NJAA Challenge just four weeks later and Abbi being threatened with disqualification on the Grand Union was sadly, an indication of things to come. Whilst this and other incidents may not have been a direct consequence of our apparent rise to fame, or at least the recent successes of Suffolk County; it certainly felt that many were indeed, out to get us. Just because you're paranoid and all that…

Our work with the county squad in 2011 wasn't done by a long chalk and for the Challenge on 1st October, I took over from Steve as project manager; I also had the added and rather dubious pleasure of actually running the event!

WINNING AT THE WATER PARK

The facilities and number of pegs available had always made Suffolk Water Park suitable for an NJAA competition and I'd submitted the required risk assessment and other necessary details ahead of the 2009 EOYM. The venue was duly accepted and I would host the event. Whilst the fishing over the four match lakes was varied and, as a consequence, any squad match plan would be a lot more detailed than usual; I'd made my submission in anticipation that the stocking levels would surely see all participants catch a number of fish and in that regard, I wasn't to be disappointed.

The change of NJAA rules regarding participants' ages meant that Abi unfortunately, would not be able to compete. Once again though, she was more than keen to help with preparations as I organized practices for each of the three weekends before match day on three of the four lakes. Ironically, the intermediates' maximum age was increased from under-19 to under-22 the following year in an effort to get more teams and anglers on the bank.

The Canal

Just seven days after the Milton Keynes match, Abi and I were enjoying a bacon sandwich and cup of tea in the café at the Water Park as several of our young anglers and their parents joined us. After paying peg fees our convoy of cars headed for the far side of the complex, close to where the Gipping winds its way towards Bramford.

The Canal at Suffolk Water Park is a long, narrow lake accommodating 20 anglers fishing from one bank towards the reeds opposite. Many years ago, I'd won a club match on the water, fishing shop bought, soft pellets at half-depth and catching small carp. By 2011 however, these carp had grown and had evidently been transferred to other lakes on the complex and the sport on the matured water was very different.

Steve Damant was with us to assist with coordination and Bradley Calver was keen to take part and share information based on his considerable experience on the venue. Like most of us though, Brad was more familiar with the larger lakes and so after a safety talk and briefing, Steve and I placed the anglers along the bank, making note of which baits they were to fish and which techniques were to be tried out in an effort to come up with an effective approach for match day. The idea was to vary the different methods and baits and see what was producing. We'd also look to make adjustments during the session and ensure everyone became familiar with successful tactics. Our aims also, were to see that all present put a good few fish in their net and were confident, should they draw the lake on 1st October. On match day, the Canal would accommodate two sections of juniors (under-16s) with the remaining anglers - four more sections - spread over Match Lake 2 and Match Lake 3.

Abi set up looking to catch silver fish close in and like the others, also fed lines in the deeper water and right across whilst Lewis Clouting based his attack around pellets. Tommy Cottrell, Jack Damant, Paul Christie and Brad were to use different combinations of worm, caster, pellet and fishmeal groundbait. I encouraged anglers to compare their findings throughout the session and we were soon able to disregard certain considerations. Abi was catching well close in, whilst Tom and Jack were taking fish from across. Later in the session, Lewis netted some good skimmers from the deeper water; Jack landed a very good rudd and Abi took a sizeable perch. A few bonus tench were also landed including one by me after a spirited fight on a white Hydro set-up as I sat on Abi's box. After his slow start, we changed Paul's approach and having fed a new line with worm, he too put a number of good skimmers in his net. The fishmeal groundbait wasn't productive and so that was dismissed. Later, Steve Damant's wife Nicky, daughter Ella and Tom's dad, Nigel joined us after the fish were safely released and as we gathered for the all-important debrief.

The day had proved more than fruitful and all were willing to share both their experiences during the session - and Abi's chocolate Hobnobs! Watching Abi and then fishing myself later, I concluded that roach and rudd could be caught close in to start with, but as the session progressed, more delicate presentation by way of lighter shotting down the line was required to keep these fish coming. Our collective agreement was that chopped worm and caster across (or in the deeper water for those that might struggle with longer pole lengths), was one of the main lines of attack. Initially though, time should be spent building a weight close in with small fish, whilst feeding and preparing the far lines. Brad in particular, endorsed this approach, given what he'd experienced during the session. With conclusions drawn and notes made, I gave details of the following week's session and looked to draft the official match plan for the lake with Abi's help and Steve's approval, in-between my school sessions.

Match Lake 1

The largest match lake on the complex accommodated 42 pegs, ample for the number of intermediate teams that were due to compete. With just three weekends available, I wasn't able to fit in a practice on all four lakes, but given the similarities between M2 and its larger neighbour; I encouraged juniors in the squad to join the intermediates on the bank of M1 on the second weekend. I felt that there'd be numerous benefits with an integrated session: not only would the juniors get the opportunity to try out my anticipated approach for M2, but that they'd also be able to spend some time in the close company of Toby and Timmy Pepper who travelled down for the session. Brad was also with us, as were Reece Page and Ashley Miller. Abbi by now had her own car and she made the journey from Benwick. Abi was also on the bank, with both Steves and a good few parents. Charlie Elton and Peter Williams attended, as did Tommy, Jack and Lewis.

With the session well underway, Abi and Abbi took a break from the fishing to chat to Ian Didcote, Steve Barraclough and Andy Neal on the opposite bank. They were filming a DVD with their sponsors, Bait-Tech and Abi had made acquaintance with several of the anglers on shoots in the course of her work with the *Angling Times*, but this wasn't before she'd stolen the show early on by landing a handsome, double figure common carp on her second cast!

As the day progressed, several carp were hooked, but not all were landed and those unfamiliar with the size and power of these fish were able to make necessary tackle adjustments. I was adamant that any team plan wouldn't be based on carp alone and encouraged the intermediates to look to catch roach and rudd close in, as well as skimmers and possibly bream on the long pole, whilst also experimenting with the feeder, pellet waggler and bomb. I spent time with Jack, looking to get him into a rhythm and catching small fish to hand. Steve Barnes managed to latch on to one of the lake's carp on the long pole, but like a few others, we never got to see it.

Many lessons were learned once again and the session ended with several anglers sitting behind Timmy Pepper who had, on his first visit to the venue, both caught well and seemed to be demonstrating exactly the sort of approach that would be required on match day. Given the large area of bank and number fishing, I felt I could have run the session better and made appropriate notes that reflected this on my planner. Nonetheless, as we debriefed in the large car park close to M1, it was once again evident that an awful lot had been gained from the day. Steve is of the opinion that anglers that fish a venue for the first time in practice have a 45-minute head start on those that haven't come match day and I don't think he's far out. Late in the day the anglers left and I made a few more notes before drawing up another lake-specific plan for the match.

Match Lake 2

On a school session-free day during the week, I'd arranged to meet James Head for a practice on M2. James hadn't been able to make the previous weekend sessions and a few hours' one-to-one would give me opportunity to run through plans for the Canal and what I had in mind for M2 itself. The evening would also give James a chance to try out Abi's Garbolino G796 pole. Abi had taken delivery of a G-Max 1000 and James was looking to upgrade from his 'barbel basher'!

Nigel Cottrell too, spent time on M2 before match day and fed back valuable information. I knew from my experiences in silver fish matches that a reasonable weight could be built by catching good roach and rudd close in on caster. I was also very confident with a groundbait mix I'd used incorporating Van den Eynde's Supermatch, Supercup and scolded pigeon droppings. After giving James a tour of Abi's pole holdall and explaining the choice of kits and elastic set-ups, I ran through our probable approach for the match and after feeding a few different lines, he dropped his rig in the water close in over his groundbait.

I already had in mind what I referred to as a 'stepped-up roach rig' for use on M2, incorporating a main line of 0.14mm or 0.16mm, with a hooklength of 0.12mm and size 16 hook (for the Canal and M3, I'd recommended main lines of 0.12mm and hooklengths of 0.10mm). The idea of the M2 rig was that should bonus carp be hooked whilst fishing for the roach and rudd, our anglers would have a sporting chance of landing them. Before match day I would make up several of these rigs and also prepared spools of spare hooklengths. I used the extremely versatile Preston Chiantis painted with a coat or two of Sally Hansen

'Hard as Nails' and added a fourth piece of silicone above the eye to prevent it being ripped from the float body, with the other three spread along the stem. There were no snags as such to worry about and the carp were of smaller average size than those in M1, so weren't too much of a problem when played close to the platforms. It wouldn't take us too long to find out whether these M2 rigs were up the job, given that number 5 elastic ripped from the top kit soon after James dropped his bait in. Neither of us should have been concerned; the soft elastic did its job in absorbing the carp's runs, the rig remained intact and the Mustad Wide Gape Barbless hook held firm. James continued to loose-feed caster whilst playing the carp and after its release, checked his hooklength, re-baited and was catching quality roach and rudd almost immediately.

The session with James went as expected and whilst we were unable to catch skimmers or bream on the long pole line; during the match itself, our anglers would have more time to try out each of their different lines and would be able to channel their efforts accordingly.

After the session, I had another match plan to draw up for Abi and Steve to check. I also fed back to Steve regarding the rigs and, as ever, had no qualms about tying as many as I could before match day, when we'd field not one, but two junior teams. Before then though, we had one more practice session.

Match Lake 3

M3 is a circular lake with all anglers fishing facing a central island; hence its nickname: 'the Doughnut'. We'd been told that double figure nets of silver fish were a possibility and carp, if any were indeed present, weren't worth considering. It was a bright, sunny morning for our final practice and after Steve Barnes and I gave a quick briefing, Tom, Jack, Lewis, Paul, Charlie and Peter made their way to their pegs and for the first time in the campaign, we were joined by Max

Rushbrook. Having been forced to shuffle teams a little, we'd drafted young Max in to ensure we had a full complement come match day. With no cadets' category in the NJAA Challenge however, and consequently no verbal coaching for that age group permitted as in the National, we looked to give Max a thorough update on everything learned during the previous weeks, whilst also ensuring he'd have the required level of confidence for the competition.

We looked for our anglers to test the theory regarding the stocks of silver fish close in and with Steve himself fishing, we built up a more accurate picture of how anglers should approach M3 if they drew it. Caster didn't really produce and Steve managed to maintain contact with small fish late in the session by fishing maggot over loose-fed pellet. Once again, practice led us to tweak our anticipated match plan.

With the boards of the island looking inviting, Tom and Jack lowered their chopped worm hookbait over cupped-in offerings and were soon into better fish on their long pole lines, whilst others put nets of small fish together. Tom included three good tench in his mixed net as the squad also banked good roach, rudd and perch, along with the odd skimmer. Abi and I spent time with Max as he looked to master the loop knot which, with his dad, Charlie's help; he'd then practise all week. We planned to give Max one of my spare poles and top kits with rigs attached. We would also furnish him with a cupping kit, spare rigs and hooklength spools for the match. Max told us later that he had indeed, practised the loop knot during the week with Charlie and had even tied it in the dark! The day's fishing drew to a close and after taking a few photographs, we debated our findings and debriefed. Before we left the Water Park, we summarized and concluded and went over final arrangements ahead of the match six days later.

In the coming days, I put the finishing touches to the match plans for all four lakes. These were A4 size documents and all fairly detailed. We would look though, for the intermediates to let their own experiences guide them once they were fishing. We were well aware that on M1, carp would be the dominant species, but also that some would sit it out for them at the expense of other fish and would come unstuck. I advised that 20lb to 30lb would be good enough for a high section placing.

On M2, again, we knew that carp would decide who took home the individual silverware; but we were after a team result first and foremost. Our plan to consider carp only as a bonus had been reinforced by Abi's observation of a club match weigh-in. Having followed the scales at a weekend fixture as I sat on her box during a practice session on another lake, she'd reported back that very few carp were included in anglers' nets. Along with their pole lines, those comfortable with a feeder rod could consider the Method for skimmers and bream and our one concession as far as carp were concerned was that later in the match, they could also underarm their feeder into the margins. None of our anglers should, if at all possible, go 10 minutes without a fish. I was confident that on M2, good nets of quality roach and rudd would be caught by our team. I was also confident of other teams blowing out as one or more of their anglers sat biteless fishing for carp; 10lb I advised, should be regarded as a minimum weight to aim for.

The plan for M3 was similar to that for the Canal. Given our experiences in practice however, pinkie would be used and fed over groundbait for roach and rudd close in. As ever, we instructed our anglers to fish both sides of their pegs; as Rob always says, one will fish better than the other. We also gave the juniors a lower target weight of 5lb per man on M3, compared to 10lb on the Canal. On both lakes, our anglers were instructed to feed their far lines and top-up periodically, but not to fish them for the first hour of the match. We found in practice that feeding these far lines initially without fishing them, really paid dividends and we felt that this tactic would be even more effective on match day. The additional advice I gave our anglers for match day, was to place their keepnets in the margins gently and to push them out with their landing net poles, rather than throw them in and disturb any resident fish unnecessarily before the start of competition; as ever, I was 'sweating the small stuff'.

All four lake-specific match plans were emailed or posted and follow-up phone calls made to ensure that they'd been received and understood. I then looked to prepare a sufficient quantity of my preferred silver fish groundbait mix for all four of our teams. I also planned to prepare separate casters for the hook, leaving some uncovered before the match to crispen up. This is a standard technique used by many match anglers that appreciate how much easier they are to hook without bursting than those kept in water during competition; their buoyancy also counteracting the weight of the hook and therefore giving a slower, more natural fall.

Additional rigs were tied and hooklength spools were topped up. With junior anglers not knowing which lake they'd be on until the draw, I prepared ice cream tubs labelled accordingly and these would be handed out by parents and coaches once the draw was complete.

In the previous chapter I mentioned critical non-essentials and when preparing for the 2011 Challenge, I looked to see the concept put into practice in our efforts to secure further team success. The basic principle is that whilst one small thing you do in an effort to improve your performance might give you only a very small advantage; a number will see an accumulation of effect. Great Britain won seven of the ten gold medals available in track cycling at the Beijing Olympics in 2008. Four years later, British Cycling's performance director, Dave Brailsford would explain his 'aggregation of marginal gains' concept on BBC Breakfast on the final morning of competition at the velodrome, as Team GB repeated their dominance at London 2012.

Back in 2011, I was keen to see our anglers benefit from what I was learning. Team matches, the like those that Suffolk were fishing, were often won and lost on returns from mid-section when just one or two fish made a difference in placings. If we could do a number of things before the match that would see some, if not all of our anglers take a few more fish over the course of the match, they would possibly, see us edge out others that didn't perhaps, make such a collective effort.

Thanks to Steve, we would have four complete teams on the bank come match day. This in itself was something several clubs and associations couldn't manage and invariably we'd beaten one or two teams even before the draw. We continued to run the risk of taking points off ourselves by having more than one team fishing in an age category; but the efforts made in giving as many youngsters as we could, valuable experience of fishing against some of the country's best young anglers were, Steve and I felt, being rewarded.

Our practice sessions had seen almost all of our squad fishing. Adam Skillcorn had not been able to get to Suffolk in the weeks leading up to the match; but when I phoned him a few days before the match he was more than happy with the team plan. Robert Murphy knew the Water Park as well as any of our anglers and he too confirmed that he was ready. As he had done at Milton Keynes, Adam would line up with Timmy, Toby and Brad in our Gold team, with Robert in our Red team, alongside Abbi, Ashley and Reece. Following his performances in practice, Jack, still a cadet, joined Sam Kennard, James, Peter, Tom and Charlie in our Red junior team. Our Gold line-up would comprise Jamie Marriott, Ollie Saunders, David Ward, Paul, Max and Lewis.

Squad preparations were dovetailed in with mine as match organizer. A month before, I'd submitted a second risk assessment and would complete another on match day. My final event and lake plan, that gave anglers and managers details of the sections and temporary peg numbers, had been emailed to Roger Drew, the NJAA Results Officer. I'd also emailed directions to the Water Park with venue rules and contact numbers so teams could arrange practices. Having cancelled my usual Friday afternoon session with Springfield Junior School, I telephoned the Water Park to confirm final arrangements. I'd also spoken to Patrick at the café, ensuring that he was aware of a business opportunity and he advised that he'd stay open later than usual to cater for post-match demand.

Temperatures Rise!

Steve and I always looked to ensure that our anglers didn't feel unnecessary or unacceptable pressure when fishing, but it was a far from stress-free Suffolk County host that was at the Water Park early on the morning of 1st October. Soon after arriving and as Suffolk's anglers congregated on the grassy parking area, I dealt with a number of issues ranging from a complaint regarding supposed interference with another team's practice, to an unjustified criticism regarding lack of signage and directions to the venue. Once again, I was not at all happy. Steve was on hand to see that what I felt was a nonsensical and purely malicious accusation of practice interference got the attention it deserved: no more. Given that this match was, in my humble opinion, the best organized NJAA event I'd ever been to and the criticism regarding signage was quite bizarre, after threatening to resign as an NJAA official there and then; I composed myself and got on with hosting and running it!

It was unusually warm for the first day of October and the Telegraph would later report recorded temperatures of 32C at Cavendish not many miles away. Along with the bait I'd prepared, I packed additional bottles of water in cool boxes, should they be needed by competitors. Indeed these would be utilized later as temperatures reached their peak. Back in the parking area and with all our anglers present, both Steves assisted with distribution of squad bait, which included premixed roach groundbait and individual supplies of dry hook casters for every Suffolk competitor, along with their feed – Sainsbury's always do well out of us for resealable food and freezer bags!

Before the draw, I called together all anglers, coaches and managers and ensured that they were aware that non-competitors should sit, or observe the match from, the areas behind the concrete peg markers. This information had been distributed before the match and I had every intention to ensure that 'my' match would be a fair one for all participating. With the briefings and draw formalities complete, all anglers headed for their sections on the various lakes. Along with the peg plan, I'd also copied a Water Park map and added notes for everyone attending. Looking back, it seems ironic that, given how well the venue fished and what a success the event was, I vowed immediately after that I'd never run another one!

Steve Barnes coordinated distribution of rigs and hooklengths once our anglers were on their pegs and one of our final jobs was to see that Sam had an appropriate team polo shirt. Our usual attendance to last minute coaches' duties was interrupted only by a threat of physical violence as someone took exception to where Steve had parked his car, albeit quite legitimately. Again, I'll elaborate no more.

With the matches for both age groups underway, Steve Barnes and Steve Damant began stewarding on M2 and M3 respectively. As a registered first aider, I'd been designated as a roving steward. Not long after the match had started, I found cause to ask a parent to move up the bank and behind the relevant concrete peg marker. As more than one adult joined him on the platform, I also advised that the intermediate angler on the peg should not be receiving assistance. For my trouble, I was subjected to a foul mouthed rant from the angler's father, within earshot of the mother of one our anglers close by.

Soon after, I found cause to ask another parent to move up the bank, this time on M2. Roger Dew had made the same request previously, but the second request saw him react, shall we say, not very amenably. I'm indebted to

Steve Damant who, on seeing the situation developing from his vantage point nearby on M3, wandered over. Steve is not small, possesses little or no head hair and sports several large and conspicuous tattoos. He'd also left his shirt on the grass by M3 and had his substantial torso on full display as he made his way over. His presence and state of partial undress, I'm sure, saw the parent in question see sense and listen to my explanation regarding NJAA rules; a short time later he sat where instructed and remained there!

In addition to the issues I experienced personally, one of our stewards was also the subject of another bizarre and informal 'complaint'. The Suffolk parent concerned was doing a thoroughly conscientious job and was working with a fellow steward from another association. It transpired that the latter was visiting the toilet and ours had, in the high temperatures, taken five minutes' rest on one of our club stools, where permitted and with all the anglers in the section clearly visible. A rival team manager however, took exception to him sitting behind his son for a short while. The accusation and intimidation were laughed off and we heard nothing further. The stewards continued with their duties and I was told later, that they were required to take action when an adult was found to be mixing groundbait in his car and walking it down to his son.

I'd been subjected to a verbal badgering at Milton Keynes and had been lambasted for supposedly phoning youngsters from all over the country and poaching them from other teams. This, along with the unnecessary upset that ensued after Abbi's pole section rolled into the canal, paled into significance compared to what Steve and I were experiencing at our own event. For the record, I never telephoned or approached any angler with a view to persuading them to leave their team or squad to fish for Suffolk. Neither Steve, nor I would stand in an angler's way should they wish to move on in order to progress and develop. My advice to managers that lose anglers is to ask the youngsters for the reason(s) behind their decision to leave. But enough already! What of more important matters... the fishing?

A Plan Comes Together...

Despite the bright sunshine, high temperatures and numbers of anglers and spectators present, the lakes seemed to be fishing well once the match got underway. Carp were being caught on M1, but as expected, not by all and for us, that was good news.

On M2, it came to light just before the match started, that one team were fielding an overage angler and later, NJAA officials (of which I was one), were obliged to disregard his weight and score. Evidently the squad in question had anglers aged under-16 fishing in the under-19s' match and an offer to swap before the whistle was turned down.

As expected, the individual winner of the junior match was to come from M2, as those on end pegs were able to cast their Method feeders to the empty corners. Once again though, several would end the match without carp – more good news for our anglers, none of which had that end peg advantage. Sam, on A4 was unlucky not to finish higher than his eventual fourth in section. Part of his recorded 3kg 720gm was a large perch. He had no carp, but was close to his target team weight as the anglers below him didn't break half a kilo. Jamie (Gold) stole the show in A section, latching on to a carp late on and taking his time to ensure that it ended up in his keepnet. It helped him to 5kg 220gm for two points and he was beaten in his section only by the individual winner of the match on one of the end pegs.

On the opposite bank, James fished an accomplished match, taking 6kg 410gm to the scales, also for two points; but he was unlucky to miss the section by just 150gm. Early in the match I'd watched Paul along the bank, catching skimmers on the long pole. Much later though, and whilst watching Jamie play a carp; I saw Paul doing the same on the far side. After several minutes, both netted their bonus fish; the stepped up roach rigs were doing their job! Steve had been close by and told me after that he could see our team plan unfolding right in front of his eyes. Paul's 5kg 430gm saw another team target weight achieved.

Sport was patchy on M3 and more small fish were being caught in the shade. Jack, who finished second in C section told me afterwards that with few small fish present close in on his peg, he'd gone across much earlier than the team plan dictated. He was though, rewarded with quality fish over chopped worm which saw him return 3kg 250gm for the best Suffolk weight on the lake. David caught well for the Gold team and he too, easily surpassed his target weight with 2kg 810gm for three points. Elsewhere on M3, Peter took the runner-up spot in C section with 2kg 280gm, thanks in part, to a large skimmer that he landed after snagging someone else's rig which was still attached to the fish! Having left young Max with his loaned kit at the whistle, he quietly went about his business. He'd not caught well in practice, but we'd spent time with him as detailed earlier in the chapter. On a hot and difficult day, Steve and I were chuffed to bits to see him take 680gm to the scales (around 1lb 8oz) for four points.

Only two of our junior anglers finished outside the top half of their sections: one from each team. It was evident that whilst other teams were winning sections, they were also carrying anglers with very low scores as the carp – just as we'd anticipated - made only a cameo appearance in the junior event.

On the Canal, the generous pegging gave Tom plenty of water and I described his weight afterwards as outrageous. He fished a steady match, returning 7kg 850gm (over 17lb) and even claimed that he hadn't realised that he was doing that well! Ollie was third in section with 1kg 400gm and in F, once again, both Suffolk's anglers were in the top three. Charlie's 3kg 650gm gave him second and

Lewis's 2kg 750gm was third with the three anglers below Lewis not breaking a kilo.

The disqualification of the overage angler did not affect the positions of the top three junior teams as Suffolk's Gold team made the podium with 18 points (18kg 290gm) and Barnsley were runners-up (16 points). The relatively comfortable winners in the under-16s' event were Suffolk County Red with a total of 13 points (26kg 840gm). Of the twelve anglers Suffolk had on the bank, Tom was the only section winner, but our plan and consistent team performances had seen Suffolk take the team trophy and our Gold team of mostly cadets, take the third spot with five points to spare over fourth. There were further celebrations as both Jamie and Jack picked up a default section winner's medal and Tom was announced as individual runner-up.

Double Top!

Things proved to be a little tighter in the intermediates' event where seven teams eventually lined the banks of M1. Steve and I felt that our under-19s were fairly evenly matched and team-wise, we'd chosen to leave things as they were on the Grand Union, but with Robert stepping in for Charlotte Gore who was unavailable. We were more than happy to see Robert back on the bank and not only because of his obvious skills on a commercial fishery and our anticipation that he'd do well. He hadn't practised with us, but had called in at the venue after one of our sessions to confirm arrangements. I'd furnished him with our plan, but Robert we were sure, would fish his own match and once he'd landed a carp or two – and we were certain he would – he'd continue to build his weight and secure good points for his team. To be fair, we had given the intermediates quite a bit of leeway, but were still looking for them to strive for the target weight. Come match day, Robert was his usual laid-back self; his demeanour was a breath of fresh air and stark contrast to the goings-on that Steve and I were having to deal with as detailed earlier.

Ashley and Timmy were pegged in the area where we'd practised on A2 and A6 respectively. Further along were Robert (B2) and Adam (B6) and continuing clockwise round the lake, were Abbi (C2), Toby (C6), Reece (D2) and finally, Brad in the trees (D6).

On the back of his Grand Union win, Ashley was perhaps unlucky not to finish higher in section. Like Reece, Ashley lost a carp after the final whistle, with little eventually separating third, fourth and him in fifth. Timmy though, picked up where he'd left off in practice and fished an outstanding match, weighing in 11kg 630gm for two points. In B, Robert had indeed managed to catch a few carp. I understand his 33kg 660gm was a new NJAA Challenge record, but the photos I have, show that he remained as relaxed throughout the day as he was on arrival; he was the same during the post-match formalities. Adam had also quietly gone about his business and whilst he didn't find numbers of carp, his 8kg 150gm after seeing the venue for the first time that day, saw him better two anglers in the section.

Things in C section were exceptionally tight and Steve Barnes, close by on M2, witnessed the faultless display form Toby, who won his section with 22kg 410gm. Afterwards, he was characteristically generous when he advised that he wouldn't have taken the section without the back-up silver fish and was particularly complimentary about my groundbait mix. Thoughts were spared for Abbi though, as she too, with Rob watching from the top of the bank, fished very well. She was unlucky to lose a very good carp under her feet as I looked on and her 20kg 750gm saw her finish fourth in section. Reece, like Ashley, rued the loss of his last minute carp and recorded 5kg 210gm for another four points. Our quiet man, Brad, had been out of sight in the high numbered permanent pegs. Whilst he hadn't exactly lit up the sky in our sessions before the match; he was always forthcoming with information (helping Abi in particular, when she fished club matches on the complex). Come match day though, like Toby, he was a class act. His 10kg 850gm was the only weight in D section to break double figures and it was befitting that his final score for the Gold team clinched the team trophy, as they finished one point ahead of JCB. Our Red team's 14 points saw them pipped to the podium by Barnsley's 12-point tally. Things could have been very different, but for lost fish; a fact not lost on Robert who took no time in pulling the many legs available afterwards!

As weights were recorded and section positions calculated, it became clear how close the final positions would be. I'd caught sight of the final results while conversing with Roger of the NJAA in the bait shop before the official presentations. As I returned to join our squad outside, Pep in particular, was waiting anxiously for news of how we'd done; I resisted though, any temptation to confirm the team result until the silverware was presented later.

Along with our junior team win, Tom's individual second and our cadets making the podium; it was equally pleasing and satisfying to see our Gold team take the intermediates' trophy. We'd won back-to-back NJAA intermediate competitions with two different teams of anglers and Robert had been crowned individual champion. Toby's individual third place and Brad's thoroughly deserved section winner's medal had seen Suffolk County enjoy another (very) good day at the office.

The event itself was also a resounding success. Roger chatted with me afterwards explaining that he believed the total weight of fish landed was easily better than any previous Challenge. My personal celebrations were tempered however, by my experiences as match host and as a steward. In putting forward the Water Park, I'd looked to run a completely fair match and in that regard, I felt I'd failed, given that a number of parents had chosen to flout event rules and my instructions. I made it clear at the subsequent NJAA meeting that whilst stewarding, in addition to others that I'd spoken to, Steve and I had also found the need to ask one Suffolk parent move back behind the concrete peg marker more than once. To my knowledge though, none of our contingent has ever sworn at, or abused a steward as they looked to carry out their duties.

Following the NJAA's EOYM, I was invited to redraft the rules in an effort to combat and reduce the unacceptable behaviour such as that seen at the Challenge and as experienced by others in previous matches. Despite the concerns of one or two regarding the implications of disqualification in such circumstances, following a lengthy debate during which, I'd received considerable support; the new rules were accepted unanimously at the 2012 AGM. I also chose to step down as Minutes Secretary at the same meeting, where Roger was good enough to propose me as an Honorary Life Member (this was a complete surprise) and this motion was also carried unanimously. I continued after, to assist Roger with drafting and editing NJAA documents when required. I remained defiant though and made it crystal clear that I would never run another national event.

Steve and I reflected on what had been an outstanding year that had brought Suffolk County six national team titles. In terms of silverware, we were the country's most successful squad and in Toby, Ashley, Jack and Robert we also had four individual champions. We'd put in an unprecedented amount of work and had managed to get more anglers on the bank in national competition than ever before. Leaving Suffolk Water Park after the Challenge, several of us called in at the Claydon Crown for a celebratory drink before moving on to the Rampant Horse in Needham Market. With us not having to travel far home, a relaxing meal at the 'Ramp' was a welcome change from the usual post-match McDonald's!

Suffolk Sport Awards

As a result of our continuing work with youngsters, and following several nominations by parents; GVAC were shortlisted for Club of the Year at the 2011 Suffolk Sport Awards. Additionally, Amy Wall - then a School Sports Co-ordinator with whom I'd worked - was good enough to nominate me as Coach of the Year. As luck would have it, I was in Bosmere Tackle when David and Christine received another letter of confirmation regarding the forthcoming ceremony. A text from Steve would later confirm that our county squad had also been shortlisted for Junior Team of the Year. In the few weeks between receiving the confirmation of our nominations and the ceremony itself, we looked to ensure that we'd be appropriately represented in all categories and made arrangements for a number of committee members, coaches, young anglers, parents and partners to attend.

Sunday October 16th saw our contingent of nominees, club officials, guests and anglers take their places at two rather large tables within the Trinity Park Conference and Events Centre east of Ipswich. After a warm welcome and introduction from Radio Suffolk's Stephen Foster, the results of the Coach of the Year category were the first to be announced and I was named one of the runners-up behind winner, Malcolm Fenton. Malcolm, England Athletics' National Coach Mentor for Heavy Throws, went on to take the award in 2012 also, when once again, I was named as a runner-up. Malcolm told me sometime after, as we chatted at a coaches' breakfast workshop with Suffolk Sport that he too is an angler; always having a spinning rod, landing net and a few lures in his car when he travels up and down the country coaching. GVAC were also confirmed as a runner-up in the Club of the Year category, with Ipswich YM RUFC named as winners.

Testaments to all nominees were read out and announcements of the winners and presentations to category winners were punctuated by a splendid meal. Tables were adorned with countries' flags, with seating denoted accordingly; we occupied Italy and Japan! Clio Aubugeau-Williams, double gold medallist at the European Rowing Championships took to the stage with a rowing machine and Zoe Newson, a junior winner at the IPC Powerlifting Championships in Kuala Lumpur earlier in the year, gave demonstrations with her colleagues.

On the night of the 2011 event, we were absolutely thrilled to see our under-18s named as the Harrod UK Junior Team of the Year. Reece, Ashley, Abbi, James, Jack and Tom stepped forward, accompanied by loud and rousing music to collect their framed certificate, glass keepsake and perpetual cup. Before we left though, Jack walked up on stage once more to take possession of the signed and framed yellow jersey worn by 2011 Tour of Britain winner, Lars Boom that was first prize in the fundraising draw.

With county coaching commitments out of the way until 2012, I continued to run school sessions. Along with those at Barking, I had my first session on the Gipping and was extremely pleased to bank a chub to order for one of Stowmarket High School's pupils. Given my overall commitment to coaching through both funded and voluntary sessions though; I was finding it more and more difficult to fit in matches, considering the travelling and amount of time and preparation I felt was required for me to be able to continue to compete at the desired level. June 2011 therefore, had seen me sample chub sport on the Gipping. I certainly didn't break any records, but it was much more convenient to fit these, sometimes quite short, but often very rewarding sessions in. I began to enjoy the change of direction in my fishing and the challenges it brought. I also had a few trips after pike after Rob introduced me to the Old Nene at Benwick. He was also good enough to take Abi tench fishing there at the start of the river season. Despite the aggravation I'd experienced on the bank when coaching the county squad, 2011 was a very successful year... and I'd also managed to catch a few fish myself!

WESTWOOD HO!

GVAC's presentation evening in January 2012 was once again very well attended. Following the awards ceremony the previous October, Suffolk Sport's Vicki Askew and Richard Neal were good enough to come along to the Limes and hand out the silverware. In addition to the usual trophies and certificates for those that took part in our club competitions; the successes of the county squad were celebrated and commemorative medals were presented to those that had represented Suffolk for the first time in 2011.

A few weeks later, on a mild, half-term day in February; I picked up Jack Damant for a promised chub trip on the Gipping. We were on the river before lunchtime and by just after dark, he'd landed three chub with the best going 3lb 5oz.

Come the Easter holidays I was coaching with Colin and Calum at Bromeswell. The weather wasn't brilliant, but the two-day project saw plenty of fish landed by those that came along.

My school sessions began after the Easter break with Springfield and Ringshall. I also ran a taster session with Chantry High School and started my occasional Saturdays with Hardwick Middle. Before long it was also time to start planning our defence of the All England Junior Pole Championships team trophy.

Purposeful Practice

With Westwood Lakes once again hosting the competition, I wanted to secure squad practice on Skylark, the lake that would be used for the team competition on 19th May. Having contacted Alex Bates at the venue, I arranged a session for Monday of the May Day weekend. Chatting to Steve Barnes beforehand, I mooted that our Red team picked itself. Although Abbi and Josh were too old to compete in the team event; Toby and Timmy were, by then, established Suffolk County regulars and their Pole Champs pedigree was nothing short of impressive. Toby had won the under-18s' individual title in 2010 and again in 2011 when he beat Timmy by just ounces. Tommy Cottrell and James Head were still eligible and although they were both revising and preparing for their GCSEs, the Pole Champs was a competition they didn't want to miss. In Toby, Timmy, Tommy and James, Suffolk County would field four previous winners in an effort to defend our team title.

Additionally, Lewis Clouting, Jack Damant and Ollie Saunders were available once again, as was Sam Kennard. At our practice session, they were joined by Peter Williams, Paul Christie, George Sundalskliev and Jamie Marriott. Swelling numbers even further, Brandon and Rohan Andrews made the journey from Norfolk with their parents, at the suggestion of Pep, Toby and Timmy's dad. Whilst Adam Swain would line up for King's Lynn on match day; he'd already stated his intentions to join his mates, Toby and Timmy and was also present for practice. Alex was good enough to allow us use of the whole of Skylark and there was plenty of room for Peter Christie, Nigel Cottrell and Nick Marriott to sample the sport alongside the youngsters.

Kestrel Lake was also free that Monday and so a few of our intermediates tagged along, looking to get to grips with fishing for the larger ide, carp and barbel next-door. The team competition would, we established, be confined to Skylark, with Hawk set aside for pleasure anglers. The accompanying under-21s' event therefore, was to be staged on Kestrel where once again, we looked to field a number of available anglers. Our final line-up on Kestrel would be: Abi Brewster, Abbi Kendall, Ashley Miller, Robert Murphy, Reece Page and Adam Skillcorn.

Given the number we had competing for places in our Gold team and with guidance from Steve, I drew up a number of Key Performance Indicators (KPIs) that would help me make the difficult decision of who would fish on match day. My final decisions were made on the bank after consultation with Steve Damant after the weigh-in. Giving credit to those that had fished the year before, acknowledging the professional approach of all those present, as well as their preparation and attitude that day; I had the unpleasant task of advising Peter, Paul, Jamie and George that their services wouldn't be required as, unfortunately, we'd not been permitted to enter a third team. I reassured all though, that they'd be considered for the teams entered in the Angling Trust National the following month.

   For practice, I'd completed my usual session planner, prepared and delivered a structured safety talk and explained the responsibilities of a licensed coach and those associated with GVAC's Clubmark accreditation. I'd completed the necessary risk assessment and Safeguarding and Protecting Children (SPC) documentation for the newcomers and, with a supply of bait distributed with the assistance of Simon Saunders (Ollie's dad) and Steve Damant; final instructions were given regarding the fishing. Rob Lincoln made his way around the anglers offering advice and come the afternoon and despite the deteriorating weather; an organized weigh-in was conducted with notes compared and information shared. The day had gone remarkably smoothly - apart from when I found myself locked out of the mini-bus!

   With several pupils from the Gipping Valley and Thurston School Sport Partnership catchment area in our squad, I had occasional use of their mini-bus and it was almost full for practice day. Partway through the session however, I'd let a couple of the younger anglers into the bus to warm up. I'd made it clear in the morning that anyone feeling the cold would be welcome to shelter temporarily in the bus and whilst most stuck to the task in hand, a few took me up on my offer just after lunchtime.

   Not wanting to run the risk of dropping the mini-bus keys in the lake whilst assisting an angler, or losing them on site as I walked the banks, I'd left them in the ignition of the bus. After all, I was unable to lock the doors if the keys were in the bus, surely; and it was only yards from where we were fishing and in full view of us all. I'd forgotten however, that when letting passengers in and out of the rear doors, the handle at the back centrally-locked the bus. The doors had obviously been closed behind those that had been inside and subsequently had locked. When I let George, the last remaining angler out, I remembered only at the last minute, that the keys remained in the ignition and just as the gap between the two rear doors closed, blind panic set in and all thoughts of suitable team tactics for match day were forgotten!

Fortunately, I'd left the driver's window open a little. This is habitual, as I usually want to allow air in if we have bait in the bus; try as I might though, I could not get my arm through this small gap far enough to reach the keys. Thankfully, help was at hand in the form of Lee Swain, Adam's dad. After trying unsuccessfully to reassure me, he left me in my state of distress; he returned sometime later though, with what looked like a partly-completed Blue Peter creation - which he'd obviously prepared earlier! Forced into the threaded section of a long bank-stick and secured by tape, was a length of coat hanger with its hook protruding. Following Lee's instruction, I stood on one of our plastic stools and angled the hook through the gap in the window. Gingerly, I manoeuvred the hook close to the key ring and then pulled it forcibly, but carefully. Thankfully, the key itself came free and still standing on the stool and with Lee, Pep and several fathers watching; I slowly retrieved the bank-stick, with the key dangling precariously from the hook, back through the window. I exhaled loudly and unclenched my buttocks as the key came through the gap. Needless to say from then on, I kept the keys in a zipped pocket!

As far as the fishing was concerned, Jack Damant and Rohan Andrews stole the show; both posing for photos afterwards with their large bream. Sam hadn't fished Skylark before, but it didn't take him long to get to grips with the lake. With no more than two or three top kits at his disposal he stripped his gear mid-session and retackled. He explained after that he felt something wasn't right and that he believed his rig could be too heavy. Without hesitation and in cold and wet conditions, he had no qualms about spending a bit of time dismantling a complete set-up and trying a different approach. Rather than struggle on with few fish to show for his efforts, he followed his instincts, invested a little time and was then rewarded with a run of carp.

Adam had shown his experience and knowledge of the venue by taking top weight and as we debriefed in the comfort and warmth of the on-site café, it was obvious that the weather hadn't dampened squad confidence. I thanked everyone for their efforts, particularly those that had made the journey to Lincolnshire, but who wouldn't figure in plans for match day. As ever, final instructions were given and arrangements confirmed before we all headed home.

Match Day

In the final day or two before the match I paid close attention to the weather forecast. It was clear that come Saturday, we'd leave mild temperatures behind in Suffolk and head towards a cold front that would come far enough south to affect Westwood Lakes. Reading other teams' reports afterwards, it was clear that some managers and anglers were caught out by the local conditions. In my final emails to the squad, I made specific reference to the forecast for the venue. Ensuring our anglers had suitable clothing for the match wasn't just another example of attention to detail that could see them put more fish in their keepnets as a result of fishing efficiently; it was something I regarded as part of our duty of care.

With 19th May also being Steve's daughter, Amelie's birthday, I was without my wingman, minder and therapist. I would just about scrape through unscathed, but once again, the fishing took a back seat to politics on more than one occasion. Lee had warned me that I was in for a bit of flack. As mentioned earlier in the chapter, Adam had approached us, wanting to fish with Toby and Timmy and Lee was, it seemed, more than happy with how Steve and I ran things and with what we and our squad could offer at the time. I wasn't proving popular with other team coaches though, as anglers, for whatever reason, chose to approach Suffolk County. The flack that Lee had mentioned materialised, but after a protracted and heated exchange of frank opinions, the day ended with a handshake between me and the team manager concerned.

  Whilst geared up for the weather, I was caught out a little by the match format. In previous years, after a fixed draw, our anglers had made for their predetermined sections. In 2012 however, our captains were advised that that anglers could be placed. It was also announced that there'd be no bankside coaching. I'd enjoyed the bank-running in the two previous competitions, but in 2012 there was a change of policy that we weren't aware of until the morning of the match.

  Our anglers were well prepared however, and I looked to ensure that we fished within the revised rules. I'm fully sympathetic with match organizers and having been in their position myself, I understand the difficulties faced and the decisions they make, for whatever reason. Unfortunately though, it seems that these rules are not adhered to by all, or always enforced when they should be. I still have my notes from the day on which I'd recorded the organizer's comment of, 'We don't want any coaching!' I, along with all the other Suffolk coaches and assistants stayed well away from our anglers as a result of the fresh ruling. Later however, I observed fathers sitting within a couple of feet of their sons for most, if not all of the match…

  The team captains were advised that two pairs of end pegs were up for grabs for the competing teams. Pegging was clockwise around Skylark and minutes later,

Toby pulled out one of them and thanks to Jack, our Gold team was pegged next door. With little time between the draw and the start of the match, a very short discussion saw Toby and Timmy head for end pegs 1 and 22. This wasn't lost on one opposing team's coach who, I was told, questioned how the brothers had managed to get end pegs. The answer was perfectly legitimately and the unnecessary jibe perhaps demonstrated that we were winning the match psychologically, even before the anglers had got to their pegs.

Tom took peg 10 and James, 31 and although I would question later in discussion with Rob, whether we should have placed Tom and James on the end pegs; Toby and Timmy knew the lakes very well and were extremely confident. It therefore seemed sensible to place immediate pressure on other teams by 'banking' two section wins. The decision was made and I was confident too, that whilst Tom and James hadn't the experience on the venue of many competing, they would still finish high up in their sections and thus secure a second successive team win for Suffolk.

As the intermediates set up on Kestrel, I received a message that an aerator hadn't been switched off in James's peg. I made my way to him and on arrival, saw him dutifully going about his business and preparing his kit; but with the aerator blowing water across his peg and apparently doing so at full blast. I reassured him that I'd take care of it and that I'd speak to the match organiser. A few phone calls later, the power to the aerator was cut and James was able to plumb up in calm water. Whilst it would be some time before the aerator's churning effect ceased; this was seen by Rob as an advantage given the better oxygenation of the water in James's peg as a result. As far as James was concerned, all he now had to contend with was the in-form Sam next-door. Back round the bank, Ollie set up next to Timmy, whilst Lewis was on the next peg to Tom; Jack, who'd had no hesitation in claiming peg 2 where he'd practised just weeks before, was next to Toby.

With half an hour to go before the whistle, I looked to park the mini-bus for the duration of the match. I'd left it close to the tackle shop initially, but with the competition about to begin, I drove it down to one of the parking areas close to Skylark. There was though, one more job to do before the whistle...

We'd set off early from Needham Lake and being fully aware of the possible effects of a fast food breakfast – as ever, we'd stopped for one on the way to Westwood – I'd added a bulk pack of Dextro Energy tablets to Hazel's Sainsbury's order the day before. These were at hand as I drove the mini-bus around Skylark with the start of the match approaching. At each of Suffolk's pairs of pegs, I stopped the bus and handed a pack of Dextro to the anglers. My instruction was that they were to take one of these a quarter of an hour before the start; the idea being to give them a boost and ensure that they were alert at the start of the match and therefore wouldn't miss any bites from 'mug' fish early on. Hopefully, as a result of the perhaps performance enhancing, but perfectly legal dietary supplement, our anglers would sneak a couple of extra fish in the opening minutes of the match. As ever, I was aware that such attention to detail could, when considered with all the efforts made in other areas of preparation, make a difference. My last minute excursion around Skylark distributing small packets of these energy tablets drew a lot of attention from the opposition and the fact that other team managers and their anglers were being distracted was an added bonus! James told me after the match that they were really nice and were, he said, all he ate during the match.

Over on Kestrel, 2011 winner and venue regular, Luke Morley was, from peg 11 Rob advised, never going to beaten. Like a good few, Luke started slowly, but soon began to put sizeable fish in his net. He fished close to the shallow, reedy area by one of the islands and eventually recorded 73lb 12oz. Suffolk's Reece Page had also drawn well (peg 23) and set his stall out to pick off ide in similar fashion from close to the island opposite. Apart from one quiet spell, he netted fish regularly throughout the match and took over 58lb to the scales. This wasn't before we had to fend off an accusation that he was exceeding the 16-metre pole limit. It was mooted that the colourful Maver graphics visible on his butt sections were evidence that he was fishing further out than permitted. However, like for instance, Garbolino; Maver poles often sport these graphics on several sections and as a company rep at the time, Rob was able to make this point quite clear to officials and measuring Reece's pole afterwards wasn't deemed necessary. Apart from that, the lengths of the assembled pole is also stated on these sections and as with many models, cutting the tips back more often than not sees them reduced. These goings-on didn't seem to faze Reece and his net was easily good enough for second place on the day.

Along the bank to Reece's left, Abi had also apparently drawn okay, but in open water. Prior to the start of the match and knowing that Abi, like me, struggles with cold hands due to our very poor circulation; I'd bottled some glycerine for her. This wouldn't stop the cold from getting to her, as she confirmed later, but would help her cope. Whilst Abi hadn't fished Kestrel before, she'd contacted Middy's Craig Butterfield, who was more than generous with his advice. She also phoned him immediately after she'd drawn for last minute advice on how to tackle that particular peg.

I didn't see an awful lot of Abi's match and although she told me later that she'd had a few fish when I found time to visit her late on; I wasn't aware that most were of considerable size. Along with ide, she'd netted some much larger carp and the odd barbel. Close to the end of the match though, a run from a powerful fish saw around eight metres of her Garbolino G-Max 1000 pole become detached from the butt sections and, after a moment or two when the sections lay agonizingly close on the surface in front of her; they slowly followed the fish out towards the island. I was on hand, but it was made perfectly clear that neither of us were permitted to enter the water and recover what was well over a grand's worth of carbon.

Abi was understandably distraught as we then made our way to the opposite bank whilst also keeping an eye on the pole as it snaked between the islands. Asking permission of the anglers close by, we took to the pontoon and although once again the sections were, for a few agonizing seconds, within reasonably easy reach; we were again warned of the consequences of entering the water. One angler was good enough to leave his peg offering his own sections as we tried desperately to recover the pole. Very shortly after however, and with water entering the butt end, the long length of pole sections disappeared below the surface. The pole was fully insured and although Rob assured me that it would be recovered later, Abi remained visibly upset. My frustrations were compounded when someone tried to make an issue of us crossing the pontoon. Later though, and with tempers simmering; at Rob's bequest, Alex Bates availed himself temporarily of his tackle shop duties and with a boat at his disposal and clad in chest waders, he was able to recover the pole, much to Abi's huge relief!

I was indebted not only to Rob and Alex, but to Barry and Gail Miller in particular, who consoled and comforted Abi before she was reunited with her pole that she'd saved so hard for. The day ended on a much happier note for her though, as she claimed the third place trophy with her 40lb 6oz. Before I left Kestrel, I also photographed Kirsty Reed's 40lb 2oz net that saw her make up the four frame places and also return home with silverware.

As a postscript, I later read of more than one top angler that had entered the water during a match and recovered their pole. In an article in *Pole Fishing*, Craig Butterfield himself wrote about how he'd swum after his pole and recovered it, before netting the 8lb carp that was still attached. He went on to win the match by 2lb if I remember rightly. I've made a note since, to have a full change of clothing handy and would have no hesitation to enter the water to recover her, or anyone else's pole for that matter. After all, swimming is one of the best forms of exercise...

In the team match on Skylark, Toby caught from early on, rotating several swims, picking off fish and building his weight methodically and clinically. For the duration of the match, left-handed Toby, thanks to our draw, virtually faced Jack, who's right-handed, next-door. The day's 'no coaching' rule seemingly didn't stop Toby giving advice to his young squad-mate during the match.

Before the match, I'd set goals for our team anglers and I believe I managed to discuss these with most, if not all of our under-18s. These were all well received and before the draw, I noted that I was looking for top two section placings from Toby and Timmy, and top threes from Tom and James. These scores would see a team tally of no more than 10 points achieved; this total I felt, with nine teams on the bank, would be sufficient for a win.

As for the Gold team, I gave Jack a target of top five and Lewis and Ollie, top six. All three were still within the Angling Trust's cadet (under-14) age group and were competing in an under-18s' event. For the record, Jack and Ollie weren't even old enough for rod licences and I'd had to seek permission for them to compete. Thanks to his own ability (and perhaps, his neighbour's coaching!) Jack duly delivered, as did Lewis and Ollie. After a slow start, Lewis landed one of the lake's large bream; much to his mum, Mandy's delight as she sat watching intently. This boost in confidence saw Lewis build his weight for target section points. From what I saw, Ollie's match was an unspectacular one, but his, like Jack's, was a tidy performance that belied his relatively tender age.

With Sam being older and more experienced however, I felt that he was more than capable of a top three placing. He actually went one better, taking a point off

James in the process. The two Suffolk boys were only beaten in their section by overall third placed Sensas A4 rod, Bradley Proctor's 29lb 14oz. I gave our Gold team a target total of 20 points. I felt that this would give them a top four finish. On the day, 17 points saw them meet their target easily and they finished 6 points ahead of locals Lincoln. Consistent team returns saw our Gold team achieve fourth place and I congratulated the boys individually after.

The fact that Toby, who recorded 53lb 2oz, would win his section was never in doubt; it was only a question of by how much. In the end, the next best weight was Timmy's 36lb 10oz. The boys were comfortable section winners, but afterwards, whilst congratulating all our anglers, I also emphasized the quality of Tom and James's performances. Rob had been aware that Adam's fourth placed net of 28lb from peg 8 gave King's Lynn a very good start and the final stages of the weigh-in proved a little nervy with the Norfolk team's angler in that section the penultimate to be recorded. There was never any real doubt however, that Suffolk would claim back-to-back team wins with a tally of just seven points. Before the presentation, Abi, having recovered from her earlier trauma and handed out some rather large strawberries as Jack offered around his chocolate Hobnobs.

King's Lynn finished runners-up with 11 points and Sensas A4 were third with 13 points. With all the results confirmed, Ollie's dad, Simon was intrigued as I noted the section returns against the targets I'd allocated on the sheets on my clipboard.

It had been a long, and at times, quite stressful day when once again issues other than fishing had detracted from my own personal enjoyment and satisfaction. Having said that, the squad had pulled off a clinical defence of their team title and for the second year running, two of our intermediates had framed in the under-21 event. Toby, this time in a Suffolk County shirt, had secured his hat-trick of individual wins in his final year as an under-18. It was therefore, with a degree of personal pride, that I looked on as our squad collected all their silverware from Alan, the venue's owner. After the traditional, if not particularly well choreographed on this occasion, post-match photos, we left Westwood Lakes. I took to the driver's seat of the mini-bus once again and thanks to the navigational skills of Nigel Cottrell, we found a convenient McDonald's!

A TRUST TROPHY!

With our Pole Champs campaign out of the way and another nameplate confirming Suffolk's successful defence of the team title on the trophy, I busied myself with organizing two teams for the Angling Trust Ladies' National. The 2012 event was scheduled to be held at Holly Farm Lakes in Leicestershire. Paperwork completed and posted; Abi and I, along with several of the girls, their partners and parents, caught a good few fish in our practice sessions beforehand.

We seemed to get to grips with the different approaches and techniques required for the two lakes, but the random draw saw most of Suffolk's anglers pegged on the lake where only smaller fish were resident. Conversely, the teams that did well had most, if not all of their anglers on the large lake where 20 of the top 23 weights came from. I calculated after, that if the match had been decided on points, Suffolk would have been on the podium. Not all the girls travelled home empty handed however, as Kayleigh Smith picked up a well-deserved section winner's medal.

I had an enjoyable opening day of the river season, catching chub on the Gipping. The largest of these fish weighed just over 4lb and was netted for me by young Sam Kennard. I bumped into Sam after driving back to Needham from the Blakenham stretch where I'd banked a chub soon after arriving. Sam promptly caught two fish on freelined meat on my rod before we moved up river to take a couple more. I returned with Abi later and she too, had a couple of reasonable fish. A week or so later I accepted Colin Booker's invitation to fish his syndicate trout water and we both landed good fish on a bright, warm day.

The Angling Trust Cadet/Junior/Intermediate National was due to be held at Lindholme Lakes at the end of June. I'd done most of the preparatory work, contacting anglers and checking their availability before collating entries. Steve Barnes however, not only agreed to take over the responsibility of organizing bait, but cleared his diary to accompany us on match day. Steve Damant meanwhile, began contacting those that required assistance with transportation of equipment, liaising with Ian Head, who once again, made available a Bristo's van.

Chris Kelly had contacted me early in the year, asking if he could enter a team of intermediates and, given that five of the six anglers he had in mind had previously fished for Suffolk County, we were happy to accommodate him. Chris advised that he'd take care of all the arrangements for his guys. This effectively gave Suffolk an additional team on the bank, alongside the other intermediate team (under-23s), plus our entries in both the junior age group (under-18s) and the cadet competition (under-14s).

Abi set to work sourcing information and her colleague at the *Angling Times*, Ben Fisk proved very helpful, as was Nick Speed. Both Ben and Nick sent emails with full details of the lakes to be fished, providing information on fish stocks, target species, preferred baits and suitable tackle set-ups etc. I collated the information on receipt and Abi contacted Sandra Drew at the Angling Trust, to confirm which lakes our different teams would be fishing. I looked then, to cascade everything to the respective groups of anglers, liaising with both Steves as match day approached.

The Angling Trust National is the most prestigious event in a young match angler's calendar and the 2012 competition saw a field of just under 250 assemble at the draw. The competition was spread over six lakes and it was agreed that, if nothing else, the day would provide valuable experience for both coaches and anglers. It was the first Angling Trust match that we'd entered at youth level and we looked to get an appreciation of how, for instance, appointed bank-runners could be deployed and utilised.

Steve and I were already familiar with the venue, but the majority of our anglers hadn't fished there before and those that had, had only sampled sport on a few of the lakes. Given the overnight stay and that we had four teams of six anglers entered, the campaign to secure silverware at Lindholme was easily our most ambitious to date. Considering the standard of competition our youngsters would undoubtedly face, we agreed beforehand that we should have realistic expectations and that a team medal of any colour in any category would be well received.

An advance party that included Toby and Timmy Pepper, Ashley Miller and Anna Blyth fished the lakes on the Thursday and Friday (late practice was permitted under that year's rules) and all caught plenty of fish on a variety of methods. On the Thursday afternoon, as I waited for the arrival of Ringshall Primary School's group at Barking, I chatted on the phone to Anna's dad, Rob as he kept me informed of how they were getting on.

A venue of a different kind that we were also familiar with was the Ramada Encore at Robin Airport, near Doncaster. In the open plan bar area the night before the match, I looked to confirm that all those that were due to spend the night at the hotel had arrived safely. Several squad members had travelled up in their own cars and some were travelling direct to Lindholme early on the Saturday. As ever, it seemed that we'd booked the majority of the rooms in the hotel and were taking up almost all of the available seating.

Notes were compared over a welcome pint or two and after a short squad meeting, I was under the impression that Jack Weatherley and Eddie Howman had departed for an out-of-character early night. Abi however, had been texting them; she advised that the pair had taken a taxi from the hotel and were sampling the local social life. It became clear on Saturday morning, that the two Harleston boys had obviously enjoyed their trip into town to engage with the indigenous population at various hostelries!

Our Ramada contingent was up and about in good time on the morning of the match. After the short journey to Lindholme Lakes, we were directed on arrival, to the temporary parking area by Oasis Lake. The number of vehicles already on site was evidence of the size of the event and with dozens of large and local associations represented, the enormity of the task in hand became very apparent. Our anglers though, whilst in awe perhaps, of the number of competitors, coaches and family members that jostled and queued in the café and bait shop; appeared in expectant mood as they waited for their captains to draw.

The rain that had been falling since we left the hotel finally stopped and intermediate captain, Chris Kelly (Red) distributed peg cards to Jack, Eddie, Dan Elliot, Steve Crowe and Robert Murphy. Ashley Miller (Gold) did the same and he, Abi, Bradley Calver, Charlotte Gore, Abbi Kendall and Reece Page also headed for their respective pegs on Loco and Bonsai. With the juniors and cadets drawing shortly after, Steve and I handed out designated bank-runner stickers. Abi had a relatively short walk to her peg on Bonsai, right in front of the café and after helping her with her gear, I moved her car from Oasis to behind the bait shop. As she spoke on the phone with Nick Speed regarding how best to approach her peg, I then joined Steve who continued with organizing the distribution of bait.

After announcing our intentions to fish Lindholme at our presentation evening, I'd had the unenviable task of ensuring all our anglers had appropriate Angling Trust membership. Individual membership numbers are required on entry forms and I sent numerous emails and made several phone calls before we achieved our target of 24. Peter Williams, one of the disappointed anglers from the Westwood practice was in our junior team, as was Anna Blyth who'd stepped in for Tommy Cottrell. Tom, whilst disappointed to be missing out on the match, was enjoying a holiday in a climate considerably warmer than where we were! Following the Pole Champs, Adam Swain was also fishing, alongside James Head, Toby and Timmy. Sam Kennard unfortunately, missed out, but was good enough to come along with his gear as reserve. For once though, no teams were short and Sam spent the day helping Steve and me with bait distribution and observing the cadets. It was quite a walk from Ian's van to where the cadets were pegged and with Abi setting up on Bonsai, Sam and I commandeered her new Matrix barrow to transport a supply of bait to Jamie Marriot, Paul Christie, Max Rushbrook, Jack Damant, Ollie Saunders and captain, Lewis Clouting.

With all the matches underway, I set about bank-running for the intermediates. Given the close proximity of many pegs and the pole sections placed on rollers behind competitors, several of our anglers couldn't be reached for fear of either fish being spooked or equipment damaged.

Suffolk's juniors faced possibly the toughest challenge of the squad. With 23 teams competing over three lakes, the local outfits were always favoured and for once, the draw bag didn't do Suffolk any favours. As Abi chatted to Nick Speed, Anna spoke with Tom Pickering. Tom was in Belgium preparing his team for the World Feeder Championships, but still found time to give Anna advice over the phone.

On Oasis, Willow and Laurels, our junior anglers worked tirelessly throughout the match and their final position of 15th didn't do justice to the amount of preparation everyone had put in before the match. All our anglers had made every effort to take on-board and digest the information distributed. I was conscious though, that I'd not been able to formulate specific, hard and fast plans for each lake. We'd not been able to practise as a squad and some hadn't even seen the venue before match day. As fully expected, northern teams dominated with Worksop taking the team trophy; Pride of Derby were runners-up and Barnsley finished third. Top scorers for Suffolk were Timmy, who took 9kg 680gm to the scales for sixth in section; Toby, with 11kg 160gm for eighth and Adam who recorded 5kg 300gm for 11th.

After speaking to Reece and Eddie on Loco initially, I wasn't able to see a lot of the intermediates' match. As I made my way carefully around the lake, I was told in no uncertain terms by one young angler, not to step over his pole sections. The stout, short-of-stature young man seemed oblivious to the fact that I was a bank-runner and rather than break his pole down for temporary storage on his rollers as he fished the bomb, chose to block the path completely with its full length. His instruction, delivered in 'blunt northern', left me in no doubt that he was not appreciative of even the slightest, perfectly legitimate bankside disturbance.

Four of the six intermediate sections were on the famous Bonsai Lake and most of our anglers were tucked away and effectively cut off by a myriad of poles that were constantly being shipped back and forth. Abi was battling to keep within a fish or two of old adversary, Jimmy Brookes next-door. She, like most others, rotated her pole lines whilst having an occasional look on the bomb or small Method feeder.

Later in the day, I walked up to Strip Pond where the cadets' match would be the first of the three to finish. I arrived after a couple of sections had been recorded and Steve Barnes informed me that our cadets were doing rather well. As ever, I took the opportunity to take some photos whilst asking our anglers how they thought their match had gone. After a few words with the parents and a chat with both Steves, I headed back to Bonsai where Abi advised that, having caught sporadically through the day, she felt that anglers pegged in the quieter area further round the bank had done much better. She also admitted to being a little nervous as Dick Clegg looked on from the veranda of the café. With the younger age groups' matches finishing earlier, several anglers were making their way back to the presentation area behind her peg. Some of them were straying from the road on to the grassed bank and Dick, she explained, was very quick to head off one spectator who wandered a little too close to the water's edge for both their liking. With the intermediates' match drawing to a close and after getting an update from the Peatmoor coaches who were seated nearby and could see a large part of that lake, I took one of my favourite photos.

Sam had settled quietly behind Abi, with cadets, Paul, Jack and Ollie and all four were kneeling on the grass to the left of her peg, as she looked to catch a few late fish down her right-hand margin. I took my camera, crept quietly towards them, knelt down, zoomed in and captured a picture which to me, epitomised how far we'd come with the GVAC Junior Academy and the Suffolk County squad. The four boys were listening intently as Abi, their older squad-mate and a licensed coach, talked them through the final stages of her match on Lindholme's famous Bonsai Lake where five times World Champion, Alan Scotthorne held the lake record.

Soon after the final whistle I helped Abi tackle down and walk her seat-box and equipment to the car. With her kit safely loaded, I found Ian Head and both Steves. I then walked round to Brad at the far end of Bonsai, looking to get some of his kit back to the van as he waited for the scales.

On Loco, Reece (18kg 600gm) and Abbi (13kg 320gm) recorded Suffolk's top scores for the Gold team with second and fourth in section respectively. Ashley too, made the top half of his section, recording 16kg 600gm on Bonsai. Abi, with 9kg 800gm was ninth in section, with Jimmy Brooks finishing eighth. The Gold team just made the top 10, 10 points clear of Boston. On the opposite bank, Chris had worked hard for 18kg exactly and was rewarded with a third-in-section placing, as too was Jack with his 22kg 500gm. Steve Crowe achieved another top half section placing with 10kg 20gm on Loco, but our intermediate performance of the day came from Dan Elliott on Bonsai. I spoke to Dan before the scales arrived and he said that he'd be disappointed if he didn't win his section. On arrival, the officials recorded his weight of 28kg 900gm for maximum points. Dan finished over eight kilos clear of a certain Oliver Scotthorne in third. He was unlucky not to make the overall top three, missing out by less than two kilos.

The Red team's tally of 57 points left us daring to hope for a podium position. Leaving the likes of Warrington, Barnsley, Worksop and Leeds in their wake - and with Steve Crowe already on the A1 and heading home for a wedding – Chris and his teammates stepped forward to receive their third place medals. Sensas A4 took the honours with 65 points, closely followed by Matrix Tameside on 62. Chris, whose contribution and efforts as team captain, I acknowledged after, was disappointed that they'd not done even better. The podium finish however, saw us achieve our target and Dan would also head home with a section winner's medal round his neck. We did though, get to even the score with Matrix Tameside...

With so many putting in such an effort before and on match day, it could be considered wrong to single out squad members. The day though, belonged to Suffolk's cadets. Only Jack had seen the venue before, yet Lewis's team finished ahead of Matrix Tameside, Smartbait Leeds and Worksop, amassing four section wins, a second and a third. Their impressive 21-point tally saw them take the coveted team cup by 6 points and Lewis's unprompted embracing of his captain's role demonstrated maturity well beyond his years. A large carp helped young Jamie to third place overall and his smile was one of the widest on the bank as he posed for photos with a full set of medals: gold for a team win, silver for his section and bronze for individual third. Ollie and Max were close behind in fourth and fifth respectively. The boys' day was made even more memorable as their medals were presented by former England manager, Dick Clegg, OBE. The Angling Trust was suitably flattering afterwards and our cadets, having lifted one of only three team trophies available, were pictured on their media release soon after.

All things considered, it had been a successful campaign. It's a round trip of 355 miles from Needham Lake to Lindholme and we'd managed to get a party of 48 - including 25 anglers - there and back in a mini-bus, 2 vans and 16 cars! There were 81 medals up for grabs on the day of competition and Suffolk brought home 18 of them.

On returning to Suffolk, I resumed my coaching work with schools. Hazel and I enjoyed a week's holiday in Norfolk and whilst away, I grabbed a couple of sessions on the Waveney. On the second of these, I enjoyed good perch sport on a float rod and centre pin reel; my attention occasionally distracted however, by frogs and grass snakes as I roved the Common.

After our break, I caught my first carp on a fly whilst preparing for a session with Ringshall Primary School and the pupils also took fish on, among other things, baked beans - I do like to vary things a little when coaching! I concluded Springfield's Friday afternoon sessions with an informal match and did the same for Castle Hill on the first Saturday of the school holidays. Six days later I sat at home watching the spectacular opening ceremony of the London Olympics. On Monday July 30th, I resumed my summer work with Colin and Calum, kicking off at Bromeswell and also running sessions at Swilland and Aldeburgh over a four-week period. Abi travelled home and joined me, along with several other coaches for GVAC's National Fishing Month event held over both days of the first weekend in August.

My fishing took a bit of a back seat over the holiday period as I divided my time between coaching and watching the Olympics. I resumed my short-session chub fishing at the end of August however and, taking advantage of a couple of weeks off banked a number of fish from the Waveney and the Gipping.

STAINFORTH SILVERWARE

Later in 2012, the NJAA National - the National Junior Angling Association's blue riband event - was scheduled for Saturday 1st September. Given that school pupils would still be on their summer break, pre-match logistics for the National would be a manageable. The venue was the Stainforth and Keadby Canal, near the market town of Thorne, South Yorkshire. Having opened in 1802, the canal is deeper and wider than many; evidence of the local boatbuilding industry that flourished from 1858, when Richard Dunston moved his yard from Torksey in Lincolnshire, to Thorne.

Steve took over the reins as project manager for this competition, but as ever, we liaised closely, exchanging emails and texts frequently. We'd mooted bread punch as a possible tactic and feedback from Barnsley Blacks' Lee Kerry was that this may be a gamble. Lee is an old friend of Rob Lincoln and being able to obtain information from an angler of this calibre and pedigree gave us confidence to approach the match with the usual level of expectation. We'd not seen the venue before and would not be able to practise. I felt that we might need a little something up our sleeve and the calculated risk we were taking with our main choice of bait was one that Lee also felt might just pay off.

With possible tactics agreed, a Friday session was arranged at Needham Lake. Steve and I were on the bank early and his kit was set up with a view to demonstrate the use of bread punch to those not familiar with the technique. With the depth of the match venue a consideration, aquarium gravel would be added to the balls of liquidised bread feed. As thorough as ever in his session preparation, Steve had a large supply of suitable gravel, plenty of prepared bread for both feed and the hook and a number of appropriate rigs. He'd also prepared hemp to add to the bread if required. After an initial demonstration and with

Steve having handed out copies of appropriate press articles detailing the required approach, the youngsters set about catching a few fish.

Needham Lake's stocks and depth gave us an opportunity to simulate what we expected to find in Yorkshire and Steve and I took turns to fish with his gear and to experiment. We varied frequency of feeding, adjusted shotting patterns and how we lowered rigs in. We also spent time with the anglers, addressing issues when bites weren't forthcoming, looking always, for them to establish a catching rhythm that would instil confidence. We followed up the Friday session with another held at the weekend and with number 2 and 3 elastics fitted in our top kits, I found the fishing thoroughly enjoyable. We didn't catch any huge fish, but consistent sport that saw us netting fish upwards of two or three ounces regularly throughout the sessions was a welcome change from catching carp at Barking.

Looking to bring everyone in our three teams of cadets, juniors and intermediates up to speed saw me back on the early pegs at Needham Lake one evening where once again, I was netting a constant procession of roach on bread punch. Jack Weatherley joined me before Steve arrived and with Jack setting up next-door, I was soon going over everything we'd learned from our previous sessions. Young Jack Damant was also on the bank, having cycled from his home and once he'd accepted my offer to sit on my box, I knew he wouldn't get off it again! With quiet admiration, Steve and I sat on the picnic table behind the two Jacks' pegs, watching as they matched each other fish for fish.

Back at Steve's the week before the match, he and I, along with Tom Cottrell and Ollie Saunders made final preparations with our squad bait. Whilst our anglers would fish bread and target roach, we were aware that in areas where these fish weren't resident, section points could come by way of perch and the possibility of skimmers being caught couldn't be ignored. In Steve's summerhouse, much of the music coming from the eighties' pop station that his digital radio is apparently permanently tuned to, was not appreciated fully by Tom and Ollie. Nonetheless, with Steve's young son, Max also assisting, we managed a productive evening's work before I dropped the two squad members home.

Steve Damant organised collection of any kit that needed transporting and we were as grateful as ever, to accept Ian Head's offer of use of a van. The day before the match, Ian's son, James orchestrated loading of the gear. Meanwhile, Tom helped organise our bait supplies before later in the day, our squad's convoy of vehicles headed up the A1 for another overnight stay at the Ramada.

The same day, Abbi Kendall and Rob Wright – then of Maver Image - were fishing the canal and in the hotel in the evening, gave us up-to-date information on how their last minute practice had gone. It was evident, Rob advised, that despite the depth of the canal, light floats were preferred and in the bar area of the hotel, tables were cleared before half empty glasses were replaced by spools of line, shot tubs and rigs as we looked to make last minute adjustments. Our approach wasn't perfect by any means, but we'd all made a considerable effort; apart from Abbi though, the squad still hadn't seen the waterway, let alone fished it!

Several of the party were up early on match day to take advantage of the hotel breakfast before we set off for Thorne. Our procession of vehicles arrived in good time for the draw at Delves Lake. This fishery is sited very close to a busy main road and, as was usual, parking spaces were difficult to come by. Maps of the match length had been distributed and Rob gave us last minute instructions on how to get to the various sections before captains for the day, Eddie Howman, Tom and Ollie returned from the draw with peg numbers 7, 10 and 2 respectively. I was to steward in B section on the intermediates' match length; but also looked to help with transporting some of our junior anglers' kit before the whistle and a little later, Nigel Cottrell was good enough to point out the location of dog mess as he and I passed each other with equipment on the tow path.

Our cadet team of Ollie, Max Rushbrook and Jack Damant didn't have far to travel to their sections close to the Canal Tavern. Our junior team of Tom, Adam Swain, James Head, Sam Kennard, Timmy Pepper and Lewis Clouting were spread eastwards along the canal with the other nine competing teams' anglers. Steve and I helped Sam set up his platform after I'd carried some of Timmy's gear to where we thought his peg should be.

For those not familiar with the waterway, permanent peg numbers are painted on the rusting metal sheets that line the canal, but on the opposite bank to the actual swims. Unfortunately for Timmy, the permanent numbers allocated for the match and also detailed on a conversion grid distributed at the draw were occasionally obscured completely by weed and rubbish. As a consequence, Timmy paced out the distance between pegs he could see, before we placed his kit where he thought he'd drawn. This situation wasn't wholly satisfactory and we were told later that Timmy wasn't fishing on the correct peg. If anything though, this was to his disadvantage and given the circumstances, we were able to nip any mooted suggestions of disqualification in the bud.

Past the juniors, Eddie, Abbi, Jack Weatherley and Toby Pepper would contest the intermediates' match with seven other teams. We also had issues with pegging in Abbi's section as Worksop's Tom Hunt, who was drawn to her left on peg 8, had a large bush growing from the bank where he was supposed to fish. As a result, and so as not to have him fish the match the other side of the bush and out of sight of stewards, he was placed very close to where Abbi should have been on peg 7. With one team not turning up, Abbi was moved a little further back down the match length to the vacant peg 6.

I would remain in, or close to, B section for the duration of the intermediates' match and Ollie's dad, Simon took on our stewarding role for the cadets; Steve Barnes did the same with the juniors. The narrow towpath in Jack's A section prevented me from leaving at any time without disturbing several anglers and so I remained within a few pegs of Abbi and saw nothing of the match elsewhere.

With the match underway, from what I could see, some very good intermediate anglers were struggling; both Jack and Abbi however, were putting fish in their nets on a regular basis. Toby and Eddie weren't though, enjoying the same good fortune. There was some consolation as Toby, with 780gm beat England's Reece Nicolson on the next peg. Despite a run of good skimmers mid-match, Abbi had to be content with third in section with her 2kg 730gm. Tom next-door, walked B section, and the match with his 3kg 600gm. Jack top-scored for Suffolk with his second-in-section weight of 740gm.

For me, the performance of the day came from Leeds angler, Ben Taylor. Ben explained to me after that he'd fed and fished squatt whilst feeding hemp regularly for the first four hours of the match on an alternative, diagonal line. With around an hour to go, he tried the hemp line and then netted a good roach after his first put-in. He felt though, that it was still a little early and held off fishing it again for a short while longer as he continued to feed. A little later his patience finally paid off as he pulled into a good fish every drop-in after reverting back to the hemp. Apart from one hiccup it seems, he fished a perfect hemp match. After starting to catch well, he changed from a 0.06mm hooklength to one of 0.08mm, but after a few minutes changed back again as bites slowed. Despite the roach feeding confidently, the difference of 0.02mm apparently made all the difference. We chatted as he loaded his kit and whilst I didn't share his taste in in-car musical entertainment, I was impressed by how he'd fished and enthralled by what he explained. Ben's performance saw his team's 11 point tally secure the team title as Barnsley finished runners-up. Worksop in third pushed Suffolk out of the frame by a single point. There was consolation for Abbi however, as she picked up a section winner's medal by double default.

In addition to the intermediates' title, Leeds took the cadets' match, but Max, Jack and Ollie didn't give up the trophy they'd won on the Grand Union easily. They battled it out for top spot with the eventual winners and pushed locals, Worksop into third in all three sections. At the presentation in the garden of the Canal Tavern, the silverware came thick and fast for the boys. Max's 630gm was good enough for third place overall and Jack and Ollie picked up a default section winner's medal each to go with their team runners-up trophies.

As in the Angling Trust event, our juniors faced possibly the most daunting task of achieving a podium finish, considering the number of local teams on the bank. I was told that some of these youngsters fish canals most weekends, all year round; but applying what we'd learned about the techniques employed through improving coaching practice was having a dramatic effect on our performances.

Lewis, having stepped up from the cadets' age group, recorded 500gm: a better weight than four other anglers in his section. Tom - Steve and Nigel explained afterwards - was in one of the areas seemingly devoid of any roach and it took him over two hours to catch. He had no choice, but to look to pick off perch with chopped worm and his 200gm saw him miss out on sixth-in-section by just 20gm (less than an ounce). Adam made the top half of his section with his 650gm and James's 1kg 170gm was good enough for fourth as he, like Tom, was just 20gm short of a higher placing. With 1kg 400gm and 1kg 160gm respectively, Sam and Timmy were comfortable runners-up in their sections.

Before the match, we were mindful that bread wouldn't be a bait that many, if any teams, had with them and as I placed kit at our anglers' pegs, I made every effort to conceal our bags of crumb and aquarium gravel. Whilst there wouldn't have been much opportunity for coaches and managers to prepare any, I wasn't about to leave anything to chance and with coaching and bank-running (supposedly) not permitted, once the match was underway there'd be little other teams could do, should our gamble pay off. Steve explained after the match how Sam was catching with comparative ease on bread, whilst others nearby looked on in frustration. The face of one coach was a picture, Steve said; evidently he stared bemused into Sam's bait bucket after seeing him bring in a fish almost every time he shipped out during a particularly productive spell.

As ever though, it was the performance of the whole team that got them on the podium. As is so often the case, every point secured was valuable. Whilst our intermediates just missed out, Suffolk's 27 points in the junior event saw locals, Barnsley, who finished on 28, head home empty-handed in fourth place. Warrington and Northwich were first and second with 19 and 23 points respectively; but along with the challenge from Barnsley, our youngsters had seen off, among others, Worksop, Wakefield and Leeds, not to mention our East Anglian rivals, King's Lynn. In addition to their team trophies, Sam and Timmy also picked up a section winner's medal each by default.

Whilst we hadn't retained any of the team titles won a year before in the same event, we had, from a difficult venue a long way from home, brought back almost a quarter of the medals and trophies available. I'm always conscious of the efforts of many teams, that go completely unrewarded at these events and I'm fully aware that several travel home with nothing. There are often teams that are expected to finish on the podium, but that miss out. At the expense of some of these, Suffolk County were the only southern outfit to make it on to the podium in any of the team competitions – and we very nearly did so in all three!

Along with our anglers and their parents, Steve and I were getting used to regular success. There was no room for complacency though, and with the next national competition being held on a venue a little closer to home, preparation would be even more thorough. Before then however, we conducted our usual post-match debrief, albeit very informally over a customary serving of fast food; on this occasion, at Peterborough Services.

DRAIN DOMINATION

My school coaching schedule through the September and October of 2012 was my busiest to date. Weekly bookings with Castle Hill and Springfield continued and fishing remained as popular as ever with Combs Middle, as three separate groups of pupils joined me for two sessions each at Barking. I concluded my season's work with Hardwick Middle School, ran sessions with Stowmarket High and also started working with pupil referral units. With the nights drawing in and the temperatures dropping, I looked to get all sessions booked in before October half-term and on one occasion ran two with different schools on the same day, staying on the bank, grabbing a sandwich and replacing rigs in-between.

On Saturday 6th October our county squad were due to defend both NJAA Challenge team titles won at Suffolk Water Park in 2011 and in Robert Murphy, we also had the reigning intermediate champion. Robert, with Jack Weatherley and Eddie Howman, would be charged with the responsibility of bringing the intermediate team trophy back to Suffolk and Steve and I considered our options for the fourth team member, as several regulars were unavailable.

Once again, Steve would be project manager for the campaign, but we'd liaise as closely as ever in the weeks leading up to the match. Considering the juniors, for Suffolk County Red, we made just one change to our Thorne line-up. Toby Pepper was back in alongside his brother Timmy, James Head, Adam Swain, Tommy Cottrell and Sam Kennard. This then gave us an opportunity to put our six winning cadets from Lindholme in the Gold team. Having checked availability, the names of Paul Christie, Max Rushbrook, Jamie Marriott, Jack Damant, Lewis Clouting and Ollie Saunders went on to the entry forms; but Steve and I were mindful that we remained short of an intermediate...

Peter Williams, with Adam Swain and Anna Blyth, had entered the Angling Trust's Talent Pathway programme. Peter was as keen as ever to impress and throughout the summer and early autumn, had fished Steve Damant's Advanced Academy matches and was doing very well in the league. With the NJAA competition fast approaching, I chatted on the phone to Abi and shortly after, put the suggestion to Steve that we ask Peter to fish with the under-19s. Steve liked the idea and Peter accepted the invitation. I had a sneaking suspicion that our Lark Angling Preservation Society rod from Mildenhall might just grab the opportunity to make a bit of a name for himself come match day. Seven days before the match, Peter was on the banks of the South Holland Drain with a number of our squad for what turned out to be a fruitful practice session.

We'd been to Holbeach two years before and a good few of our youngsters had experience on the venue. We also knew how fickle and occasionally difficult the water could be and were wary of accepting overly positive reports on how it was fishing. I didn't have a complete understanding of how big tides and rainfall levels could influence fish movements in the area; nonetheless, on the last day of September we looked to familiarise ourselves fully with how the drain was fishing.

On the bank reasonably early, we spread our anglers along the drain as Rob Lincoln prepared to demonstrate. Given the nature of bank, Steve had sourced several platforms for those that needed them. I'd completed a risk assessment and made note of the steep drop down to the bank; the prevalence of brambles and the speed of traffic on the road along which, we'd all parked, were also recorded on my paperwork and mentioned when we addressed the squad. In our briefing, I made everyone aware of the speed of occasional passing vehicles, having had first-hand experience as I moved the mini-bus! I also placed a platform for Paul, but not before I tested the depth of water close in whilst hanging on to his dad, Peter's arm. Taking a small step (unintentionally) too far with my left foot as I hung on; my wellie and most of one leg of my jeans disappeared below the surface and Paul looked on as his father wrestled with his county coach. My life didn't exactly flash before my eyes and Peter's efforts to save me from a complete dunking weren't helped by our uncontrollable giggling. Eventually though, we composed ourselves and Paul tackled up safely on his platform. I made my way back up the bank, emptied my wellie and wrung out my sock!

As thorough as ever with his preparation, Steve had a spare pair of socks with him – he'd seen me fall in before! I hung my wet sock over the windowsill of the mini-bus and laid my wellie on the driver's seat with its open top facing the sun. I then pulled on Steve's socks and changed back into my trainers. The one wet leg of my jeans would dry through the day and I turned my wallet inside out to dry on the bus's dashboard. On match day, I'd ensure I had a change of clothing with me! (Had I not said I was going to do just that at Westwood?) In an apparent effort to demonstrate the potential hazards noted on my risk assessment even further, I managed to dive, headfirst, towards Tom's tackle after tripping on a bramble stem as I descended the steep bank behind his peg. Making adjustments to a rig, Tom turned his head and assumed a look of quiet bemusement as I came to a stop, spread-eagled on my stomach with my head very close to his roller and butt section of his pole. Eventually, I regained a modest level of dignity and managed to avoid further mishap for the rest of the practice.

To our left, Worksop also had a number of anglers practising and we were conscious too, that several locals were keeping an eye on how we were getting on. It wasn't as though we had an awful lot to hide and it transpired later that Worksop's youngsters were faring much better than we were; taking more fish and of a better stamp. As ever with our practice session though, in addition to giving some of our anglers the opportunity to fish an unfamiliar venue, several things were noted during fishing and Steve and I, along with Steve Damant, Simon Saunders and the other parents present passed tips along to the anglers.

As our practice session unfolded, Rob felt that the noise of hemp was attracting fish and we quickly distributed supplies of the bait, and at that point, looked to keep what we were up to from anyone watching. Closest to the Worksop guys, Jamie's dad, Nick caught well; but the roach weren't present in any numbers and Lewis was one of the few that found fish of any of size. It was evident too, that big fish weren't showing and those that cast feeders to the far bank found only occasional roach. Local reports confirmed that large bream that we'd seen caught in 2010 were conspicuous by their absence and before match day, Steve and I agreed to change our feeder groundbait from fishmeal to a sweet mix; giving our anglers another small fish option, should things be particularly tough.

Before our debrief and journey home, Steve and I discussed sport with Worksop's team manager, Neil Nicolson. It had been suggested that the match could be moved along the drain where roach were more numerous. We were led to believe however, that the bank was even less safe on the alternative stretch and Neil, Steve and I agreed unanimously that there were enough fish present for the match to go ahead where originally scheduled and this information was passed back to the match organiser.

With no overnight stay required on the Friday before the match, I ran my usual afternoon session with Springfield. That evening, I collected the mini-bus before exchanging texts with Steve. I arrived at Needham Lake on the Saturday morning very early and before too long, all expected were on-board. Several parents were also taking cars and most were already on the road by the time we left.

Our pre- and post-match refreshments for the South Holland are usually taken at McDonald's at Long Sutton, but on this occasion we had to forego breakfast. Those that know the A17 will be familiar with Sutton Bridge and on that particular morning its temporary opening and consequent road closure delayed our arrival for the draw. A text message was sent confirming that we weren't far away and when we finally arrived, I let everyone off the bus. I then set about finding a safe place to park on the road running alongside the drain. At this point, things obviously weren't going as smoothly as I'd have liked and only after passing a long line of cars did I then find sufficient grass verge on which I could park the bus safely. I was quite a way from the draw, but after checking and locking the bus, I made my way to where Steve was distributing bait.

For whatever reasons, very few teams had made the journey to Lincolnshire and the intermediates' competition saw just us and the host side, King's Lynn on the bank. Attendance wasn't much better in the junior event, with only King's Lynn, Worksop, Stoke Angling For Everyone (SAFE) and our two teams present. Nonetheless, there was still a match to be fished and two team titles to be won. Worksop were a very good side and they'd done better than us the week before and King's Lynn, on a local venue, would surely take some beating; most, if not all of their squad had ample experience of fishing the drain in the East Coast Winter League. With the small number of teams present, the draw formalities were over quickly, before I encountered yet another problem...

Given the steep bank and the need to place platforms, a previous request from Steve for more setting-up time had been acknowledged and accepted. As I made my way up and down the drain distributing spare hooklengths and rigs however, it became evident that the start time had not been put back, and some of our anglers were nowhere near ready. With several needing more time and with other team coaches raising the issue as well; I got on the phone to Steve and also made my feelings clear to match organizers. One or two local anglers, familiar with both the venue and layout of the permanent pegs made it clear to me that they were ready; but others weren't and I put it to more than one official that anglers' safety and welfare should come above everything else. A short while later (and with my toys back in their pram!), it was confirmed finally, that both juniors and intermediates would have an additional half-hour to prepare.

Steve was, as ever, dealing with these issues better than me, but I attempted to relax a little after the extension of preparation time had finally been confirmed. It was then though, that we received a message from Nicky Damant that Lewis was on the wrong peg. Lewis's confusion had been brought about by a permanent peg being left out (and quite rightly) due to the presence of a wasps' nest. With just a quarter of an hour to go and with poor Lewis looking more than a little concerned, we didn't stand on ceremony. As Lewis looked on, his dad, Glyn, along with Steve, Steve Damant, Rob and I set about moving his kit to the correct peg. With so many of us mucking in, the move took no time at all and we reassured a bemused, but now slightly less concerned Lewis, instructing him to compose himself and to take his time when re-plumbing. To be fair, his look of worry disappeared quite rapidly as he realised how quick we were in getting his platform levelled again and all his kit set up on the correct peg. We were indebted to Nicky for spotting a potential problem.

We looked to address and rule out as many potential pre-match problems as we could and aimed to have our anglers as relaxed as possible for the start of competition proper. On this particular day however, things weren't going brilliantly and on top of everything else, it had been Steve's turn to get a bit of a dunking. Not only had I washed his socks from the week before, but I had with me, a full change of clothes which were made available as he'd taken his turn to get intimately acquainted with the South Holland Drain!

With Lewis on his box in time for the whistle - and with Steve in dry clothes - the match got underway. I had, once again, been assigned stewarding duties, but with excellent visibility and there being no need for adults to be present on the bank behind anglers, the role wasn't exactly onerous. When practising, we'd noted that even if we crouched down and made only quiet conversation behind any of our squad, bites tailed off. I made a point of advising our anglers to instruct anyone that came behind their pegs to leave immediately. During the competition though, none found this necessary.

Whilst we're used to matches starting quietly, this one was something else; sometime in, we were all playing 'spot the fish'! We weren't fully aware at the time as to the reason for the slowness of sport, only that reports were being received of a concentration of roach further along the drain close to a bridge and where the presence of several cormorants gave their location away. The region had experienced heavy rain in the 48 hours leading up to the match and we established after that an increased salt content in the stretch, possibly as a result of the prolonged downpour and higher tide; had resulted in the roach moving en masse. To be fair to the hosts, it was only a day or two before the event that the fish had apparently disappeared and if the contest had been staged two days before, I'm certain things would have been very different.

Although the roach had vacated the match length in numbers, one or two anglers were catching small fish. I saw Peter catch early on and word came along the bank that Timmy and Ollie had also had a few. In our practice session, a few of our anglers had caught what we presumed were bleak, although Steve had his doubts regarding species identification; locals had been overheard referring to 'sunfish', a term which, at the time, meant nothing to us. On the bank on match day, we were no wiser and we assumed that the fish being caught were bleak. Only later, after I'd found time to do a bit of research, did I establish that the fish being caught were perhaps sunbleak (Leucaspius delineatus). It seems that this species have a tolerance of brackish water which also results in increased swimming activity. In the week after the match, I submitted a short report to the Environment Agency; but my photos weren't of a sufficiently high resolution for them to establish beyond doubt, that sunbleak had taken an apparent liking to both our anglers' groundbait and their squatt hookbaits.

The match continued and as I sat chatting with Neil Nicolson he explained that, from what he'd seen and heard, our Gold team were winning the junior event; they had apparently, all caught. Worksop themselves, had just one 'catcher', as had SAFE. With an hour to go, Steve and I were under the impression that a couple of our Red team were still fishless. In the intermediates' match, Peter and Robert had caught, but in-between them, Luke Wrozek, the England angler guesting for King's Lynn, certainly hadn't. Jack was fishless and believed that Eddie was too. I established late on though, that Eddie had in fact caught a solitary fish; but he'd not admitted this to the King's Lynn steward and wanted to leave Jack thinking that his customary pre-match bet with his Harleston club-mate was still safe.

Aware that we had three intermediates with fish, the team trophy looked likely to return to Suffolk. Late in the day, Steve and I discussed whether the lack of wind may be having a detrimental effect on the fishing. Whether it was or wasn't, given how well our anglers were doing, we agreed that the final whistle couldn't come quickly enough and the last thing Suffolk needed was for a few fish to put in an appearance. Eventually though, the final whistle was blown and as the weigh-in started, we were as certain as we'd ever been, that Suffolk County would lift both team trophies – the attendance of a fat lady with a microphone, on this particular occasion, weren't required.

Having passed a message to the parents of our junior anglers that they should ensure that scales were zeroed absolutely correctly, given that so little had been caught; I assisted with recording the intermediates' returns. First to be weighed was the King's Lynn's Tom Cockle and he was credited with just 10gm. Next to weigh was Peter and when I asked how many fish he'd caught, he advised that he'd lost count; on the day, he was possibly the only angler that had! He tipped over a dozen small fish into the weigh-net and I recorded 110gm for an easy section win. To cut a long story short, no other King's Lynn anglers caught and with Robert Murphy in C also taking several fish, he too picked up a section win. I was feeling a little mischievous after weighing Robert's net in, knowing that Eddie had taken a fish when other stewards were blissfully unaware. Jack was also none the wiser and his face was a picture when he realised he'd been duped by Eddie and that he now owed him not an insignificant amount of money - courtesy of a solitary fish of unknown species that weighed less than half an ounce!

Three of the four King's Lynn anglers incurred an extra penalty point for a blank and ahead of their total of 11 points, Suffolk County were easy winners with 6. Peter, still a junior, was individual winner and Robert, champion the year before, was runner-up.

In the junior event, only one angler each from Worksop and SAFE managed to catch, both of them in F section where Timmy (Red) recorded 100gm. Ollie (Gold), pegged next-door, was close behind with 70gm. There were further section wins for Timmy's teammates: Sam, Tommy, Adam and Toby, as young Paul pipped James in A. Working back along the sections, Max, Jamie, Jack and Lewis all secured second-in-section placings and whilst King's Lynn anglers also caught, they incurred a blank in the section where Adam and Jamie managed to find fish. Timmy took the individual crown with Ollie runner-up and Toby third. Tommy and Sam finished fourth and fifth respectively as Suffolk took a clean sweep of the top five places. Suffolk County Red were junior team champions with 7 points, as the Gold team took the runners-up spot with 11, comfortably ahead of home side, King's Lynn on 17.

After the presentation the whole squad, apart from Jack Weatherley who'd left for a social engagement, posed with the two team trophies and their individual silverware.

There was a low turnout for the event, but all things being equal, we'd have expected no more than perhaps one of the team titles and a smattering of individual keepsakes. King's Lynn knew the water very well and we'd managed to schedule just one practice session in, the same as Worksop. A number of our anglers hadn't seen the venue before practice, yet no home side angler had beaten ours in any of the intermediate or junior sections. It could be argued that, because we found the sport so inconsistent in practice, we were perhaps, better prepared for how tough things would be on match day. We had ensured our anglers fished very fine with small hooks and we had discarded any thoughts of catching big fish by concentrating on a squatt approach. I'm sure too, our final groundbait mix was as effective as any on the bank and possibly better. Steve's project management was as professional as I'd become used to and we received considerable support Steve and Nicky Damant, Nigel Cottrell and Simon Saunders. In practice, our anglers had watched Rob closely and despite the change in conditions and lack of expected target fish, they'd all stuck to the task. Once again I was convinced that our holistic approach and attention to detail had made all the difference. Suffolk County had won both NJAA Challenge team titles, back-to-back and on completely different types of venue... Ron Dennis CBE once said, 'You may find this difficult to believe, but winning isn't as easy as it looks.'

As the October half-term holiday fast approached, my school sessions continued with some momentum and I was named a runner-up for the Suffolk Sport Coach of the Year award again. Steve, Hazel and I attended the awards ceremony with, among others, Olympic and Paralympic bronze medallists respectively, Anthony Ogogo and Zoe Newson. The first Saturday morning of half-term saw me on the banks of the Gipping at Needham Market with Tony Scott and three of his Castle Hill Junior School pupils. In addition to catching small rudd on a float rod and centre-pin reel set-up, we were very pleased to bank two chub on the link leger rod. It was an unseasonably cold morning and the second chub was photographed in a heavy sleet shower. Not long after we headed for a hard earned bacon roll and cup of hot tea at the local sandwich shop.

I missed the half-term coaching with Suffolk Coastal which Colin ran with a reduced number of participants as I'd been called up for two weeks' jury service. Between September and November I also enjoyed three productive pleasure sessions on Needham Lake, taking 36 bream in total. I'll add that, after setting up and feeding for the first of these sessions, I slipped on the wooden revetment and fell in! On clambering out of the lake, I had to retrieve my cap with my landing net, but didn't recover my Optonic that had also gone in attached to a snapped bank-stick until I returned the following day. Fortunately, the peg I'd fed was still free and I banked 18 bream after topping up the previous morning's feed.

Taking advantage of the spare time I had available I grabbed short sessions on the river and took an unexpectedly good bag of fish at Great Blakenham with the Gipping coloured and rising. In fact I moved my box up the bank twice during the session and although struggling with cold fingers, my perseverance was rewarded with a double figure bag of mostly dace, with several fish topping 8oz. I was fortunate enough that Friday afternoon, to catch the river just right and took all fish on a float rod, centre-pin reel and stick float tactics that were far removed from those I'd employed during all those years as a club match angler.

I also resumed my chub fishing and before the year was out, enjoyed a trip to one of the Norfolk Anglers' Conservation Association stretches on the Wensum in the company of fellow coach and NACA member, Martin Burgess. I'd met Martin briefly when coaching at the NACA Open Day and he also attended the same Level 2 course as Abi; we met again at the launch meeting of the River Waveney Trust. On our second trip together early in 2013, we both banked chub over four pounds, taking nine fish between us during a thoroughly enjoyable day when the weather remained kind and temperatures stayed favourable.

Over the winter, in anticipation of another season's coaching, I stripped down and retied well in excess of 100 pole and whip rigs of varying lengths for GVAC's venues. I topped up my hooklength boxes for the school sessions and prepared a selection for the county squad for whom, it had been another, very successful year.

Our January presentation evening, despite the severe winter weather, was well attended with Suffolk Sport's Vicki Askew and Richard Neal on hand once again to present silverware.

Soon after, I took a trip to Cudmore Fisheries in Staffordshire, accompanying Peter Williams who was progressing well in the Angling Trust's Talent Pathway programme. Peter, Adam Swain and the other Pathway anglers were attending a bloodworm and joker session on what had been, for a good few years, the Fish O'Mania final venue. On Saturday 2nd February, both did very well to cope with the bitterly cold conditions and thanks to what I'd learned several years before on the Chesterfield Canal, I was able to give Peter some guidance beforehand, as well as pick up a few tips from Adam, who'd received some coaching from Alex Bates at Westwood Lakes.

The cold spell continued, but I did manage to find time to make the most of a one very mild Tuesday in early March, before temperatures dropped once again. Having banked a couple of chub to over four pounds on cheese paste the evening before on the Gipping at Blakenham, I enjoyed a short day on the river back at Needham. Keeping mobile, I fished swims on both the GVAC stretch close to Needham Lake and those on the free water through the town. Using a short float rod and my centre pin reel loaded with 6lb line, I landed half-a-dozen chub on steak, fished over breadcrumb and fish that I'd cut up, having on a previous trip, had cause to clear up some discarded pike bait and other rubbish that had been left on the bank by a couple of inconsiderate individuals. The water level was very low and although ongoing flood prevention work had required the removal of numerous willows and alders; in the evenings, Steve and Jack Damant were enjoying similar good sport as they too, banked a number of reasonable chub.

Back on the bank again a couple of days later, I experimented with my approach and was pleased to land fish to over four pounds again on my first session with an-line maggot feeder; two floating, flavoured rubber maggots on a size 16 hook resulting in their downfall.

Determined to fish the last day, I was back on the Gipping at Blakenham, fishing a deep swim where I felt the splash of my heavy feeder would be tolerated by the chub. After almost two hours' casting and feeding, a very short tug of my quiver-tip saw me retrieve a bitten-off braid hooklength. A little bemused, I switched sometime later to cheese paste on a substantially bigger hook and first put-in, contacted a fish that proceeded to take line against a tight clutch. Eventually, the fish came to the surface and it wasn't the large chub that I'd hoped for, but a reasonable sized pike. After removing my size 4 B983 crimped-barb hook, I caught sight of two brightly coloured imitation maggots attached to a size 16 Wide Gape Specialist, just inside its mouth. Whilst I was disappointed not to have landed further chub, I was happy that I'd been able to recover my hook from a previously unseen fish. I released the pike after taking a couple of photographs and fished on into dusk, but saw no more action. It was though, an eventful end to my river season.

Come 7th April, I was with Adam and Peter again on the Talent Pathway programme, this time at Packington Fisheries in Warwickshire. Later the same month, I travelled to Gloucester with Peter and his grandmother, June. He, and around 25 other hopefuls attended the England Under-18s' trials event on the Gloucester Canal. Unfortunately,

Peter wasn't in Steve Sanders' choice of 10 that progressed to the final selection day and after a near-400 mile round trip, we put any disappointment at the back of our minds and focused on issues closer to home once again.

BACK TO BOSTON

With the daytime temperatures improving just a little, I managed couple of club matches in April and May. At the first of these Wednesday fixtures at Hinderclay, I bumped into Jeannette Halliday. Having returned my keepnet, I noticed Jeannette practising on one of the other lakes. Chatting as she packed her kit away, I asked whether she'd heard anything following the England Ladies' trials. Whilst at the time she hadn't, I was delighted to hear two days later that she'd been picked for the squad and was off to Slovenia with them for the World Championships in August.

With the GVAC AGM out of the way, Steve Barnes, Steve Damant and I were at Barking early on the morning of Saturday 4th May for the first of our Fish Club sessions. I'd come up with the concept and format with a view to see under-14s from both my school groups and our Junior Academy progress to a standard that might see them able to compete in national competitions as cadets. With Lewis Clouting and Paul Christie now too old for the under-14s' team, we were looking to work with younger and less experienced anglers in order to fill their vacant positions.

Having enjoyed Springfield's company on the Friday afternoon, I greeted Aston, Ciaran and Curtis again the next morning, as they joined Ben from Needham Market Middle and Jack, Ollie, Max and Amelie in the classroom. After a short briefing and introductions, Jack and Ollie observed as the rest of the group set about learning how to tie a figure-of-eight loop knot. Nail clippers and loop tyers were distributed and despite the initial looks of trepidation, it wasn't long before our white picnic table was covered with various examples of the aforementioned knot. I discussed and explained tackle preparation and methods of storage as the participants continued to practise their knots. Jack and Ollie then assisted me with distribution of top kits, landing nets and bait, as a couple of the adults sampled the fishing.

Meanwhile, and with my video camera running, the two Steves took over with the classroom group and explained and demonstrated how to attach hooklengths, loop-to-loop. All of us later adjourned to the pegs nearby, looking to conclude the session with some fishing. We debriefed and all agreed how enjoyable and successful the morning had been. We'd been looking to put something of this nature in place for years and finally we'd got around to it. Later in the day, I watched the video recordings back with interest, as I prepared my planners for the two remaining sessions, scheduled for the Saturdays of half-term week.

Following Saturday's Fish Club, I was at Needham Lake very early on the Monday morning. With three teams entered in the All England Junior Pole Championships, we were heading for practise on Skylark at Westwood Lakes ahead of our defence of the team title just five days later. Steve Damant and I had spent a great deal of time planning the day and on Sunday evening, we'd mixed around six kilos of groundbait as all of the kit was being dropped off for loading on to the van and as Jack kept everyone supplied with fresh cups of tea.

We were looking to arrive at Westwood before 9 a.m., but the young, male driver of a Vauxhall Vectra that hit us as we crossed the Fiveways roundabout at Mildenhall put paid to that. We were delayed for the best part of two hours, as two police officers took statements from me and then the parents that were travelling in the bus. Eventually, and with Steve having tied up the loose bumper of our vehicle, we were given permission to continue on our way as they questioned the driver of the Vauxhall further.

I took little comfort, but perhaps a degree of relief, from a phone call received around an hour later. Nigel Cottrell answered the call whilst I was driving and having pulled over at McDonald's near Long Sutton – an outlet which we all knew well – he passed the phone over to me. The police advised that they were looking to prosecute the other driver for careless driving and were happy that I was blameless in respect of the incident. Thankfully, no-one was hurt. Given the circumstances and the speed of the other vehicle, things could have been an awful lot worse. A couple of months later I received a letter advising that the driver of the Vectra had been prosecuted and found guilty of Careless Driving. He was fined a total of £180 and received six penalty points on his licence.

Eventually we arrived at Westwood. Lee Swain was holding the fort and Ian and James had unloaded the seat-boxes, pole holdalls and other kit from their van. Young Finlay Bulbeck had joined the squad and along with Adam Swain and Timmy Pepper, was set up and fishing as Steve got everyone organized. I visited the shop on site and paid our peg fees before joining the rest of the group soon after. A short demonstration by Adam was followed by a quick question and answer session and all were fishing by noon. The sun was shining and plenty of fish were caught in the favourable conditions.

A few hours later and assisted by Fin's dad, Steve; Lee weighed the anglers in before we debriefed and gave final instructions. After spending a good part of Tuesday filling in an insurance claim form at Stowmarket High School and then obtaining a quote for repair of the mini-bus; I looked ahead to our third All England Junior Pole Championships at Westwood.

Working with Springfield's pupils on Friday afternoon and having prepared most of their kit and bait on the Thursday, I collected the mini-bus in the morning. That evening, Steve D mixed a supply of groundbait for the teams. Taking advice from Pep and Alex Bates, we'd switched from a sweet fishmeal to red krill mixes. I'd also divided up and bagged the venue's pellets purchased on practice day. These were mostly micros, but with some 4mms to be mixed in. Those travelling on the mini-bus once again, dropped their kit off at Steve's, but with Ian unavailable, Nigel would drive the Bristo's van. Tom and James would assist with loading and unloading.

At around 5.45 a.m. on Saturday, I pulled in at Needham Lake where Steve and his son, Jack were already waiting. Steve Barnes arrived soon after, as did the rest of the mini-bus passengers and we were soon on the road, heading to collect Peter Williams and his grandmother, whom we were meeting at Homebase at Bury St Edmunds – a safer alternative to the Fiveways roundabout pick-up!

Following discussions between coaches, parents and anglers, our final line-up would be: Tom Cottrell, James Head, Timmy Pepper and Adam Swain (Suffolk County Red); Paul Christie, Lewis Clouting, Sam Kennard and Peter Williams (Suffolk County Gold) and Jack Damant, Jamie Marriott, Max Rushbrook and Ollie Saunders (Suffolk County Cadets).

In the under-23s' individual event, we fielded seven anglers; once again, more than any other squad. Along with Brad Calver, Abbi Kendall, Robert Murphy, Toby Pepper, we had Finn Bulbeck and Brendan Strowlger. Living not too far from Westwood, Brendan was keen to fish, but his former team, King's Lynn, weren't participating. After chatting to Lee and noting that the age limit for the individual match had been raised, we were happy to accommodate Brendan. Completing our entry of under-23s was Jess Knights. Jess was eligible for team selection, but had been unable to attend squad practice. She had however, visited the venue on the Tuesday and after we chatted on the phone a couple of days before, she fished Kestrel with a deliberate view to compete with the older anglers on the same lake the following Saturday and the time she put in in practice with her dad would stand her in good stead four days later.

Gone With the Wind

We'd left Westwood Lakes after practice with the venue bathed in warm sunshine. Only a gentle breeze ruffled the surface of Skylark and Steve D and I agreed it was the warmest we'd known it on the complex in our half-a-dozen or so visits. Unfortunately, the conditions flattered to deceive and whilst we'd always been aware of the increased effect of the wind on Lincolnshire waters and parts of Westwood in particular; I later felt that we were still caught out on match day. I had suspicions that, with the relatively large team entry and with some top northern sides taking part, we may just see our crown taken from us. I kept these thoughts to myself obviously; always wanting to be as positive as I could be in the company of our anglers.

At the practice debrief however, I did challenge all those present to be honest with themselves and to ensure that they put maximum effort in as they prepared for competition. Looking back and discussing issues with Simon Saunders on match day, I felt I'd been a little hard on them and had been perhaps asking too much. One or two were busy with exams at school and my desire for the team to continue to do well at a high level, possibly got the better of me. The incident with the Vectra on the way to practice didn't help and I was certainly not in the best frame of mind as I addressed the squad. After though, I got on with the task of transporting a number of our anglers, their parents and coaches both back from practice and to Westwood again for the match itself. I'd also offered to take the vehicle in for repair early on the Monday after the match and it was then, sitting alone in the bus that I felt extremely uneasy and a little nauseous. I admitted how I felt to Simon a day or two later and we discussed how it may have taken some time for me to realise the potential seriousness of the collision and the consequent shock may have been delayed whilst I was focused on the competition and my allocated duties.

As far as match was concerned, Steve Barnes and I had taken a bit of a step back and were looking to do a little less for the anglers. This was a deliberate attempt to see them take more ownership with kit preparation. I did though, tie eight rigs early on Thursday morning and prepare a large number of hooklengths for the less experienced members of the squad.

At the draw, it became obvious that bank-running would be permitted again and there was no mention of the no coaching rule that I'd seen flouted blatantly twelve months before. Our coaches and assistants however, prefer to allow the anglers to fish their own matches with as little interference as possible – for the sake of their enjoyment if nothing else – and it was perhaps, inevitable that given the conditions, we'd relinquish the coveted wooden trophy come the presentations several hours later.

We'd been able to place our anglers in sections in 2012 and we prepared for the same again this time around. Max travelled direct to the match with his dad, Charlie, and we advised him after practice, to prepare to fish Hawk. With Hawk hosting one section of the team event and with the lake being perhaps, a little less daunting than Skylark, Charlie and Max were in agreement. We asked Paul to do the same for our Gold team and he and Peter were therefore able to make their way there with tackle, before the main rush after the draw. Knowing the venue reasonably well, I'd managed to park the mini-bus in a central car park on arrival. With the van beside the bus, we were also able to despatch Steve Barnes to register our arrival as Nigel, Tom and James unloaded the van.

Lee Swain had not only kept us informed regarding which lakes were to be used for both the team and individual match, but also how the draw would take place. As the area around the on-site tackle shop and cafeteria became clogged with vehicles just before 9 a.m., we'd already parked up and had placed our anglers' equipment along the bank in their designated sections. We'd advised Adam and Timmy that one of them should fish Hawk as that they knew it better than either Tom or James.

Eventually, the two Steves and I made contact with all our intermediates, as well as the under-18s that had travelled direct to the venue. With the team and individual draws complete, Lee headed for Hawk with Adam and his kit. Lee had also persuaded the match organizer to allow an hour and a half setting-up time. In addition to giving our squad plenty of time to tackle up, this also gave young Jamie time to complete his paper round with his dad, Nick before the drive to Westwood. With Jamie placed in A section, I sent a text to Nick advising him of Jamie's peg number (11). One of my last jobs before the start of the match was to ensure Jamie had his supply of groundbait and venue pellets. I'd distributed rigs to Max and Paul and before the whistle went, Steve Barnes had managed to assist Max at his peg.

Hawk is smaller than Skylark, but the wind was still proving more than a little troublesome for the younger and slighter framed. Word reached me soon after the start however, that Max and Paul had caught fish. Adam caught immediately, having fed a mixture of groundbait and soil and his worm hookbait was grabbed before his float reached the water when he lowered his rig in at the start. Later, Charlie advised that it was a pleasure to watch Adam a few pegs along from Max, as he picked off fish from the far shelf. Adam went on to finish second in his section behind an England trialist on the favoured end peg by the footbridge.

On Skylark it was a slow start for most, but from close to the mini-bus I watched Timmy on the opposite bank in A section taking fish. The wind was affecting presentation considerably though, and in many cases prohibiting competitors' ability to present bait long; this was something we'd achieved with comparative ease in practice. It was also decidedly chilly and although we'd checked the forecast and I'd advised our squad to note the temperature drop from practice, several were struggling with the conditions; me included and I wasn't fishing! The Suffolk County parents and coaches were all sporting evidence of sun- and wind-burn from the Monday. Five days later, we were plunged into wintry conditions and many youngsters were forced to fish the deeper water and the margins as a consequence.

As a further example of our frustrations, I watched Jack hook a good fish to his right, only then for it run to his left and tangle with his young neighbour's line. They both looked bemused as I separated their rigs half-way between their pegs. Whilst Jack hadn't enjoyed the best of practice sessions, he was a changed young man on match day. Despite losing that first fish and also pulling out of several others that were possibly foul-hooked – an occupational hazard on Skylark – he remained calm and unfazed. Soon after, Abbi's boyfriend and recent Hotrods signing, Rob Wright joined us as we watched our cadet. Rob remarked immediately, that most of our anglers weren't fishing heavy enough and needed 4 x 16 rigs and to be fishing overdepth to achieve the presentation desired.

  The wind, if anything, was strengthening. On numerous occasions, Steve Damant and I walked over to the areas immediately behind the anglers to replace rollers that were being blown over repeatedly along the match length. Rob continued to chat to Jack and after a few minutes made a visit to his car and returned with a heavier rig. We watched as Jack placed it on one of his kits and shortened the line between pole tip and float as Rob looked on.

  Steve Barnes and I had compared notes, having asked the organizer about stewarding and, as mentioned earlier and unlike the year before, we agreed that we were able to both coach and bank-run. We also agreed later that this led to a much more relaxed atmosphere on the bank, albeit that some parents remained unclear as to what rules were in force. Rob meanwhile, continued to coach Jack and Jack was an eager subject. Slowly but surely, he began to put a few fish together and as Rob left him, he had a definite air of confidence about him – even more so than usual!

  To the back of us on Kestrel, I'd spoken to most of our anglers and some were faring better than others. Jess, although drawn on unfancied peg 8, had been advised by Lee exactly where to fish. Further along on peg 11 however, Abbi was struggling to fish long in the wind. Brendan was catching opposite and young Finn was holding his own against much older opposition.

Word had reached me via Lee that Brad had unfortunately arrived for the match without a pole! His dad, Brett explained that Brad had removed his pole from his holdall to check his top kits etc. but that they'd then driven to Westwood without it. Finn's dad, Steve had then retrieved a spare from home and I watched Brad putting it to good use; although things were quiet on Robert's peg. Completing our line-up of intermediates was Toby on peg 7. Probably the best angler in our squad, Toby had won several recent Westwood opens and whilst I photographed him landing fish later on, they were not of a consistent size to trouble those that were doing well.

Jess on the other hand and on only her second visit, had arrived at Westwood, happy with the required tactics and tackle set-up and I was on hand to see her land a large carp. Soon after, I weighed a barbel for her of 7lb 12oz. Not long after that, I weighed another and as I left her, she continued to take fish.

Back on Skylark, most of our anglers were finally catching, but some were finding the going extremely tough. The one thing I'll say about all of them though is that they stuck at it and I only ever see them leave their seat-box for one reason, Lewis being best placed of all of them to visit the Portaloo between Skylark and Kestrel!

With more than three hours of the match gone, I finally succumbed and headed for the cafeteria for a hot cappuccino, treating Sam's mother, Sue and Peter's grandmother, June to a hot chocolate. As I left the girls to it, looking to get down to Hawk before the match ended and grab some photos of our anglers there, Peter Christie advised me that Jack had landed a very large carp. Almost immediately I received a text from Steve Barnes advising the same; it had been weighed at 13lb 12oz and returned immediately. That battle scarred fish – several hooks were removed from its mouth and fins - helped Jack to second place in section, as he beat both James a few pegs along, and Peter opposite. He went on to pick up a well-deserved default section win prize and was by far the youngest angler called up in the presentations.

As I arrived on Hawk I saw Max playing a modest sized barbel; I say 'modest', but it was bigger than all of the ones I'd ever caught! I then grabbed a couple of photos of Adam and with the sky turning darker by the minute, I took another from behind Paul's peg. I chatted to Peter for a few minutes, ensuring that Paul was okay before beginning my walk back to Skylark. As I crossed the footbridge once again however, the heavens opened.

In the few short minutes it took to walk to the minibus, I got drenched. My thoughts though, as I took shelter on the veranda of one of the lodges, were for the youngsters fishing in the bitter cold and almost horizontal rain. The shower wasn't prolonged however and by the time I'd opened the back of the mini-bus and donned my leggings, the rain had stopped! There wasn't much of the match left and the downpour was queue for several intermediates to pack up. Robert arrived at the van with his trolley loaded and for once, he'd not emptied the lake. Abbi wasn't far behind him, but speaking to Chris, Jess's dad; it was evident that she had had a much better match. She'd ended up with four large barbel and as the scales arrived at her peg, he produced his note of their weights, all of which had been witnessed as required. After weighing her second net and calculating her total weight, Jess was confirmed as runner-up on Kestrel. I offered my congratulations as she'd ensured that Suffolk County would be represented in the frame of the individual match for the third year in succession and in every Pole Champs held at Westwood.

Returning to Skylark, Steve Barnes updated me on the anglers' fortunes and teams' scores. It was evident with an hour or so to go, that Sensas A4 were going to take the team trophy. Barnsley too, were looking very good. The presentations got underway and Timmy and Jack were handed their section prizes as Adam was also named third on the day in the team match. Jess was also presented with her runner-up trophy and finally, the team positions were read out, as tradition dictates, in reverse order.

Our Gold team were announced in tenth spot, shortly before our young cadet team were confirmed as seventh; whilst the day was tinged with a degree of disappointment - if only because we'd set ourselves such a high standard in recent years - this was one result that we could take some satisfaction from.

Having enjoyed a comfortable practice session fishing the far shelf, James had struggled a few pegs along from Jack. To be fair to James though, like most of our squad, he'd not benefited from one-to-one coaching as our bank-running was minimal. I did manage to get a shot or two of James catching and having tackled down, he dutifully set about loading his dad's van with squad kit. Pegged in an area he's come to know well, Tom finished just in the top half of his section however and we calculated our Red team tally of 21 points long before the presentations were made. It was with some relief therefore, that three teams were announced in joint fourth on 23 points. As we always say, fourth is the position no team wants to finish in. Shortly after, Suffolk County were confirmed in third place and Adam, James, Tom and Timmy stepped forward to receive their trophies. Worksop finished runners-up and, as expected, Sensas A4 were easy winners.

I'd chatted with Simon whilst sheltering from the wind and rain during the closing stages of the match and we'd agreed that, if we'd been told back in 2007, that our squad would progress and develop and win 10 national titles in a period of just 17 months, we'd not have believed it. We'd come to expect a lot from our squad and perhaps justifiably. I'll admit to an ironic smile as we prepared to leave Westwood, given our feeling of disappointment when they'd just won eight trophies and prizes. I worked out after that there were 22 available and we brought back 36% of them!

We pulled into McDonald's at Long Sutton and it was soon evident, as I sat with Steve Barnes and James, that if anyone else was disappointed, they weren't letting it affect their appetite!

With Peter having received confirmation of funding for his Level 1 coaching course, we were keen to see him attend, even though it would rule him out of selection for the Angling Trust National at Tunnel Barn. Adam was disappointed to say the least, that a geography trip meant that he too, was unable to participate and Jess would be attending her prom on the 29th June. Nonetheless, looking at the squad sheet, we still had seven eligible juniors and were looking too, for two under-14s to join Jack, Jamie, Ollie and Max to defend our cadets' title. The emails I'd sent out after the first Fish Club would hopefully see us in a position to make suitable selection.

THE ONLY WAY IS ESSEX

The 2012 Angling Trust Ladies' National had proved to be a huge personal disappointment. The two lakes used for the match at Holly Farm in Leicestershire had very different stocks and much larger fish were landed by the anglers pegged on Trotters; whilst virtually all those on Gils struggled to compete. Given the random draw and with the team event decided on total weight; the Suffolk girls came away with just Kayleigh Smith's section winner's medal to show for their efforts in both practice and on match day. With the 2013 event scheduled for Coleman's Cottage near Witham in Essex however, I felt that the girls might perhaps, make it on to the podium for the first time.

Well ahead of the match, I contacted Jayne at Coleman's and she confirmed that Stepfield Lake had been booked by the Trust. Abi then started to source information and very soon we began to get an idea of what we could expect in terms of the fishing. With the venue just an hour's drive away, I looked to put together a few practice sessions.

Les Thompson, the 2012 £50,000 Maver Mega 'Match This' winner had qualified for the Fish O'Mania final early in 2013 at Coleman's and was more than helpful with information. Stepfield, we established, was the newest of the lakes on the complex and reports of how it was fishing were mixed. We found out later that Stepfield is actually two separate lakes of an 'L' shape; one within the other and separated by a similar shaped burr running down the middle. Anglers fishing the different banks of Stepfield effectively face each other over the burr.

I'd always approached working with the ladies a little differently to when coaching the youth squad. I was reluctant to pick teams and with eight anglers available once again, whilst selection of a perhaps stronger group of four may have given us a better chance of a medal, I still wasn't prepared to compromise on any level of enjoyment. I was also well aware of the standard of matches some of the squad fished on a regular basis and looked to facilitate first and coach second, and only if required.

Speaking to the girls, they were happy to remain in the fours from 2012, but with young Anna Blyth unavailable, Nuala Gray stepped in. Abi and I had met Nuala and her husband John (both coaches) at White Acres. Nuala, from near Milton Keynes, had been let down at the last minute in 2012 and despite practising at Holly Farm, fished as an individual on match day. After I'd confirmed with Anna's dad Rob, that his daughter wasn't available for Coleman's; Nuala, who knew Anna, jumped at the chance to be part of the squad. At this point, I had my two teams and prepared the entry forms.

At the Suffolk County EOYM in 2012, it was agreed that £100 be donated to the Ladies' National entry fees. This was in memory of the late Barbara Mackie-Morrison, former secretary of both Saxmundham Angling Club and Suffolk County. The girls were then good enough to post me their balance cheques and, as ever, I was keen to get take care of the paperwork in good time in an effort to confirm entry.

With all cheques apart from one received, I contacted Abbi Kendall and admit to being disappointed to hear that she'd be fishing with the England girls: Sam Perkins, Sam Sim and Emma Pickering. After talking the matter over with Steve Barnes however, I understood the reason for Abbi's decision and accepted fully, her ambition to be part of the England set-up. I wished her well, but losing such a good angler from the squad was a huge personal disappointment. Also, I was immediately aware of the strength of the team she was now part of. I had though, little time at that point to worry about the match and had the more pressing issue of finding a replacement. Once again, I called upon Nuala for assistance.

Abi and I had met Leanne Knott at White Acres in 2011 and after double-checking the 2012 Ladies' National results, I knew Leanne had fished as an individual. At that point, I didn't know whether she'd been snapped up by a team for 2013 and so telephoned Nuala who advised that she not only knew Leanne reasonably well, but was also sure she'd be available for the team. Nuala then offered to contact Leanne on my behalf and I was extremely pleased to receive confirmation just a few days later, that we once again, had a full complement of eight anglers. Not only that, Leanne was very quick to let me have the information I needed for the entry forms and also to get her cheque to me.

With our Gold team of Judy Ford, Jeannette Halliday, Jess Knights and Nuala already confirmed, we now had our Red team: Abi, Kayleigh, Charlotte Gore and Leanne. I posted the forms and cheques and contacted Coleman's again to confirm some possible practice dates. I appreciated that one or two squad members might not be able to visit the venue before match day, given where they lived and taking into account their other match commitments, but came up with a couple of weekend dates that suited most. After exchanging emails and telephoning Jayne, I managed to get two sessions arranged on each bank of Stepfield. Charlotte and her dad, John confirmed that they'd look to travel up from Kent to practise separately as they would be on holiday and not be able to join us. Dennis Willis and Judy also planned to get at least one additional session in, along with squad practice. John was also good enough to email me valuable information on the venue well ahead of our planned practices.

By this time, Abi had moved in with her boyfriend, Lewis Porter, Group Media Manager for Fox International. Living in Langtoft, north of Peterborough, she'd popped home for the weekend and we travelled to Coleman's early on Sunday 26th May for the first squad session. Several of the Suffolk girls were already enjoying breakfast when Abi and I arrived. Sophie Hill, individual winner in 2012, also greeted us. Like several of the competitors, we'd met Sophie at White Acres where Abi had drawn between her and Sam

Sim on the first day of the 2011 Solero Festival. Sophie asked if she could tag on the end of our practice and the girls and I were happy to accommodate her; the more we had fishing, the better we'd be able to recreate anything like match conditions.

With breakfast out of the way and day tickets purchased, we made our way to Stepfield's higher pegs. Speaking with Dennis, we looked to split the girls with husbands, partners and dads fishing in-between. We then agreed to tackle up and have a period of fishing, before a short match. Everyone caught and with a few different rigs, lines and baits tried, we then placed our keepnets.

Jess in particular, had caught well in the initial hour or so, but after placing the nets, sport became noticeably slower for most. Sophie was on the lower end of the stretch with spare pegs to her left and after a few hours' fishing topped the returns. Leanne and Jess also did well and Dennis explained afterwards that he'd spent some time watching Abi next-door in an effort to keep up with her! I felt I'd overfed my skimmer line, but enjoyed the session catching roach, rudd, perch, small barbel and ide close in on caster. My weight though, was well below most and silver fish were immediately discounted as an option in the match, unless it was particularly hard. We debriefed and I agreed to enquire about fishing the following weekend on the lower pegs. Jess and her dad stayed on to have an hour or so on the opposite bank, after Dennis had had a look at tactics employed in the match there earlier. Abi had started a part-time cake making business and with an order to fulfil, she and I gave our apologies and headed back up the A12.

Exchanging emails with Jayne at Coleman's during the week, I then made a few calls and Nuala and John, Judy, Abi and I agreed to meet up again on the following Sunday. Given how popular the venue is with match anglers, we were grateful to fishery owner Gerry, who was good enough to find us space on the low numbers on 2nd June. With the venue closed to competitors from the

Monday, this would be our last opportunity for the girls to practise.

I chose not to fish at this second squad session and having spent time during the week tying rigs and hooklengths, assisted Judy and Nuala, and looked also, to observe the two matches that would be taking place. As John and the girls tackled up in the warm sunshine, plenty of fish could be seen cruising in the upper layers.

I passed out rigs where required and once the session was underway, it became very clear that the fishing was better on this side of Stepfield, just as John, Charlotte, Dennis and Judy had previously experienced. I made my way back and forth between Abi, Judy and Nuala and took several photographs of the girls playing fish. I also took a few more panoramic shots of Stepfield to email to Kayleigh and Jeannette during the week, along with my final update. Before the session finished however, I found time to sit on Abi's new Matrix Superbox and land a few fish on her G-Max 1000 pole. Once again, we debriefed, and after helping the girls return their kit to their cars, I made sure we were all aware of the draw time for the match that was now just six days away.

During the last few days before the event, I emailed the whole squad, confirmed final arrangements and ensured I had plenty of spare rigs made up for both sides of Stepfield, along with hooklengths for any of the girls that would need them.

Better Late Than Never

Early on match day, I loaded the car and Abi and I enjoyed a trouble-free journey to Coleman's. Arriving in plenty of time before the draw, I checked for everyone's arrival. I moved between tables in the café, greeting those in our squad, whilst also noting the presence of the usual big names and fancied teams. Meeting up with John Gore, he explained that he'd fished the day before, as Charlotte watched. Rob

Wright had also fished, with Abbi looking on, whilst Alan Scotthorne sampled sport with wife Sandra another interested spectator.

Talking with all the girls, I reiterated that low numbers would obviously be preferred and recalling my experiences in the GVAC Evening Series some years earlier, chatted with Jess and Chris in particular, about how delving deep into one of the corners of the draw bag might see them pegged on the coveted left-hand side of the lake.

I'm never completely relaxed on these occasions and along with the usual apprehension and anticipation before a draw, I was a little distracted by the fact that we were one angler short as the stewards called the girls forward. I'd not seen Kayleigh, but knew that she'd travelled down the evening before and that she'd stayed nearby. With the draw taking place, I took a call from her; she'd missed a turning and had found herself on the opposite side of the complex. After checking the post code noted and giving her details of where the entrance to the fishery was located, I advised her that I'd let match organisers know she as on her way.

Meanwhile, the rest of the Suffolk girls had already drawn and Jess and Abi were on the low numbers. In fact Jess was on peg 3 with just one angler to her right. On her left however and on peg 5, was Sam Perkins. Abi had pulled out peg 24 and Nuala, on peg 9 was also on, what we'd found to be, the better side of the lake. Judy (peg 53) and Leanne (peg 50) had drawn in the area where we fished our first practice session, with Jeannette at the near end of the same bank (peg 60) and Charlotte at the other (peg 36). Charlotte would have England's Helen Dagnall for company close by. The draw could have been better for the girls, but it could have been a lot worse. We had two from each team on either bank of Stepfield and scanning the lake after helping Abi to her peg with her kit, it seemed most other teams had a similar split of anglers. Fishing as Doncaster AA, Abbi Kendall and Sam Sim had both drawn high and were pegged near Judy and Leanne, whilst teammates

Emma Pickering and Sam Perkins were on the left, more favourable side of the lake.

The draw bag had not though, been kind to 2012 winners Starlets. Only Sophie Hill (peg 11) was on the coveted left bank, with her three England international teammates, Julie Abbott, Helen Dagnall and Sandra Scotthorne all having drawn high. Conversely, Warrington AA had three of their team on the left half of Stepfield and so could, I felt, prove hard to beat on the day. The one small blessing was that their best angler, former World Champion, Wendy Locker was on peg 45. From what I could see, the remaining teams had two on each bank and the teams to overhaul, or at least, keep in touch with in our efforts to secure a team medal would be, I felt, Doncaster and Warrington.

There remained though, the small matter of making sure I actually had two full teams on the bank. I still hadn't seen Kayleigh and admit to being just a little concerned as I sought out one of the organisers. I needn't have worried and they confirmed her arrival and that she'd drawn close to Abi. I headed straight to her on peg 27 met up with her mum, Linda. As unflappable as I've always known her to be, Kayleigh had made her way to her peg with her kit and was going about tackling up. With Abi and Kayleigh pegged near to each other and with match organisers asking us not to wander the bank whilst the match was underway, I looked to spend most of the match some way behind the pegs, close to the footpath in the trees.

Before long, the match got underway and I was pleased to see Abi's nerves settled with a couple of early fish. Kayleigh too, began to catch well and a couple of hours in I compared notes with Linda, confirming that both girls were doing okay. Looking across to the opposite bank, I could also see Leanne netting fish regularly, but it was evident that some on that side weren't faring as well.

Making my way along the footpath, I noted Emma Pickering catching consistently and could also see that

Sophie was doing well for Starlets. Among those I found opportunity to chat to whilst watching the match take shape was local match angler Paul Bird, who was tasked for the day with supporting and coaching Warrington's Pat Geary. Paul advised that the middle area of that half of Stepfield, where Emma was pegged, was very productive and whilst Abi and Kayleigh were pegged off what he felt was the best area; he was complimentary as to how well Abi in particular was doing. Later on in the match, I also had a few words with Alan Scotthorne, debating the format of the match and chatting about how Sandra was doing on the far bank. Talking to others as I made my way through the trees and back to the toilets at the café, the bankside grapevine confirmed that Sam Perkins was doing very well.

    Back from the café and seated comfortably on my Fox Royale carp chair, I watched as Abi played a reasonably large fish with her usual confidence in her rig and top kit. Within a minute or two she'd netted it. She then spun round on her box with the fish cradled in the landing net. She beckoned me over to, as I thought, have a look. As I approached, she asked quietly which keepnet she should put the fish in. The fish in question was a large tench and with designated nets for silver fish, carp and F1s, she wanted to ensure she followed the fishery's rules. A quick discussion with others watching confirmed that it should go in with the silver fish. Minor drama over, she resumed fishing and I assumed my place back on my chair, noting how often she seemed to bag herself a bonus tench in matches.

    Hearing the final whistle, I had no idea how either of Suffolk's teams had done. With bank-running restricted and with the match decided on total weight, rather than section points; it would not be until I'd managed to get an idea of individual returns, that I'd be able to work out whether Suffolk County might make the podium.

    The anglers on the far bank were weighed in first and Abbi Kendall topped the returns with 17kg 240gm.

Fishing worm, she'd taken an exceptionally good weight, and with some very good anglers around her. On her first visit to the lake, Jeannette in our Gold team had more than doubled her neighbour's weight, with 11kg 280gm. Whilst Judy had found the going as tough as in the first practice; she was in good company as England's Julie Abbott also failed to make double figures from the same area. Sam Sim had also topped 17kg and it was a foregone conclusion that, as expected, Doncaster, with three England girls in their line-up, would take gold. For Suffolk County Red though, Leanne's 14kg 160gm and Charlotte's 10kg 380gm had, I felt, put us in with a shout of a team medal for the first time in the event. Leanne had almost doubled Julie Abbott's weight and Charlotte had managed to stay within a kilo of Helen Dagnall. Warrington's Wendy Locker had done very well, but I'd not seen her teammates on the lower pegs catching at any rate. Charlotte and Leanne's combined return was also, I quickly calculated, a shade better than that of the two Mark One Sensas anglers on the far bank. As Gerry and the match stewards began weighing in the low pegs, heading for Abi and Kayleigh towards the far end, it was game on!

Meeting the scales part way along Abi's bank, talk was of 'the young lass' who'd had 25kg and catching up with Chris, I was able to confirm Jess's weight of 25kg 630gm. Chris also confirmed that she'd beaten Sam Perkins by around four kilos. John advised though, that Nuala had struggled for a good deal of the match on peg 9, but I was hoping that both, along with Judy and Jeannette would be able share any squad success in the form of a Red team medal (I was becoming more confident that they'd made the podium) as well as perhaps, individual silverware for Jess.

The scales reached Sophie and having fished the match in the same area the week before where she'd also done well, she weighed in 24kg 720gm. Local angler, Elizabeth Larkin had topped 21kg from peg 2, but until the scales reached Emma Pickering on peg 21, no other nets took the scales past the 20kg mark. It was no surprise however, to see Emma record 32kg 500gm for what would prove to be top weight on the day.

Abi's neighbour recorded a weight of 17kg 560gm before Abi's own net was confirmed at 20kg 520gm and it was around this time that Rob Lincoln had a word in my ear, advising that Abi was lying sixth, with only the top six going through to Ladies' Fish O'Mania…

Abi's weight was almost double that of the Warrington angler to her left and with mixed emotions, I then watched Kayleigh weigh in. Kayleigh, as she always does, had fished a very tidy match and had also caught a few fish from her long line late on, when many others struggled for bites. I was convinced she'd better Abi's weight, but the scales settled at 17kg 440gm. Whilst Fish O'Mania qualification hadn't entered my head at any stage before Rob mentioned it, I'll admit to a considerable level of nervous anticipation as the final three anglers' nets were weighed. Having noted two returns of around eight kilos and one of one of just under fourteen, all indications were that Abi had qualified for Fish O' Mania. I'm always one to wait for official confirmation, but I also knew that Rob wasn't usually far out.

As Abi chatted with other anglers, I made my way back to my car with her kit and returned to help Kayleigh, chatting to competitors and confirming weights whilst doing so and mentally calculating team totals. Before heading for the presentations, I was convinced that Suffolk had secured a bronze medal. I knew we'd beaten Starlets, but was unsure about Warrington. Walking to the café, I was stopped by Abi, who had picked up a text from Les Thompson. Abi initiated the exchange of texts, advising that she believed she'd qualified for Fish O'. She told me not to repeat aloud what the text said as she handed me her phone; I'll just say that the second word was 'awesome'!

Before long, the presentations got underway and with no default prizes at Angling Trust events, Abbi Kendall and Emma Pickering each received their section winner's medal and Emma was then announced as National Champion. Jess was confirmed as runner-up and the highest placed under-21 and recipient of the Claire Dagnall Memorial trophy.

Team-wise, Suffolk Gold were out of contention, finishing with a similar overall weight to Reading Angling Team Hydro. Mark One Sensas were also announced before the top three teams, closely followed by Warrington with 57kg 80gm. I knew then, that Suffolk had a team medal and on hearing Starlets being called up for bronze with a total of 58kg 160gm, the silver was one better than I'd anticipated a short time before. A medal of any colour for either team was our target and I'll admit to being more than a little emotional (I don't think I was alone) as I watched the girls step forward. Doncaster lifted the team trophy with an impressive 88kg 770gm.

A fundraising draw then took place and I handed my prize of a bag of roach groundbait to Abbi Kendall for her match the following day. Jeannette busied herself assisting as part of the England Ladies' squad and a couple of months later she returned from Slovenia with a team gold medal around her neck!

After the obligatory squad photo, I thanked Nuala, Judy, Jeannette and Jess; Charlotte, Kayleigh, Leanne and Abi for their efforts. I also thanked husbands, partners and parents for their support.

I left the car park of Coleman's Cottage knowing that two the six 2014 Ladies' Fish O'Mania finalists would be Suffolk County anglers. After the heartbreak of Larford in 2010, the nightmare of the Kennet and Avon in 2011 and the bad draw at Holly Farm in 2012; Abi not only had a team silver medal, but had also qualified for the prestigious Sky Sports match. Before we set off, we scanned the results sheets and noted that she'd made the top six by 2kg 340gm. I advised her that it was the large tench that had probably seen her through. Ironically, she'd edged out three times champion Denise Yeomans (formerly Hudgell). Denise, whom I'd chatted to earlier in the day, had beaten Abi from the next peg back in 2010 at Larford.

After unloading back home, I grabbed a quick photo of Abi with her medal. I was soon back on the bank working with schools and attending to maintenance duties with GVAC. With me putting all my efforts in with the ladies, Steve had agreed to manage the campaign for the Angling Trust Cadet/Junior/Intermediate National at Tunnel Barn on the final Saturday in June. Before then though, and in-between school coaching and practices, I managed to get on the Gipping and bank my first chub of the river season.

COVENTRY CAPERS

On my return from Coleman's Cottage, I spent time preparing press releases for local papers and newsletters, along with the customary GVAC website report. After the elation of the match on the Saturday and the realisation of what the girls had achieved, it was back to the day job during week. Meanwhile, Steve Barnes was making final plans for practice ahead of our trip to Warwickshire.

Like many other competitions we'd entered, bringing back silverware from an event scheduled on a venue such a distance away was going to be a challenge. The near-300 mile round trip to Tunnel Barn saw us discount practice, other than on club waters. We accepted that most of the squad would be tackling up on match day, never having seen the complex before, let alone fished any of its lakes.

Whilst Steve organised a couple of get-togethers at Barking, young Finn Bulbeck and his dad, Steve travelled to Tunnel Barn from their home in Lincolnshire and fed back comprehensive and valuable information. Dennis Willis, with a friend working at the fishery, also contributed to our endeavours to formulate some kind of plan and Abi was able to tap up her contacts as usual. Before too long, Steve was building ideas of how the squad could approach the match and at the first practice session proper on 15th June, addressed those on the bank at Barking.

I was with Hardwick Middle School that bright and breezy Saturday morning and set up near the classroom on the carp lake ahead of the pupils' arrival. The school would fish the far end, with the county squad on the earlier pegs. The sessions dovetailed well and after Hardwick left around lunchtime, I joined Steve along the bank. Steve and Finn had travelled down from Lincolnshire and gave details of what they'd discovered in Warwickshire.

We convened again eight days later and Aston, Ciaran and Curtis of Springfield Junior School came along to experience a county practice session. Several parents were also with us and after Steve's thorough briefing, the fishing and a debrief, he gave final instructions ahead of the match that was to take place the following Saturday.

Having cancelled my Springfield session, I was with Steve by late morning on the Friday, assisting him with final bait preparation. With an insurance claim on-going and the memories of the incident in the mini-bus still fresh in my mind, I chose to take my own car to Tunnel Barn and many of our squad were heading westwards on the A14 as Steve and I finished sorting bait late afternoon. With Sam Kennard and his mum, Sue having arrived, we loaded up and minutes before our departure, I checked the post code of our overnight accommodation.

I knew of the Travelodge Steve had booked and also knew how difficult it was to find; I regretted immediately, not having liaised with him more closely regarding our accommodation. Sam jumped into my Astra and Sue kept Steve company for the journey and everything went well until minutes from our destination, when I chose to follow the instructions of my sat nav, rather than Steve's rear bumper! What ever possessed me to think that using the same sat nav as when I couldn't find the place before, would see me doing anything other than drive around the same square mile or two of Coventry, wrestling with the same one way system and road closures without finding it again this time?

I circled central Coventry, treating Sam to the many sights it offers unfamiliar visitors on a Friday evening. Not all of these were pleasant and after parking and phoning Steve, we waited in a less-than-salubrious area and I instructed Sam to lock his door as more and more drinkers spilled from the many pubs and clubs, on to the pavements all around us. We sat waiting for Steve to lead us to the hotel – which of course, he'd found without too much difficulty.

Several young Suffolk County anglers and parents were gathered in the open plan bar area and it soon became clear that I wasn't the only one to experience difficulties finding the place. As Steve gathered everyone for a somewhat delayed team meeting, I dealt with another major headache – what to have to drink, given there was no cask ale available. In the end, I settled for a bottle of Budweiser as Steve gave instructions to the squad and answered questions, before soon after, most headed for bed. Sam was certainly in need of a decent night's sleep as he'd been up most of the night before tying rigs whilst on a school camping trip.

Up until now, things weren't straying too much from plan. Those of us staying in Coventry had had issues with finding the Travelodge, but we were used to overcoming a few distractions and occasional mishaps that challenged our meticulous planning for such campaigns. We would soon find out however, that virtually everything that could go wrong during this campaign was going to, and really through no fault of our own.

Around midnight, one of our mums fell on the pavement outside the hotel entrance, sustaining a nasty bump on the head and cutting her elbow. She was though, grateful to be rescued and assisted back inside by three individuals that resembled many of those that Sam and I had observed hours earlier, a little worse for wear on the street nearby. I'll not elaborate further on the poor lady's identity; we gave her enough stick the following day and continue to pull her leg even now. I will though, continue to describe events and confirm that after I'd dressed her arm, Steve took her to the local hospital. With Sue, a nurse, in attendance also, we insisted that she get checked out and I reassured her son that we were sure she'd be fine and that we were just taking appropriate precautions. We knew that Steve's return trip to University Hospital Coventry wouldn't be a quick one and I resigned myself to the fact that I was to get even less sleep than I usually did the night before a big event.

Any interim rest that I believed I was to manage before Steve's return was curtailed quite abruptly, when the hotel fire alarm sounded sometime after Steve's departure. We all assembled outside the front of the hotel, somewhat bleary eyed and not too long after retiring. With no fire drill scheduled (it was by then, around 1.30 a.m.) and with bemused hotel staff also gathered on the pavement, we deduced that the persons responsible were, to put it politely, ne'er-do-wells. Eventually, we all made our way back inside and around 3 a.m.; our mum and her Suffolk County cadet son were reunited. Most of our party had long since tucked themselves up in bed once more and Steve and I settled down in our room; but not for long…

I'll do my best to describe subsequent events delicately, but those staying on the same floor as Steve and me will know more of what then transpired. Given the noise from the corridor, it wasn't long before I was out of bed yet again, this time to remonstrate with those causing the disturbances. It seemed that more than one room was being used not only by an excessive number of guests, but for more than purely rest and relaxation, shall we say. Given also, the frequency of these disturbances, Steve too, got up and made his feelings quite clear to those we felt were responsible for our sleep deprivation. With the arrival of more than one member of staff, eventually, at some time around dawn, we believe we may have gone to sleep!

An hour or two later (or possibly less!), we'd got the kettle on and after downing coffee and strong, sweet tea respectively, Steve and I checked the room as we left. We were then greeted in the corridor by a police officer guarding one of the rooms!

In the bar area a quick head count confirmed who'd already left and soon after, we assembled at Tunnel Barn. Several of the squad had had just a few of hours' sleep and Barnes and Brewster, considerably less!

There was no time to dwell on the events of the night before (or indeed, most of the morning so far) and after the formalities of the draw, Suffolk's anglers made their way to their sections. We'd agreed some months before to field cadet and junior teams and forego intermediate participation. Whilst we knew the juniors would be up against it considering the number of teams competing, we were always quietly confident that we might see our cadets return to the podium. Sandra Drew of the Angling Trust advised me later that the seven teams entered in the under-14s' category was a competition record and whilst our youngsters faced stiff opposition, we prided ourselves on working with the whole team in an effort to secure good section points throughout. Before the match started, Steve and I assisted our two new cadets, Callum Murton and George Faiers at their pegs and after last minute checks and distribution of extra bait tubs, I prepared to bank-run for our under-18s.

Whilst we would certainly never rely on luck, it was clear that our juniors needed a degree of good fortune if they were to secure any silverware. Several teams had practised repeatedly in the run-up to the event and one we knew of had had six sessions on the different pools. Conversely, we had little experience at Tunnel Barn and Finn, who'd practised on several of the small lakes, found himself fishing on one he hadn't visited. Bank-running was difficult, given the restricted access on some of the pools and the inevitable problem of poles blocking pathways. Steve Bulbeck and I, along with other parents did our best to pass information along where we could, but it was clear that no single method or particular tactics, even on the same pool, were bringing fish to anglers.

Nonetheless, Suffolk did particularly well in a couple of the 21-peg sections. Sam Kennard, despite his lack of sleep, finished second in his and was unlucky not to go one better. Timmy Pepper's usual polished performance saw him very unlucky also, not to take maximum points as he won his lake comfortably; he fell foul though, of a split section. The considerable effort from everyone involved with the juniors, was rewarded by just a modest overall team placing. We always looked though, to fish as a squad and therefore turned to our cadets for a chance to bring home the team silverware that we had become used to picking up in every competition.

Bank-running for the cadets, Steve was able, as ever, to give accurate details of how our six anglers had got on. Despite not having his glasses with him, George had banked a few fish from close in where he could see his float and from further out, striking when Steve, looking over his shoulder, told him too! There were back-up scores from Max Rushbrook and Jack Damant who, after a slow start, landed some reasonable sized fish. Leading the charge for Suffolk though, were Ollie Saunders, Jamie Marriott and Callum.

Ollie took the heaviest net of Suffolk's cadets, finishing second in section. Jamie grabbed another section winner's medal to add to the one from Lindholme and I was on hand to see Callum weigh in for another maximum score. Callum had made the most of an inviting corner peg and included a coveted barbel in his seven kilos. With our individual anglers' scores tallied, we dared to hope for a team medal. We knew that Matrix Tameside/Bait-Tech had won; but we were looking for not only the squad to have something to show for their collective effort, but also silverware as suitable reimbursement for overcoming everything that fate (and drunken hotel guests) had conspired to throw at us during the previous 24 hours. As one mum explained to me that she'd dented her car backing into a tree as she attempted to park back near the presentation area, my desire to see her son, Steve and everyone else involved, rewarded for the work put in, increased significantly. It's at times like these that, given an option, I'd take team bronze; as I've mentioned before: no-one wants to finish fourth.

I took several candid photographs of our party as they gathered close to where the trophies and medals were laid out and before long; the Angling Trust officials began to announce section winners and individual placings in the cadets' match. Jamie and Callum stepped forward for their section medals and shortly after, Ollie was named as individual runner-up. The team placings were announced in reverse order and this particular coach breathed a sigh of relief as, with four down and three to go, Suffolk hadn't been mentioned. I'll admit to mild elation therefore, when Worksop were then announced in third with a total of 29 points. Suffolk County, on 30 points, were then called forward as runners-up. Whilst Tameside were indeed confirmed as comfortable winners on 38 points, there was a postscript to this somewhat eventful campaign.

Steve Damant told us afterwards, that he'd chatted to one of the Tameside coaches who'd explained how our getting the better of them at Lindholme had served as a wake-up call for the highly motivated and sponsored outfit. This was, for us perhaps, appropriate consolation after three national competitions without a win. Whilst we'd relinquished all the team titles won in 2012, we had succeeded in bringing team medals back from all three of the events Suffolk County had competed in in 2013.

The Tunnel Barn campaign was the last outing for the county squad in 2013. The NJAA National was scheduled on the River Weaver and competing would entail a journey of considerable distance. With several of the young squad starting at new schools that week also, the decision was made not to enter, or to consider the NJAA Challenge, usually held on the first weekend in October.

With the county matches out of the way, I busied myself with my schools and saw through, what Jonathan Wilson had begun, by running the county's inaugural Sainsbury's School Games match at Suffolk Water Park. This was won, incidentally, by Jack Damant, Ollie Saunders, George Faiers and Max Rushbrook, fishing as Needham Market Middle. Max had agreed to make up the Needham foursome, given that Combs Middle didn't enter a team and our four cadets saw off the challenge from both their Suffolk squad-mates and several older, high school teams. Jack also won the individual event easily, with a mixed net from M3.

Later in July I worked with Colin Booker, coaching adults on consecutive Wednesdays at Bromeswell, Manor Farm Lakes at Swilland and Trimley Lakes near Felixstowe. Funding for sessions with Suffolk Coastal had been channelled towards older participants and I relished the challenge of working with a different demographic.

A week after completing these sessions, I was tackling up for a match on the carp lake at Barking. Whilst not competing regularly in matches, I did, in 2013, fish occasional events in the Midweek League. Having struggled at Hinderclay earlier in the year, I managed two seconds at the Needham Lake fixtures and was extremely pleased to win at Barking. There were just nine of us fishing and being more than familiar with the lake and what baits do well at different times of the year given my regular coaching there; I was quietly confident. I took 125lb 14oz to the scales for an easy win. Former club skipper, Bob Gunn was second with 59lb 7oz. What made the match even more enjoyable was that I'd caught all my fish on a float I'd designed and made myself. Changing to a smaller size after netting two carp, I took a further ninety-seven, plus a few silver fish, on the same float; after weighing in, Ray Catling pegged next-door, promptly bought five off me there and then. I stripped my rigs down after returning home and rinsed the floats I'd used under the tap. I went on to sell the entire first batch, including inadvertently, the one I'd won the match with!

My summer school sessions finished late in July. As lead coach, I then found myself on the banks at Barking most Saturdays for sessions with the Junior Academy and the Advanced Academy competitions. The former were as popular as ever and included our National Fishing Month day when Abi travelled back to assist and our local coaches were joined by Dennis Willis, Judy Ford and Martin Burgess from Norfolk.

I returned to work with the schools in September with a smaller Springfield group and took the boys to Needham Lake and Suffolk Water Park; I also included two roving sessions on the Gipping to conclude their autumn programme. I was back on the bank with Amy Wall and Combs Middle School as well. I also ran five sessions with a pupil referral group and a match for Stowmarket High School. With Tony Scott of Castle Hill, I attended a Pike Anglers' Club event at Barham Pits and following his successes with the club over the summer and at Tunnel Barn, Callum promptly banked the only two pike of the day and for his trouble, took home a tackle voucher and T-shirt. The day was all the more pleasing as Callum landed his fish using a rod and reel set-up of mine and that hadn't seen the light of day for many years.

  I concluded my school coaching before half-term at the end of October and assisted the Eastern Angling Centre of Excellence (EACoE) with a session at Swilland during the short break. My coaching year finished with my having delivered over 70 sessions with almost a third being on a voluntary basis.

Sometime before the rescheduled GVAC AGM late in November, I made the decision to step down as a committee member. I'd been the treasurer for over 21 years and had served as an officer of the club for more than a year or two beforehand. Wanting to vary my future coaching and being aware that Abi was due to compete at Fish O'Mania, I also stepped down as GVAC's lead coach. I relinquished my paid maintenance work which had become more and more physically demanding. All of this, I did with a clear conscience, given my previous longstanding commitment to the club and what I felt I'd achieved. I wasn't about to pack up coaching though and having met Jason Skilton of the Pike Anglers' Club and Ron Dalton of the Lure Anglers' Society at Barham, set about bringing an all-day, junior event to Needham Lake. It was, I felt, time for a change.

A WINTER OF DISCONTENT

The winter of 2013/2014 was the wettest on record; but the Gipping being unfishable on several occasions was merely a minor personal inconvenience compared to the misery and despair that the consequent floods brought householders and business owners in other parts of the country that were affected much worse.

After the school half-term at the end of October 2013, I threw myself into pole float making. By then I was posting floats up and down the country and requests from customers saw me design and modify several different patterns. I continued to fit in odd chub sessions, but also targeted the Gipping's perch on the float.

In November however, a visit to my doctor resulted in me being referred to West Suffolk Hospital for removal of a mole on my back. Thankfully, this proved to be a non-malignant, basal cell carcinoma. After the operation however, I was advised not to do anything that may cause the stitches to split. For fear of a fall on the wet banks of the Gipping, I chose to spend my time making and selling floats and stayed off the bank. All seemed to be going well with the dissolving sutures until one Saturday evening I managed to split the wound whilst laying on the settee watching *The Inbetweeners Movie*! Eventually, I managed to get an appointment with a nurse at my local surgery the next morning, but only after describing, in front of other patients, what had happened and in quite graphic detail.

The next two months saw me visit the surgery at least twice weekly, so that my wound could be redressed. For fear of further damage, I took the nurses' advice and didn't fish during this time.

Hazel and I put our house on the market before Christmas. For various reasons, we'd made the decision to move and just a few weeks later in January, we accepted an offer after only a handful of viewings. Very keen to relocate and after the initial disappointment of losing a house that we'd seen ourselves; we had our offer accepted on another property not far away and started to plan the move.

Come February, I received the all-clear from the nurses and with packing well underway, I grabbed an afternoon session on the Gipping at Blakenham; this was my first chub trip for some time. The river had come down in-between heavy bouts of rain and was looking good. After feeding and fishing two swims however, my landing net was still dry. Missing several sharp bites in one spot, which I put down to small fish that I'd seen in that location in the summer; I moved to my 'banker' swim and was rewarded first cast, with a reasonable fish on cheese paste. By this time I was listed on the Laguna Fishing Products website as one of their consultants and bait testers. I incorporated their Pristex brand's 'soak and coat' bait activator in all my pastes when after chub and also used it as a dip with artificial maggots and casters. Using the flavoured activators gave me complete confidence in my baits and on that late season afternoon, this was seemingly justified as I landed my first fish of the session.

After unhooking and photographing the fish however, I slipped when attempting to return it via my landing net. So keen was I to protect the fish, I took the fall on my bottom and right arm whilst holding the fish aloft with my left. Recovering a little composure and after releasing the fish safely, I wiped myself down; despite a degree of pain in my wrist and hips (and despite also, my thoroughly wet backside!), I decided to fish on until after dark. I was aware that my fishing time would be at a premium in the coming months and didn't want to waste an opportunity to bank another fish or two, just because I was wet, uncomfortable and in a lot of pain!

After feeding more samples of what a Laguna consultant, Christian Barker refers to as 'posh' cheese paste; I baited up again and cast out. I expected things to be quiet for a time and that's how they were, until around 5.50

p.m. when the starlight bite indicator showed a dramatic drop-back on my rod tip. A few minutes later, I weighed and photographed a chub of 4lb 7oz and after returning the fish, packed up and headed home.

During the evening, I wasn't in a huge amount of discomfort following the fall. After retiring to bed however, I woke up at around 2 a.m. with severe pains in my right wrist. Not having had much sleep the rest of the night, I telephoned NHS Direct and later, Hazel dropped me off at Accident and Emergency at West Suffolk Hospital. An X-ray showed only the healed break following a football injury and the conclusion was that I'd damaged the ligaments of the same wrist. Once again therefore and whilst my wrist healed, my fishing was curtailed. It wouldn't however, be in plaster whilst we continued packing belongings in anticipation of our move. Hazel came to collect me from hospital, but only after I'd watched Team GB secure bronze medals in the women's curling at the Winter Olympics, with an assortment of patients, porters and other hospital staff, on the large, wall mounted television in the waiting area.

After just one session, my fishing once again, took a back seat. Following the pike day at Barham however, I was working with Jason Skilton and Ron Dalton with a view to put on the Junior Lure Day at Needham Lake. The day after the river season closed, coaches from as far afield as Kent, Hertfordshire and Leicestershire arrived early at Needham, followed soon after by over 20 keen youngsters. Among the coaches, we had Ron's fellow England lure squad members and father and son team, Gary and Sam Edmonds. The bright conditions resulted in difficult fishing, but a number of modest sized pike were banked and Aston Lander and Max Rushbrook took home the main prizes for their afternoon captures. Three months' planning and preparation had gone into the day and all participants left with goody bags, DVDs and fishing magazines.

The day was something a little different and one which saw me out of my usual comfort zone, but learning from some of the country's best lure anglers. Noting that a picture of his new heroes adorned the cover of one of the magazines handed out, Aston made a point of grabbing Gary and Sam's autographs before he left. The event was my first coaching session of 2014, but I then stepped back to concentrate on preparing for the house move. I tackled down most of my rods and packed my float making kit away. With the new property requiring a substantial amount of work, my priorities would certainly change in the coming year.

Back in 2013, Hazel and I had started working for Animals at Home, hosting dogs whilst their owners were on holiday etc. We also did a little dog walking, covering for, and assisting our agent. It was in the back of my mind that I may need to reduce the amount of coaching work I did; considering the move, the work that needed doing at our new home and how busy we were becoming with dogs. In April 2014 we received the news that Hazel needed to undergo a reasonably serious operation after which, she'd need to rest for some weeks. Around this time, I took the decision to stand down from the Suffolk County committee.

In-between hospital visits and packing, I did fit in some fishing, visiting Marsh Farm, near Saxmundham. My enthusiasm for catching perch hadn't diminished since the previous autumn and having banked some good ones in matches at the venue, I decided to go back and target them with a specialist approach. During my first session, I dispensed with fishing worms, as even whole lobs attracted the attentions of small fish. I found that prawns picked out the better fish. Fishing a whole king prawn I found, was the best way to single out good perch. In-between the perch however, I banked a string of roach- and rudd-bream hybrids on the same baits. During my few sessions in April and May, I banked hybrids to well over two pounds which fought incredibly hard, on both float gear and light, running leger rigs on Avon rods. I also landed perch approaching the same weight, so thoroughly enjoyed the sessions.

We finally moved on 22nd May and the day after, we received a phone call requesting that Hazel go into hospital for her operation the following week. Some six weeks or so later, we finally received the news that not only had the operation been successful, but that no further treatment was necessary. We continued with our work on the house and I resumed coaching again.

Hazel and I threw ourselves into the work on the new house and its garden – and I threw myself off a ladder as I attempted to clear the conservatory guttering! I sustained a particularly nasty gash on my shin, having fallen with my leg entwined with the ladder as I came down on to the paving slabs around one of the ponds. After falling also, on the stairs whilst carrying a large, heavy box of belongings from upstairs to the conservatory; I had another trip (no pun intended!) to West Suffolk Hospital. Examination and X-ray showed only a severe sprain and no fractures. Heading Hazel's strongly worded advice to take things just a little bit easier, I resumed work on the house, and the back garden in particular, but at a slightly slower pace.

It had been a difficult winter, given the stress of the move and the worries of Hazel going into hospital – not to mention my own trips to West Suffolk. I'd stepped down as an officer of both GVAC and Suffolk County. We were now living in varying states of disarray in our new home, but looked forward to when the work we were undertaking would be finished. I looked forward too, to both coaching and fishing without the additional pressures associated with committee involvement.

GIRLS ON FILM

Early in 2014, I took the decision not to commit to travelling with the young Suffolk County squad to either the All England Junior Pole Championships or the Angling Trust Cadet/Junior/Intermediate National. For once, I put my family before my fishing and given the house move and Hazel's hospital visits; was comfortable with my decision. As it transpired, we completed just two days before Pole Champs Saturday and Hazel went into hospital for her operation the following Tuesday.

      The Angling Trust event was scheduled to be held at Makins Fishery, necessitating a Friday departure and an overnight stay. With everything else going on, I started my usual summer term's work with Springfield Junior School very late in the summer term. With Cameron pinching my car for his long weekend at the British Grand Prix at Silverstone (we'd purchased a Nissan X-Trail just before we moved), and with Abi due to compete at Fish O'Mania; I was to miss a couple of Fridays with the school. Able to fit in just four sessions, I was on the bank with the pupils at Manor Farm Lakes, Swilland, as Suffolk's youngsters prepared to head to Warwickshire.

      Steve Barnes, despite running GVAC and also picking up my slack after I stepped down as an officer on the county committee, saw to it that Suffolk were represented at Westwood Lakes. Suffolk had lost anglers to other teams and I'm sure communicating my early decision not to be involved at the Pole Champs led to these youngsters looking elsewhere. I'd previously been heavily involved in organizing the squad for this event and my stepping away whilst not in a position to give an indication of whether or with what level of commitment, Suffolk might compete; I feel resulted in former squad members looking to secure a place with other teams. The offer of a place with a high profile, sponsored squad is understandably attractive and for the reasons already outlined, I'd dropped the ball, so to speak. Whilst this resulted in Steve taking a younger and less experienced contingent to Westwood; it also meant that for this fixture and the forthcoming Angling Trust National, he'd be able to give some a chance to put on a Suffolk shirt for the first time.

Thanks to Steve's drive, determination and time management skills, two teams of four Suffolk County anglers were on the bank come May 24th. Jack Damant captained Jamie Marriott, Ollie Saunders and Peter Williams; whilst Max Rushbrook skippered Paul Christie, Ciaran Gardner and Callum Murton. Jack's team did well, with Callum third-in-section as he took points off Barnsley and Worksop's anglers. One poor section placing saw the team miss out on a podium place which, as Steve explained afterwards, would have been a massive achievement considering the strong opposition and challenging conditions. The squad returned from the Pole Champs without team silverware for the first time under our management; as ever though, valuable experience was gained by all on a day when the weather and conditions were apparently, particularly unpleasant.

Some weeks later I joined Steve, Paul Sargent and Charlie Burgoyne on the bank at Barking. Taking Saturdays off from work on the house, I helped them with preparing the cadets for their trip to Makins the last weekend in June. These Saturday sessions were already underway by the time I was able to commit three consecutive weekends to working with the youngsters. The final line-up for Makins would be: Max Rushbrook (captain), Ben Aldous, Amelie Barnes, Kezia Denny, Curtis Jay and Aston Lander. Max was the only angler in the team to have fished for the county previously and a substantial amount of work was put in to get everyone to a level at which they could compete. The efforts put in by the coaches though, were matched by the enthusiasm of the team and whilst, as with the Pole Champs, it was clear that a podium finish was unlikely; this fact wasn't evidenced from the attitudes on the bank at Barking.

As mentioned previously, I was working with Springfield as the squad headed for Makins on the last Friday in June. Along with Suffolk's team of cadets, Peter Williams captained a junior team comprising himself, Paul Christie, Jamie Marriott, Callum Murton and Ollie Saunders. Despite every effort by Steve to find a replacement for those that chose, for whatever reasons, not to fish; the juniors tackled up at Makins one short. With nothing to lose, the five team members attacked their swims, effectively fishing as individuals in an effort to gain a top six finish overall and secure a place at Junior Fish O'Mania in July. This was a tall order, given that none had seen the venue before and when the final results were distributed, it was a disappointment to see that Suffolk County weren't apparently listed. As if to rub salt into the wound, the lake where Suffolk had no competitor threw up a number of the best weights. The cadets, with a full complement of anglers, fared a little better. All caught and but for a couple of section results, could have achieved third place, rather than fifth.

I exchanged texts with Steve that weekend and congratulated him on the amount of work he'd put in ahead of both the Pole Champs and the Angling Trust event. He'd taken a group of inexperienced youngsters to Makins for their first taste of top level competition. Curtis and Aston had attended GVAC's school projects with Springfield Junior School and Ben with Ringshall Primary. They'd fished alongside Amelie and Kezia in the Junior Academy and had finally 'graduated' and put on their Suffolk shirt for the first time. Max by now, was an old hand with several years' experience and with numerous National Junior Angling Association trophies and Angling Trust medals to show for his commitment. A couple of events without silverware would not detract from what GVAC coaches had achieved in previous years and the club's angling development model remains the envy of many. GVAC now had a proven track record of taking youngsters who'd not fished before, working with them through school projects, bringing them on through the Junior Academy and then seeing them represent their county in national competition.

My perception, which I shared with Steve, was that if anything, Suffolk County's record of success in the previous years had only reduced any pressure on the coaching staff. I felt that we no longer had anything to prove in a sport where, I believe, some coaches' desire to win (and perhaps also satisfy sponsors), can ride roughshod over development and progression. Whilst admittedly not being involved as a lead coach at either Westwood or Makins, I took a completely philosophical view of the results. It was extremely disappointing not to have a complete team of juniors at Makins and I felt for Steve. Rarely, if ever, had we been able to rely on the complete list of anglers listed on our team entry forms; but this was the first time our squad had arrived on match day an angler short and it hurt. On a positive note however, Paul was now an integral part of the county coaching set-up and Charlie too, had become a reliable and committed member of the team. Later, in the school summer holidays, Gary Bennington, another club member who'd come up through the ranks so to speak, joined us at Barking for the two National Fishing month events. Without committee pressures, I was thoroughly enjoying being back on the bank coaching.

Sometime after the 2013 Angling Trust Ladies' National it became clear that I'd be able to field just the one team of four in the 2014 event. Given the long return journey to the venue, I took an early decision not to travel to the match. We were, as mentioned, preparing to move house and Hazel was waiting to go into hospital. Judy chose not to fish and Abi had a christening to attend that weekend and was also baking the cake. By now, Jeannette was an integral part of the England set-up and after putting Jess forward also, had been asked to compete for another, more high profile team, standing in for anglers with commitments elsewhere. These arrangements were made with my full knowledge and blessing after I'd talked things through with Jeannette, acknowledging the opportunity for Jess to further her ambitions and raise her own profile. With the match scheduled for Boldings Pools in Shropshire, Abi obtained a little information from Les Thompson, which I passed on to Charlotte Gore, Nuala Gray, Leanne Knott and Kayleigh Smith, who would be representing Suffolk this time around.

With their individual forms and cheques posted, I agreed to fund their team entry, as thanks for their efforts in 2013. The girls posted me cheques for their county subs and their pools; other than complete and post off the team entry form, I did very little in the way of preparing for the match itself.

On match day, I was at home working on the house, but was conscious that, around 180 miles away in Shropshire, the girls were competing. I left it until early evening before I made a telephone call to John Gore to see how they'd got on. He and Charlotte were already heading home when they took my call, 'hands free'. John almost casually relayed the news that, in addition to Kayleigh's individual triumph, Suffolk County had won team gold. I listened as John and Charlotte gave brief details of how Kayleigh had taken the match apart and how the back-up weights of the rest of the team had also seen them clinch a narrow victory. When the call ended, I contacted Steve Barnes, before also telephoning Dave Gladwell to pass on the news.

Not long after, I telephoned Kayleigh, seeking permission to pass on her contact details to the *Angler's Mail*, who'd telephoned Steve. After agreeing to an interview for a follow-up feature, I chatted to Kayleigh at some length about the match itself. Maintaining a reasonably steady catch rate throughout the competition, she'd caught F1s, carp and barbel and returned 43kg 550gm, almost doubling the weight of the second placed angler.

Discussing the team match, it was a typically modest Kayleigh that acknowledged immediately, the importance of all three of her teammates' weights. With the outcome being decided on total weight, Kayleigh's runaway victory had obviously put Suffolk County in a good position for a medal. However, there were some very strong teams on the bank and the foursome of Sam Perkins, Emma Pickering, Sam Sim and Suffolk County 'old girl', Abbi Kendall was, we knew, going to take some beating. Charlotte, Nuala and Leanne though, returned weights which, when added to Kayleigh's, saw Suffolk claim gold by a margin of 1kg 810gm – the equivalent of a 4lb carp! This was one of those occasions that illustrated how important the weight of every member of a team can prove to be, even in an event decided on weight, rather than section points. As Kayleigh said herself after the match when reflecting on the team result, 'It just goes to show how every fish counts.' She concluded by saying, 'My day could not have gone any better and it is a memory that will live with me forever.'

Kayleigh's win at Boldings saw her qualify for the 2015 Ladies' Fish O'Mania final and just over four weeks later I was helping Abi prepare for the 2014 event.

As part of her preparation ahead of our trips to Cudmore, Abi stayed behind after a coaching session with the cadets and spent a couple of hours with me at Barking as we looked to ensure that her casting was still up to scratch. I spent time with her, as she cast her Method feeder repeatedly to the opposite bank, simulating fishing towards the island on Arena Lake. Later, she warmed up for her Fish O'Mania debut at the annual pairs' match with her *Angling Times* colleagues. As I was at home re-elasticating her G-Max 1000, she was giving my old Shimano Speedmaster a workout at Decoy Lakes near Whittlesey. Whilst she claimed after, somewhat tongue-in-cheek, that having the weight of one of her nets of carp reduced was all part of a male conspiracy that saw her and her partner for the day, Thom

Airs finish runners-up behind Steve Fitzpatrick and Richard Grange; she was obviously pleased with how she'd fished and was seemingly looking forward to Fish O'Mania.

On the Tuesday before the match, Abi and I arrived at the venue for a couple of days' practice. After speaking to fishery staff we made our way to the area of Arena, allocated for both the ladies' event on the Saturday and the junior match on the Sunday. As we looked across the lake late that morning, we could see a good number of competitors from the main event catching odd fish; but as I helped Abi prepare her kit and bait, it was already evident that there weren't an awful lot of large fish being banked. As Abi set about plumbing up, I began casting a bomb to the island and clipping up. The circular island is the same distance from each peg, but I checked by casting from most available swims to be on the safe side. Finding the distance across consistent, I clipped up her three Method feeder and bomb rods ready for match day and later in the session, she took a few small fish across, her casting practice at Barking seemingly having been of benefit.

We approached the practice session cautiously and Abi certainly didn't over-feed; the fishing though, was still hard. Chatting to locals, we established that there were no longer any barbel in the lake and whilst some carp were large, there were fewer present than previously. We also established that the pegs allocated for the ladies' and junior events were the least productive. Our opinion also, was that the prevailing wind was taking fish, carp in particular, to the opposite bank of the lake. Nonetheless, Abi plugged away on several different lines and took a number of roach, skimmers and small tench. We'd had a long drive to Staffordshire, followed by preparation and fishing, and late afternoon we packed everything away before heading for a nearby Travelodge. As I drove to our accommodation, Abi chatted to Les Thompson on the phone, updating him with how the lake had fished and discussing Wednesday's approach.

After a meal out the night before and Abi's choice of healthy, grab and go breakfast, we were back on the bank reasonably early the next day. On a different peg, Abi tackled up and before long, was fishing and rotating several lines. On several occasions during the session, I wandered to the top of the bank, taking time to watch some of the finalists practising for the main event. Later in the day, we spoke to a number of competitors and their runners and, as usual, they all knew Abi!

By just after lunch we'd concluded that fishing on match day, at least in the area where the ladies' pegs were located anyway, was going to be hard. We agreed that a chopped worm and caster approach was needed to put silver fish in the net, but that additional lines for carp would need to be fed from the early stages, with a view to picking one or two off later in the competition. As we packed Abi's kit away that afternoon, it was our belief that there would be few, if any carp caught in the ladies' match and that silver fish would prove to be crucial. We would be proved right come Saturday teatime.

Having dropped Abi off in Langtoft, I arrived back home late on Wednesday, but after a couple of nights in my own bed, we were heading back to Cudmore. Taking time on the road with a break or two from driving, we pulled in at Cudmore late on Friday afternoon. Neither the ladies nor juniors drew for their pegs and it was Les who'd established and advised Abi that she'd be on peg 5 come Saturday. After arriving back at the venue and managing to find a parking space, we wandered up to the lake and took a few photos. There were now areas roped off with barriers in place and large boards with sponsors' logos adorning the slopes behind the main competition pegs. One of the two access paths for spectators was behind Abi's peg and behind her and to her left would be the main presentation area and scoreboard.

We then walked back to the main car park and sat chatting to Sarah Collins from Get Hooked On Fishing, along with Fox consultant, Rob Hughes, who'd be one of the bankside presenters for Sky (naturally Abi knew them both!), as the main draw took place in a marquee close by. We then departed for our Travelodge and Abi telephoned Les. Our final job the night before the match was to mix Abi's groundbait and with this done, we enjoyed a meal together before getting our heads down.

Early next morning we purchased our breakfast from the service station adjacent to the Travelodge. We'd looked to check everything ahead of the match and I'd approached the day with my usual mixture of thoroughness, apprehension and nerves! Following a short drive to Cudmore, we pulled up at one of the entrances and showed Abi's car park pass to an official. We then made our way to what we'd established beforehand was the competitors' car park, only to be told on arrival that we couldn't leave our car there for the match. We unloaded Abi's considerable amount of kit and bait and carried it all to her peg. Each time I walked back to the car I had to fend off circling officials, assuring them that I was merely unloading as my daughter was a competitor – in an environment where many of the country's top match anglers were gathered, I obviously looked out of place! It had dawned on me by then, that if I was to be made to park my car in the public car park accessed some way further along the road, I'd have to fight my way through traffic leaving the venue later in the day, to get back to pick Abi up again. Still, as instructed, I left her with her kit and, as the sun crept higher in the sky and temperatures rose; I duly drove around to the public parking area.

Having pulled up on the other side of the complex, I spoke to the officials manning the area set aside for spectators' parking. After I then explained my concerns about being able to get back to Arena later, they were good enough to allow me to park the X-Trail adjacent to the temporary Blue Badge area. After thanking them, I then left to walk the considerable distance back to the lakes, and mentioned that I'd not seen any other competitors bringing their vehicles over.

Sweating somewhat by the time I got to Abi's peg; I caught up with Les, who'd arrived some time earlier. A previous Fish O'Mania finalist, Les had seen it all before and was a calming influence on both of us as the time approached when she could start tackling up. I left them at her peg and took the short walk to one of the portable toilets. Chatting to a couple of the other lady competitors on my way back, it was clear that not everybody had taken kindly to the parking instructions and all had found parking close by. After raising this issue once again with an official, I was told that there had been some confusion and that I could now park in the area by Arena as we'd been led to believe when Abi had received her priority pass. After advising Abi and Les, I made the journey back to the spectator's car park to retrieve the car. Sometime later I managed to find a space in the area allocated that was, by then, all but full of competitors' and stewards' cars, Sky vans and VIPs' vehicles. As I made my way back to Abi once again, one of the officials, who'd recognised me from earlier, stopped me to apologise for the miscommunication.

Spectators were now arriving in quite large numbers and as I arrived back at Abi's peg, she and Les were busy preparing for the start of the match as Abi's boyfriend, Lewis, looked on. With Les sponsored by Matrix (Fox's match brand), Lewis knew him well.

The area from behind Abi's right-hand side to where Jess Knights was on peg 2 had been closed to public access by barriers, given the close proximity of a hedge. Lewis and I though, were able to take up temporary residence on two of my coaching stools inside the barriers. One of Abi's final jobs before the start of the competition was to chop her worms and not wishing to pass up an opportunity to learn, I listened intently as Les instructed his young charge for the day on how to prepare a choice of baits for the hook and for feeding. Shortly after, she checked her bait tray one final time before picking up her cupping kit ready for the 'all in'.

The ladies' event got underway, five minutes before the main competition. With all her lines fed, Abi shipped out to six metres and after a few minutes banked a small fish on chopped worm. Roach and small skimmers then came steadily and whilst they were of no significant size, she was putting fish in her net - something I could see, not all competitors were doing. At intervals and under Les's watchful eye, she continued to feed her various lines and, resting her chopped worm and caster swim, went out to 13 metres just after the half-hour mark. She'd been regularly feeding this line via a catapult with hard pellets, as well as occasionally topping up her margins with loose groundbait via a cup. With forty minutes gone, she laid her shallow rig in over her pellet line and immediately her pink Matrix number 12 elastic pulled from her top kit. All too soon however, the elastic retracted and the carp responsible was free once again. At times such as this, nothing needs to be said and an exchange of glances was sufficient. We would debate afterwards, whether the fish had been foul-hooked, but Abi quickly got back to the job in hand, landing occasional fish whilst also feeding all her various lines.

With an hour of the competition gone, the scales arrived behind Abi's peg and Les carried her catch over to the waiting stewards, having ensured her second net was secure and ready for her to use as she continued fishing. Her first hour's net of 1kg 10gm was recorded and the fish placed in her 'keeper' net along the bank before Les returned to his chair. With all six girls recorded I checked the weights on the steward's board and noted that Abi was marginally ahead of her five fellow finalists. However, Emma Pickering and Sam Perkins were breathing down her neck with 980gm apiece with Sophie Hill next-door, close behind.

The match continued to unfold and I noted that Sam Perkins was now catching quicker from her small fish line than she had been previously. I remember thinking that Abi wouldn't be able to keep pace with Sam or Emma if it became a skimmer match; but given the way the lake had fished in practice - at least in the area the ladies were pegged – I remained happy with her tactics. Apart from everything else though, I was exceptionally pleased with how she was fishing. I knew that she would certainly be nervous to a degree, but felt that once she was fishing and was catching a few fish, that she'd be okay. She was though, feeding very tightly with her catapult, whilst holding her pole and whilst she'd done this in many matches before Fish O'Mania, she was grouping her feed very tightly, despite the increasing number of spectators that gathered behind her peg, several of which made a point of asking me how she was getting on. Under Les's guidance, she appeared smooth and unhurried and wasn't making any mistakes, despite fishing under more pressure than ever before.

After two hours, Abi was overhauled by both Sam and Emma. In the third hour though, the course of the ladies' match changed as Sophie 'mugged' (her description to me afterwards) a carp. This was a game changer and the other competitors now had to consider their options. As far as Abi was concerned, I still felt she'd fished tactically correct and her weight of silvers may prove crucial, if she could latch on to a carp. After three hours the scoreboard confirmed what all of us watching already knew: just one carp from any competitor in the final hour could decide the match…

I could see Emma catching good skimmers on peg 1 consistently and Sam too, was doing well; but Abi and Les focused on the task in hand. With just over half an hour of the contest remaining, Abi's float lifted as a large fish picked up a bait fished hard on the bottom on her long line, lifting the group of small bulk shot close to her hook in the process. Once again, the Matrix number 12 stretched from her top kit as the fish kited to her right. Calmly - so it seemed to us sitting behind her - she swivelled slightly on her box and followed the fish, which came up off the bottom before causing a large swirl just under the surface. I took a deep breath and sat on my hands as I looked at Lewis. The carp then began to make slowly for the central island. Abi kept her pole low and close to the water, but after an agonizing few moments, the fish was off. The hook had pulled and the chances of Abi picking up the winner's cheque had seemingly slipped away with the fish. Emma, also now playing a carp down the bank to our right went on to lift the winner's trophy for the second year in succession.

The final results for the ladies' event were as follows:
1st Emma Pickering (Peg 1)   7kg 50gm
2nd Sophie Hill (4)   4kg 610gm
3rd Sam Perkins (6)   4kg 270gm
4th Abi Brewster (5)   2kg 300gm
5th Jess Knights (2)   610gm
6th Liz Larkin (3)   570gm

In a match that was eventually decided by just one carp, Abi had managed to hook two. The second of these was, from what I saw, a very large fish. Whilst I'm unsure whether it was large enough for her to close the gap between her and Emma, I'm certain that both lost fish would have been; but that's fishing. Andy Geldart won the main competition and took home £30,000. Just as Abi had done, Andy fished for roach and skimmers during the first couple of hours of the match, before switching attention to his carp lines. Daniel Brydon, with a late run of fish, finished runner-up and in addition to his cheque for £5,000, received a further £1,000 for the day's biggest fish (4kg 980gm). A large group of supporters had travelled from Norfolk to watch Daniel and several we knew had also stopped behind Abi's peg to ask me how she was getting on.

    With the ladies' match over, Les, Lewis and I commiserated with Abi. I may be biased, but I felt she'd fished an outstanding match. We began packing her kit away as Emma and Sam's runners continued fishing, acting as 'stoppers' for the main match which continued for a further hour.

Eventually, with all her gear cleared, Abi took some time out to walk the bank as the pressure of the day finally seemed to take its toll. We could hear the cheers from behind Daniel's peg away to our left as he landed odd fish in the closing stages of the match. With all of Abi's kit loaded into my car I thanked Les and after speaking to a few competitors and spectators, made my way to a local pub car park where Lewis and Abi had arrived in his van. We then transferred her kit so that I could drive straight home rather than via Langtoft. I stared thoughtfully into a cappuccino at more than one service station en route home, contemplating what might have been. Despite obvious frustrations and disappointments however, being part of Fish O'Mania - and on a day when a record crowd was later confirmed - was a fantastic experience and I felt privileged to be part of it. Above all else, I was, and remain, extremely proud of how Abi fished.

Six days later, a session at Suffolk Water Park concluded my summer term's work with Springfield. As it was also the final session of the school year, I treated Charlie, Ethan, Marcus and Patrick to a McDonald's on the way home. During the summer holidays, Hazel and I continued working on our house, but I also made time to help out at GVAC's National Fishing Month events.

REFLECTIONS

Late in 2014, I looked back at my forty years of fishing and considered what I might have achieved. As alluded to in my introduction, my angling 'career' has been far from spectacular (thus far anyway!). However, GVAC has been delivering voluntary sessions for young people for over 20 years and the Junior Academy continues to thrive. The fresh enthusiasm of the likes of Gary Bennington and Charlie Burgoyne, themselves former junior participants at the club; the new impetus of Paul Sargent and the continued work of a small number of dedicated coaches and assistants will see this continue, I'm sure. Whilst I'm no longer a committee member, I feel proud to remain a club and county coach. In the autumn of 2014, I delivered my 200th school session, a landmark for both GVAC and me.

As a lead coach with the young Suffolk County squad from 2007, I shared their disappointment and triumph, frustration and joy, as they progressed from participating to competing, and from competing to winning. The period between May 2011 and October 2012 when the squad won ten national team titles, not to mention the individual successes, was very special. I don't believe Suffolk County will enjoy such a level of success again. However, having been an integral part of the coaching set-up at the time and looking back at what GVAC has also achieved domestically; I feel the club coaches can continue to take pride in what they do, but without the pressure to deliver in competition that we may have felt in past years. As the cliché goes, we've 'been there and done that'. The emphasis on enjoyment, when working with young people in any sport surely, must come above everything else.

In 2014 my own fishing took a complete change of direction. In a year when I didn't fish any matches, I enjoyed trying new techniques and catching (or at least trying to catch) species that I've given little attention to before. I became more involved with Laguna Fishing Products and their sister company, Pristex and continued to test liquid and powdered bait activators as one of their consultants, liaising with their MD, Chris Wilson. This was all new territory for me, but as with my coaching work, I was looking to challenge myself. I incorporated Pristex bait activators and additives in my chub and perch fishing. I visited venues where I'd coached before, but not fished myself. During a morning session after roach at Bromeswell and whilst testing an amino additive from Pristex, I banked a large carp on a float rod and centre pin set-up. Fishing specifically for big carp is not something I've ever done and I aim to give the species some attention during the warmer months in future. I started to prepare for these sessions by making my own boilies using the Pristex range of flavoured base mixes and bait activators.

In the early autumn of 2014 I joined the Peterborough and District Angling Association and I look forward to catching a good barbel or two from the Nene and to perhaps sampling the bream fishing at Ferry Meadows.

Inspired by the Team England members that came along to our lure event in March and having incorporated some drop shotting in a session with Springfield and with the pupils having caught reasonable perch on the method; I'm looking to gain more experience in the discipline before delivering technique-specific coaching sessions. In November I sampled fishing with jigs in the boatyards on the Broads and caught my first perch on the method in the company of Martin Burgess. Given the roving nature of both drop shotting and lure fishing, and the variety of colourful 'jellies', 'craws', rubber worms and shads used to tempt target species; the techniques will, I know, appeal to younger participants. Wandering a river or lake with a rod and minimal amount of tackle is something that I'm appreciating more and more myself as I get older – stark contrast to the 'kitchen sink' approach of my match fishing years!

At the end of 2014, Steve Barnes looked to continue driving forward the work with Suffolk County's young cadets and Paul Sargent had an ambitious calendar of events planned for the GVAC Junior Academy. My continued work with schools, PRUs and occasional work with local councils, whilst also supporting Steve and Paul indicated that a good deal of my time would continue to be spent on the bank whilst health permits.

I look forward to continuing to develop and hopefully progress as a coach. I've committed to continue working with GVAC, as well as delivering more varied sessions personally, including classroom based activities with school groups. As I write, there's still a great deal of work to do on the house and this, with my coaching, will undoubtedly take up large chunks of my time. I hope though, to set and achieve new personal targets and experience the different aspects of fishing neglected during all the years I was preoccupied with matches. I have to continue to manage the symptoms of CMT (motor and sensory neuropathy), which I'm well aware, are becoming more pronounced with age. With consequent reduced energy levels, the change of direction with my own fishing has been borne as much out of necessity as desire. I'm sure though, I can contribute positively to my sport and its development, even if it's more frequently from behind a desk as time passes.

A legacy has been created at GVAC and I'm proud to have been associated with a small, but extremely proactive club that has achieved so much. As mentioned, coaching with the county squad in particular has been extremely challenging at times and recalling some of these experiences brought about this book's title. The level of the Suffolk squad's success and the enjoyable memories I and others have from the many trips up and down the country for both matches and practice however, have made the considerable collective effort worthwhile. After recounting details of our campaigns and having penned anecdotes from many national competitions in the previous pages; I'll give my final chapter over to those that have done the catching; a tribute from those that did the coaching...

SUFFOLK COUNTY SILVERWARE (2007 TO 2014)

After the NJAA Challenge in 2003 when Ian Reynolds was crowned Intermediate Champion on the Bridgewater Canal, the young Suffolk squad weren't seen together on the bank for four years. Then, as we looked to pick up where Andy Wilson-Sutter had left off and to build on his groundwork; it wasn't too long before the county's anglers were featuring in results once again.

When writing this book, I'd always intended to include an 'at a glance' record of the squad's successes, but I didn't envisage detailing such a degree of achievement over a relatively short period of time. It was though, an absolute pleasure putting this short chapter together.

As a squad coach, I made a habit of ensuring that I obtained a copy of all the relevant results of events before leaving venues, and accessing the information on-line where I could soon after. Having also prepared, or at the very least, edited all of the press releases and website reports whilst directly involved with coaching and managing the squad; I found I could recall most of the information from memory. Nonetheless, I checked hard copies, referred again to website records and also contacted parents to check trophy engravings in an effort to ensure that everything detailed below is correct. Section winners, I found, were too numerous to list, but I believe I've managed to namecheck these anglers in the preceding pages.

The following pages are testament to everyone connected with coaching, managing and assisting the young Suffolk County squad during the time I was involved. I hope that those, whose names are featured, will take as much enjoyment and pride from looking through the record as I did when collating it.

2007
NJAA Challenge (Great Ouse, Ten Mile Bank)
Intermediates
Individual Runner-up: Rob Foulger

2008
NJAA National (Kennet and Avon Canal)
Intermediates
Individual 3rd: Chris Kelly
Juniors
Individual Runner-up: Robert Murphy

2009
NJAA National (Lindholme Lakes)*
Top Girl: Alice Bullock
Best Reserve: Jack Damant

NJAA Challenge (Grand Union Canal, Milton Keynes)
Intermediates
Team 3rd: Abi Brewster, Alice Bullock, Abbi Kendall and Jack Weatherley
Individual Winner: Abbi Kendall

2010
All England Junior Pole Champs (Dents of Hilgay)
Team (Under-18)
Team Runners-up: Abbi Kendall, Ashley Miller, Robert Murphy and Reece Page

NJAA National (South Holland Drain, Holbeach)
Intermediates
Team 3rd: Abi Brewster, Abbi Kendall, Ashley Miller and Reece Page
Individual Winner: Abbi Kendall
Juniors
Individual 3rd: Sam Kennard
Youngest Competitor: Jack Damant

2011
All England Junior Pole Champs
(Westwood Lakes, Boston)
Team (Under-18)
Winners: Josh Balodis, Tom Cottrell, James Head and Abbi Kendall
Individual 3rd: Josh Balodis
Individual (Under-21)
Runner-up: Robert Murphy
3rd: Ashley Miller

GUSAC (Grand Union Canal, Milton Keynes)
Team 3rd: Olivia Bullock, Lewis Clouting, Tom Cottrell and Sam Kennard

NJAA National (Grand Union Canal, Milton Keynes)**
Intermediates
Team Winners: Charlotte Gore, Abbi Kendall, Ashley Miller and Reece Page
Team Runners-up: Bradley Calver, Timmy Pepper, Toby Pepper and Adam Skillcorn
Individual Winner: Ashley Miller
Juniors
Team Winners: Tom Cottrell, Charlie Elton, James Head, Sam Kennard, David Ward and Peter Williams
Individual Runner-up: Peter Williams
Individual 3rd: Sam Kennard
Cadets
Team Winners: Paul Christie, Lewis Clouting and Max Rushbrook
Individual Winner: Jack Damant
Youngest Competitor: Max Rushbrook

NJAA Challenge (Suffolk Water Park)
Intermediates
Team Winners: Bradley Calver, Timmy Pepper, Toby Pepper and Adam Skillcorn
Individual Winner: Robert Murphy
Individual 3rd: Toby Pepper
Juniors
Team Winners: Tom Cottrell, Jack Damant, Charlie Elton, James Head, Sam Kennard and Peter Williams
Team 3rd: Paul Christie, Lewis Clouting, Jamie Marriott, Max Rushbrook, Ollie Saunders and David Ward
Individual Runner-up: Tom Cottrell

2012
All England Junior Pole Champs
(Westwood Lakes, Boston)
Team (Under-18)
Winners: Tom Cottrell, James Head, Timmy Pepper and Toby Pepper
Individual Winner: Toby Pepper
Individual Runner-up: Timmy Pepper
Individual (Under-21)
Runner-up: Reece Page
3rd: Abi Brewster

Angling Trust Cadet/Junior/Intermediate National
(Lindholme Lakes)
Intermediates
Team 3rd: Steve Crowe, Dan Elliot, Eddie Howman, Chris Kelly, Robert Murphy and Jack Weatherley
Cadets
Team Winners: Paul Christie, Lewis Clouting, Jack Damant, Jamie Marriott, Max Rushbrook and Ollie Saunders
Individual 3rd: Jamie Marriott

NJAA National (Stainforth and Keadby Canal, Thorne)
Juniors
Team 3rd: Lewis Clouting, Tom Cottrell, James Head, Sam Kennard, Adam Swain and Timmy Pepper
Cadets
Team Runners-up: Jack Damant, Max Rushbrook and Ollie Saunders
Individual 3rd: Max Rushbrook

NJAA Challenge (South Holland Drain, Holbeach)
Intermediates
Team Winners: Eddie Howman, Jack Weatherley, Robert Murphy and Peter Williams
Individual Winner: Peter Williams
Individual Runner-up: Robert Murphy
Individual 3rd: Eddie Howman
(Trophy awarded to winner only)
Juniors
Team Winners: Tom Cottrell, James Head, Sam Kennard, Timmy Pepper, Toby Pepper, Adam Swain
Team Runners-up: Paul Christie, Lewis Clouting and Max Rushbrook
Individual Winner: Timmy Pepper
Individual Runner-Up: Ollie Saunders
Individual 3rd: Toby Pepper

2013
All England Junior Pole Champs
(Westwood Lakes, Boston)
Team (Under-18)
Team 3rd: Tom Cottrell, James Head, Adam Swain and Timmy Pepper
Individual 3rd: Adam Swain
Individual (Under-23)
Runner-up: Jess Knights

Angling Trust Ladies' National
(Coleman's Cottage, Essex)
Team Runners-up: Abi Brewster, Charlotte Gore, Leanne Knott and Kayleigh Smith
Individual Runner-up: Jess Knights
Claire Dagnall Memorial Trophy: Jess Knights

Angling Trust Cadet/Junior/Intermediate National
(Tunnel Barn Farm, Warwickshire)
Cadets
Team Runners-up: Jack Damant, George Faiers, Jamie Marriott, Callum Murton, Max Rushbrook and Ollie Saunders
Individual Runner-up: Ollie Saunders

2014
Angling Trust Ladies' National
(Boldings Pools, Shropshire)
Team Winners: Charlotte Gore, Nuala Gray, Leanne Knott and Kayleigh Smith
Individual Winner: Kayleigh Smith

*Fishing as a guest for Leigh Ospreys, Alex Gissing received a third place team trophy.

**Olivia Bullock, fishing for Milton Keynes, took home the Top Girl silver salver and a team runner-up trophy.